EARLY MAN IN THE NEW WORLD

THE MACMILLAN COMPANY
NEW YORK · BOSTON · CHICAGO
DALLAS · ATLANTA · SAN FRANCISCO

MACMILLAN AND CO., LIMITED
LONDON · BOMBAY · CALCUTTA
MADRAS · MELBOURNE

THE MACMILLAN COMPANY
OF CANADA, LIMITED
TORONTO

TURNING POINT

The weapon of Folsom man as it was found in 1927 between the ribs of an extinct form of bison. In the face of long and violent opposition to early man in the Americas, this discovery proved he had hunted animals that were peculiar to the Great Ice Age. This and subsequent finds established his presence in North America 15,000 to 25,000 years ago. (Courtesy of the Denver Museum of Natural History.)

EARLY MAN

IN THE

NEW WORLD

———◆———

KENNETH MACGOWAN

With Drawings by Campbell Grant

And these are ancient things.

—I Chronicles, 4:22

THE MACMILLAN COMPANY

New York 1950

For permission to quote passages from their respective pub-
lications grateful acknowledgment is made to the following
authors, publishers, and literary executors:
J. B. Lippincott Company: Aleš Hrdlička, "Early Man in
America: What Have the Bones to Say?" in *Early Man,* ed.
George Grant MacCurdy (copyright, 1937, by The Academy
of Natural Sciences, Philadelphia); The Macmillan Company:
William B. Scott, *History of Land Mammals in the Western
Hemisphere,* rev. ed. (copyright, 1937, by The American
Philosophical Society); G. P. Putnam's Sons: Earnest A.
Hooton, *Apes, Men, and Morons* (copyright, 1937, by G. P.
Putnam's Sons); Rinehart & Company, Inc.: Robert H. Lowie,
The History of Ethnological Theory (copyright, 1937, by
Robert H. Lowie); Charles Scribner's Sons: Roland B. Dixon,
The Racial History of Man (copyright, 1923, by Charles
Scribner's Sons) and *The Building of Cultures* (copyright,
1928, by Charles Scribner's Sons); Whittlesey House: Harold
S. Gladwin, *Men Out of Asia* (copyright, 1947, by McGraw-
Hill Book Co., Inc.); University of Toronto Press: Earnest A.
Hooton, "Racial Types in America and Their Relations to Old
World Types" in *The American Aborigines,* ed. Diamond
Jenness; Yale University Press: Earnest A. Hooton, *The In-
dians of Pecos Pueblo* (copyright, 1930, by Yale University
Press).

First Printing

PRINTED IN THE UNITED STATES OF AMERICA

TO

GEORGE C. VAILLANT

PREFACE

During 1941 and 1942 my work in the Office of the Coordinator of Inter-American Affairs included the preparation of some educational films upon archaeological work in Mexico and South America. As a result I came to know and esteem the Director of the University Museum, George C. Vaillant. To my surprise and pleasure, when he learned of my interest in American archaeology, he proposed that we collaborate on a prehistory of the New World. When the war prevented active work together by taking him to Peru, I prepared what would have been the first two chapters of our book—the place of early man in the story of pre-Columbian America. Upon Vaillant's untimely death, I decided to study the subject more intensively, to add material on the Great Ice Age and early man in the Old World as well as the New, and to expand the two chapters into a book that I might dedicate to the man who had done so much for American archaeology in the twenty years of his work—George C. Vaillant.

Since this book is not the result of personal work in the field, but rather the product of the kind of research that is nothing more than reading and talking, I am in the debt of many men and books, and a welter of papers, pamphlets, and periodicals. I find it hard to believe that in any other branch of science so many overworked men and women would be so ready to give their time to talk and correspondence with the amateur. I am deeply indebted to more than two score who have gone out of their way to answer questions, lend books, or give reprints of papers. In listing them here I am more than certain that I have inadvertently omitted some: Edgar Anderson, Ernst Antevs, Ralph L. Beals, Junius Bird, Robert Braidwood, Henry J. Bruman, Kirk Bryan, George F. Carter, R. A. Daly, Helmut de Terra, Loren C. Eiseley, Richard F. Flint, James Gilluly, Harold S. Gladwin, M. R. Harrington, Frank C. Hibben, Frederick W. Hodge, Harry Hoijer, Earnest A. Hooton, W. W. Howells, Frederick R. Johnson, Arthur R. Kelly, G. H. R. von Koenigswald, Alex D. Krieger, Alfred L.

Kroeber, M. M. Leighton, Theodore D. McCown, George G. Mac-
Curdy, P. C. Mangelsdorf, Paul S. Martin, Hallam L. Movius, Jr.,
Raymond W. Murray, N. C. Nelson, Charles W. Phillips, Cyrus N.
Ray, E. B. Renaud, Frank H. H. Roberts, Jr., Alfred S. Romer, Irving
Rouse, Curt Sachs, Carl O. Sauer, E. H. Sellards, Herbert J. Spinden,
T. D. Stewart, Wm. Duncan Strong, Griffith Taylor, Bella Weitzner,
H. M. Wormington, and Clark Wissler.

Next to the scientists who provide knowledge, stand the librarians
who help to preserve it and make it usable. I am peculiarly indebted
to a number of these: Miss Margaret Currier, Librarian of the Peabody
Museum, Cambridge, her assistant Miss Jessie Bell MacKenzie, Mrs.
Ella L. Robinson, Librarian of the Southwest Museum, Dr. Lawrence
C. Powell, Librarian of the University of California at Los Angeles, his
most cooperative staff, and particularly one of its members, Miss Hilda
M. Gray, whose expeditions into the equal mysteries of stacks and
bibliographies saved me many hours of labor and I can't guess how
many blunders.

I am particularly indebted to Frank H. H. Roberts, Jr., of the
Smithsonian Institution, the outstanding authority on early man in
North America, for his reading, checking, and challenging of the
manuscript, and to M. R. Harrington, who read and criticized my first
draft. I also owe much to a number of men and women who read
various chapters on which they had special knowledge: Edgar Anderson, Ernst Antevs, Robert Braidwood, Henry J. Bruman, Loren C.
Eiseley, James Gilluly, Harold S. Gladwin, M. R. Harrington, Robert
F. Heizer, Earnest A. Hooton, Alex Krieger, Alfred L. Kroeber,
Theodore D. McCown, Ernest S. Macgowan, Hallam L. Movius, Jr.,
and H. M. Wormington.

I am especially obliged to Campbell Grant, amateur of anthropology
as well as artist, for the many illustrations.

Finally, in the typing of the manuscript and the checking of the
many references I have been fortunate in having the aid of Miss
Frankie Porter and of Joe Pavalko.

Since I am not adding a repetitive bibliography to the almost four
hundred references that I cite, I should like to list a few of the sources
which I have found most useful and which should prove so to any

reader who may wish to pursue further various aspects of the subject:

Frank H. H. Roberts, Jr., "Developments in the Problem of the North-American Paleo-Indian," *Smithsonian Miscellaneous Collections,* 100:51–116 (1940), and "The New World Paleo-Indian," *Annual Report of the Smithsonian Institution for 1944,* 403–433.

H. M. Wormington, *Ancient Man in North America* (Denver Museum of Natural History, *Popular Series no. 4,* 1949).

E. H. Sellards, "Early Man in America: Index to Localities, and Selected Bibliography," *Bulletin of the Geological Society of America,* 51:373–430 (1940), and 58:955–977 (1947).

Raymond W. Murray, *Man's Unknown Ancestors* (1943).

Early Man, a symposium edited by George Grant MacCurdy (1937).

The American Aborigines, a symposium edited by Diamond Jenness (1933).

George Grant MacCurdy, *Human Origins* (1924).

Miles C. Burkitt, *The Old Stone Age* (1933).

W. J. Sollas, *Ancient Hunters and Their Modern Representatives* (1924).

W. B. Wright, *Tools and the Man* (1939).

André Vayson de Pradenne, *Prehistory* (1940).

Edith Plant, *Man's Unwritten Past* (1942).

Hallam L. Movius, Jr., *Early Man and Pleistocene Stratigraphy in Southern and Eastern Asia* (1944).

Earnest A. Hooton, *Up from the Ape* (1946).

W. W. Howells, *Mankind So Far* (1944).

Roland B. Dixon, *Racial History of Man* (1923).

R. A. Daly, *The Changing World of the Ice Age* (1934).

Richard F. Flint, *Glacial Geology and the Pleistocene Epoch* (1947).

Frederick E. Zeuner, *Dating the Past* (1946).

Robert H. Lowie, *The History of Ethnological Theory* (1937).

K. M.

University of California,
    Los Angeles, Calif.

CONTENTS

Preface   vii

Chapter 1.   THIS SUDDEN NEW WORLD   1

A Secret Laboratory of Culture. Time-Tests by Travel, Tongues and Physiques. From the Old Stone Age to the New. From Tools and Bones, Fossils and Rocks.

Chapter 2.   THE ROAD OF EARLY MAN   9

How New Was the New World? A Passage from Asia to North America. Men Out of Asia—and All the Continents. Bering Strait—Free Way to the New World. Three Roads to the South—with One Detour. Problematical Roads to the New World. Ware Dogma!

Chapter 3.   THE DEAD HAND OF THE AGES   23

Conflicts and Confusions. The Problem of the Ages. The Bronze Age—a Phantasm. Wood, Bone, and Shell Ages. Dividing the Stone Age—the Old and the New. Activities of the New Stone Age. Agriculture—Test of the Neolithic. First a Food Gatherer, Then a Hunter.

Chapter 4.   THE GREAT ICE AGE   36

Our Part of the Geologic Time-Scale. The Glacial Hypothesis Appears. The End of the Great Ice Age. River Terraces and Beach Lines. The Cause of Glaciation.

Chapter 5.   EARLY MAN IN THE OLD WORLD   51

Archaeology, a New Science. Mortillet's Cramping Classification. Enter the Eolith. Flake vs. Core Industries. Dating Early Man in Europe. Chellean and Acheulean Man. Ancient Man in Java and China. The Progressive Neanderthal. Homo Sapiens—New or Old? Solutrean Flint Workers Invade Europe. Weapons and Tools—from Hand Ax to Arrowhead. The Danger in Universal Time-Scales.

Chapter 6.   WHAT THE BONES HAVE TO SAY   91

Early Man As Adam's Progeny. Science and Religion Embattled. Reaction, Led by Science. The Red Herring of the "Primitive Skull." The Mystery of the Missing Bones. South America Provides the First Skulls. North American Skulls and Bones. Early Man Not Solely Mongoloid or Indian.

Chapter 7. THE ARTIFACTS OF EARLY MAN 108

Artifacts from Heaven. The Folsom Point—Unique and Potent. Americans Hunted Animals Now Extinct. Two Other Folsom Sites—Clovis and Lindenmeier. Another Fine and Ancient Point—the Yuma. The Plainview Point. A New Point —and Sloths—in Gypsum Cave. Old Lake and River Sites. Sandia—Older Than Folsom. The Milling Stone Appears. A Paucity of Art Objects. Hand Axes in the Americas. Early Man in Mexico.

Chapter 8. EARLY MAN AND THE
GREAT EXTINCTION 140

A Twofold Problem. Myths and Mammoths. Archaeological Evidence of Recent Man and the Mastodon. Sloth and Camel in Dry Caves. The Folsom Bison Not Extinct? The Mystery of Extinction.

Chapter 9. PYGMIES, AUSTRALOIDS, AND
NEGROIDS—BEFORE INDIANS? 152

The Mythical Indian Race. Racial Definition—the Field of the Physical Anthropologist. The Cephalic Index—and Others. What Skull Measurements Tell Us About Early Man. Europe Recognizes the Australoid in America. Hooton and Dixon on Early Invaders. A Potpourri of Races. Pygmies Before Australoids in the New World? Australoids, Negroids, and Men from Europe. No Mongoloids till 300 B.C.

Chapter 10. DID THE INDIAN INVENT OR
BORROW HIS CULTURE? 175

Diffusion vs. Independent Invention. Bastian's "Psychic Unity." Complexity an Argument for Diffusion. Dispersion As Well As Diffusion. The Trap of Time. Escape from the Trap. Dead Alexander Invades America. Independent Inventions Neither Parallel nor Diffused.

Chapter 11. THE INDIAN IN AGRICULTURE 197

Inventions—Some New, Some Old. American Plants and Their Cultivation. When and Where Did Our Agriculture Begin? The Indian's Accomplishment in Agriculture. How Old Is Corn?

Chapter 12. PUZZLES, PROBLEMS, AND
HALF-ANSWERS 210

The Pendulum Swings. The Puzzle of the Skulls. The Puzzle of the Querns. The Puzzle of the Points. Was Our Early Man a Solutrean? Or Was the American Aurignacian or Magdalenian? Chopping Tools Instead of Hand Axes in Asia. Spinden's Neolithic Blockade. Was the First Migration Interglacial? Geological Evidence and the Pluvials. In Sum.

References in the Text 225

References as to Illustrations 248

Index 253

ILLUSTRATIONS, MAPS, AND TABLES

Turning Point—Folsom and Extinct Bison Frontispiece
The Treks of Early Man from His Homeland page 4
Out of Noah's Ark and over Bering Strait 11
The Land-Bridge to the New World 15
A Great-Circle Route to North America 16
Migration Routes 19
Glaciers and Ice Fields as Barriers to Early Man 22 and 23
The Life Story of the Earth 37
The Ice Fields of the Last Glaciation 41
The Age of River Terraces 43
The Four Great Glaciations 47
Glaciation Through Warmth 49
The First Hand Ax Found and Recognized 52
A Time Scale of Early Man 54
The "Dawn Stones" of Early Man 55
The Major Paleolithic Cultures 59
Man's First Perfected Tool 60
Ancient Implements of Bone and Wood 62
Java Man—*Pithecanthropus erectus* 65
Gigantopithecus—Giant Ancestor of Man? 66
Three Types of Old World Man 68
Man's First Spear Points 69
Percussion Flaking 70
The Second Step in Flint Knapping 71
The Third Step—Pressure Flaking 72
Sculpture of the Old Stone Age 74
How Blades Were Split Off a Core 76
Upper Paleolithic Tools 77
Three Aurignacian Types 77
The Meaning of Scrapers 78
The Tanged Point 80
A Laurel-Leaf Solutrean Point 81
A Tool to Make a Tool 82
A Magdalenian Harpoon 82
The First Illustration of a Blade 82

The Spear-Thrower As Used by Early Man   page 83
The First Paintings   84
Bowmen from Africa   85
Archers from Spain   86
Magdalenian Engravings   87
A Chart of Old Stone Age Cultures   88 and 89
A Spear Point Found Near Trenton, N.J.   109
The Lake Lahontan Point   110
The Making of a Folsom Point   111
The Minute, Ribbonlike Flaking of a Folsom   112
The Finest Flint Work of Early Man   113
A Map of the Chief Sites in the Southwest   115
Burials in the Old World and the New   117
Flint Knapping of the Old and New Stone Ages   118
Two Points of Plainview Type   120
A Gypsum Cave Point   121
Three Early Points from the Borders of Extinct Lakes   122
An Abilene Point   123
A Sandia Point Compared with Two Solutreans   125
Cochise Milling Stones   127
An Animal Head Carved from a Fossil Bone   130
A Sculptured Foot Carved from a Mammoth's Tooth   130
A Hand Ax of the Black's Fork Culture   131
A Hand Ax and a Chopping Tool from Texas   133
A Broken Pestle from Gold-Bearing Gravels in California   135
The More Important Sites of Early Man in the New World
                         136, 137, 138, 139
Mammals of the Ice Age in North and South America   141
Prehistoric and Modern Bison   147
The Mongoloid Fold   153
The "Twin" Nature of the Races   155
The Cephalic Index   156
The Dispersal of Head Types   157
Three Types of Skulls   159
Early Man vs. the Mongoloid   161
The Migrations of Early Man   166
From the Old World and the New   172
From Burma to Melanesia to America?   177
Fishhooks from Tahiti and California   178
Diffusion or Independent Invention?   179
Circumpacific Navigation?   182
Bearded White Gods?   190

The Equatorial Counter Current page 192
The Indian's New World Products 199
The First Illustration of the Corn Plant 203
"Turkie Corne" 205
A Seventeenth Century Picture of Corn 206
Corn of 4,500 Years Ago 207
Yuma Chipping in Siberia 214
Hand Axes and Chopping Tools of the Old World 217
A Chopping Tool of Northwestern India 218

EARLY MAN IN THE NEW WORLD

A Note on Notes

There are no footnotes in this book. A catch-all for the author's afterthoughts and for the corrections provided by friends who have read manuscript or galley proof—as well as a place for legitimate references—they are often a nuisance and always a typographical eyesore. The reference numbers in this book direct attention only to the sources of quotations, facts, or theories. They do not lead the reader to supplementary text material. Therefore, he may ignore them unless he wants to pursue the subject further for himself, or to verify the authority for what may seem to him an implausible statement.

1

THIS SUDDEN NEW WORLD

*Of all animals, we men are the only
ones who wonder where we came from
and where we will go.*

—W. W. HOWELLS

A Secret Laboratory of Culture   By 1943 Timbuctoo was surprisingly close to Keokuk. Boys from Brooklyn stared up at Roman columns in the African desert, and Marines swapped a package of cigarettes for the spear of a stone-age man in New Guinea. Physically ours was indeed one world.

In a different sense it was one world before Columbus sailed, but a very limited world. Europe, North Africa, and portions of Asia made up all that Columbus knew and all that he expected to know. He intended to find a new road to the Indies; that was all. It would be a road across his own one world.

Then suddenly this world of his was two worlds. A new hemisphere appeared like a comet from outer space. It was a land and a people utterly unknown, utterly different. It had lived and grown for thousands upon thousands of years, sealed off to itself, unique. We search for some fit comparison, and find nothing adequate to describe the discovery of this secret laboratory of experiment in human culture.

Perhaps I should not have said that the New World had been "sealed off to itself." I might better have said "sealed off from Europe." The culture which the Spanish Conquistadores found in the

1

Americas owed nothing to that world from which they had come. What the Americas owed to Asia is another matter—in fact, the matter of this book.

One thing is clear. The Americas were indebted to Asia for man himself. Man—even one type of man—did not originate here. A small primate, the extinct Notharctus, left his bones—but no descendants—in our Southwest. The New World has no great apes; there are no indications that it ever had any. Its monkeys are quite out of the running. They have four too many teeth, their nose is flat, and they are cursed with a prehensile tail.

The New World owed something more to Asia, of course; but how much, is uncertain. Most anthropologists believe that man crossed Bering Strait with a very meager kit of culture. He brought, at various times, the spear-thrower, the bow and arrow, the dog, the boat, the strike-a-light, some kind of clothing, but not a great deal more. Almost all his culture—pottery, weaving, agriculture, masonry, metallurgy—he had to invent for himself in the New World; at least, that is the general opinion. A few anthropologists say that men out of Asia brought quite an array of culture traits; but these migrants were late comers, and most of them crossed the Pacific by boat.

Only a few students now deny that men had been crossing over from Asia through twenty or more millenniums before the birth of Christ. Some of them were what we call Indians—most of them, no doubt; but, before the Indians came, there seem to have been other immigrants. It is the purpose of this book to tell you what is known or believed or hazarded about these earliest men of the New World.

There are two chief problems: When did these men come? and What were they like?

It is a curious fact that, if we look at the rich variety of men and languages and cultures which was spread from end to end of two whole continents when the European came, we get some vague idea of how long man had been in the western hemisphere but no idea at all of what he was like when he anticipated Columbus by discovering the New World. Through the haze of time, we can see the general outline of Indian civilization, and many details. Much of this is clear and concrete, most of it is natural and understandable in terms of our

Americas, and all of it is striking and extraordinary. But, for our present purposes, the best it does is to tell us that many millenniums of time must have been required for its development. It tells us nothing about the men who preceded the Indian, the primitive savages who discovered the New World. These men who first journeyed from Bering Strait to Cape Horn were not the men who made the Maya civilization, and they came long, long before. But by studying both the Indian and his predecessors we may gain some hint of how long ago this was.

Time-Tests by Travel, Tongues, and Physiques Somehow or other, by this route or that, the migrants from Asia drifted across to the Americas, down the two continents, and out to their uttermost limits. Of the many possible tests of man's age in the New World—some good, some not so good—one of the least accurate is a guess at how long it would take men and women, encumbered with children, to walk—and to eat their way—from Bering Strait to Cape Horn. It has been estimated that they might have covered the 4,000 miles from Harbin, Manchuria, to Vancouver Island in from 20 to 1,000 years; the time involved really depends on how fast and in what direction those wild animals moved upon which early man depended for food. As the country widened out, then narrowed in Central America, and widened out once more, there is no knowing how long the trip to Cape Horn may have taken. Our migrants would have had to camp and hunt as they went, and at first they would have moved only as the pursuit of game spurred them on. There would have had to be time, too, for increase in numbers—among themselves as well as among later invaders—to create pressure of population, and force the earlier men to the peripheries of northeastern America, Florida, and Lower California, and push them across jungled Panama and Amazonia and toward the bleaker and less desirable parts of South America. The various invaders multiplied as they moved, and it is anybody's guess how many people were crowded into America by 1492; one authority says 8,400,000, another 50,000,000 to 75,000,000.[1] It took much time, of course—many millenniums—to breed so many men and cover so wide a space.

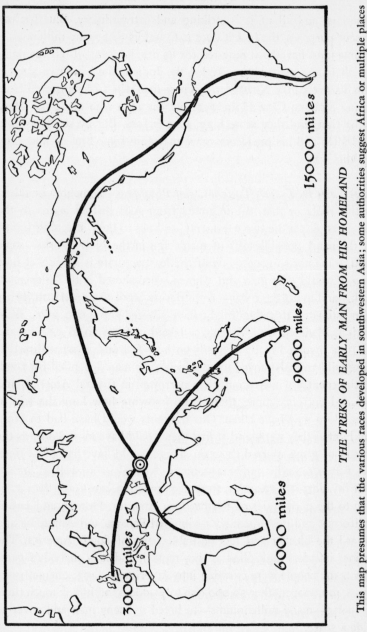

THE TREKS OF EARLY MAN FROM HIS HOMELAND

This map presumes that the various races developed in southwestern Asia; some authorities suggest Africa or multiple places of origin. The journey of early man from Bering Strait to the tip of Cape Horn was a matter of 10,000 miles.

3000 miles

6000 miles

9000 miles

15000 miles

Other things suggest a long sojourn for the Indian in the New World. Consider the matter of language—"the archives of history." The Indian, writes N. C. Nelson, "had been at home in the New World long enough to have evolved about 160 linguistic stocks or language families, with 1,200 or more dialectic subdivisions." [2] Alfred L. Kroeber says that North and South America "contain more native language families than all the remainder of the world." [3] Some of this diversity could be due to migrations from different linguistic areas of the Old World. It might also be accounted for by the theory of Franz Boas that among early primitive peoples there was great diversity of language, and that single tongues began to spread widely only when conquering and proselyting groups won a certain amount of power and dominion.[4] John Harrington, an American linguistic authority, believes that the diversity of Indian speech argues a very long residence in the New World—"at least 20,000 years, perhaps three times that." [5] Edgar B. Howard states: "Considering that the languages of the New World lack evidence, outside of Eskimo, of any identification with Old World languages, the conclusion appears to be that human contact between the two continents was very remote." [6] If there is no such identification, then even the last migrants came at a very early date indeed, or else all the members of all the tribes that were left behind in the Old World perished without linguistic trace. It is possible, of course, that resemblances have merely not been recognized.

In addition to differentiation of language, there is differentiation of physique. When we in the United States think of the Indian, we think of a tall man with high cheekbones, a hawk-nose, and a bronze-red skin. Actually the American Indian is probably more varied in height, face, and color than the whole White racial stock.[7] More than that, his somatic constitution—the inner man in a physical sense—varies greatly. By 1492 the Indian had adapted himself to eight different climates from arctic to tropic, from arid to humid, from sea level to the 14,000-foot heights of Peru. This would take time, much time. Albrecht Penck, the great European glacialist, thinks 25,000 years hardly long enough.[8]

The civilizations which the Indian developed in the Americas—the

Maya, Aztec, and Inca cultures—provide another test of how long man had been in the New World before Columbus came. This test is no more exact than those I have already mentioned, but it suggests quite a long sojourn.

From the Old Stone Age to the New   While the physical man was adapting himself to all manner of climates, the mental man dragged himself up from the hunting life of the Old Stone Age to the invention of writing and the perfecting of an accurate calendar. On the way —and as slow, necessary steps in his progress—he developed agriculture, and invented or perfected the arts and crafts of pottery, weaving, dyeing, metallurgy, sculpture, poetry, painting, architecture, city planning. In his agriculture he utilized irrigation, discovered fertilizers, and developed twenty exclusively American plants which now supply more than half of the world's provender. He was the first to write numbers through the use of zero and numerical position. He practiced trepanning—the removal of a piece of skull bone to relieve pressure on the brain—and he discovered how to use certain medicines and narcotics. In his textiles he employed all the weaves known to us today. He contrived efficient methods of government. He proliferated into 368 major tribal groups, and developed fifteen culture centers of distinct individuality.[9] In the United States he left 100,000 mounds as the product of one of his cultures; in Middle America, 4,000 ceremonial cities of stone. He practiced most types of religion except atheism. Certain things that he made resemble things of the Old World; most are peculiar to him and his life. Of Indian culture traits Clark Wissler remarks that "the range in variety and individuality seems even greater in aboriginal America than in the primitive Old World." [10]

Progress is slow in the stone age. It seems to have been particularly slow in the Old Stone Age, or paleolithic period, when man spent half a million to a million years learning to chip stone and hunt and gather food efficiently. Things went much faster in the New Stone Age, or neolithic period, when he was learning to grow plants and make pottery and polish stone tools. To move from the beginnings of agriculture to the beginnings of metallurgy, which ended the neolithic, may have taken as little as 700 years in the Old World and certainly not much more than 7,000; 2,300 seems a safe guess.

Progress was slower in the New World. The Indian reached the New Stone Age later, and he may have stayed in it longer than man did in the Old World. This can probably be blamed on the peculiar fauna of the western hemisphere. In all of the Americas there were no animals to domesticate except the dog—which the Indian probably brought with him—and those dubious objects of husbandry, the turkey, the bee, the Muscovy duck, the llama, the alpaca, and the guinea pig. Because there were no sheep or cattle, the Indian had no pastoral life and no milk and butter. He had no beasts of burden except the dog and the llama; he invented no wheeled cart. It was not entirely his own fault that he remained essentially a man of the stone age even though, toward the last, he had perfected a metallurgy of copper, silver, gold, platinum, and bronze.

The story of the Indian's spread through the Americas, his variation in language and physique, and his building of the civilizations of Peru, Central America, and Mexico argues that he came to the New World many millenniums before the birth of Christ. You may point out that the argument is too general, too inexact in outcome, but you must remember that behind the Indian lies an earlier migrant. We are on somewhat firmer ground when we turn to the evidence we have of this migrant's tools, his hearths, and his bones. For they are related to the fossils of extinct mammals and—more important—to certain kinds of earth and rock.

From Tools and Bones, Fossils and Rocks   The tools and the hearths and the fossils are plentiful, and some years ago this proof of man's antiquity seemed to be enough. The great and spectacular mammals whose remains were associated with early man in the Americas, as well as in Europe, were thought to have vanished with the glaciers of the Great Ice Age. Therefore, early man in the Americas must also have lived in that period. Now, however, a number of scientists believe that the American mastodon, along with a number of other animals that are now extinct in the New World, survived the Great Ice Age here. This would still leave us, let me remark, with an American whose antiquity is quite respectable.

The best proof of the age of early man is, of course, geological. If we can date the earth and rocks in which we find his tools, we can date man, too. And we can date him with relative accuracy. Unfortunately, we have none too much geological evidence in the Americas, and what we have is none too firm.

Yet, between tools and bones, fossils and earths, we are beginning to know quite a little about when man reached the New World and about how he lived.

2

THE ROAD OF EARLY MAN

*I have been a stranger
in a strange land.*

—EXODUS 2:22

How New Was the New World? We moderns were not the first to ask the question: Just how new was the New World on October 12, 1492? Or how old?

For a time, it was a very ancient world to the Spaniards. It was the Indies of the East, and they thought they had discovered nothing more than a new way of getting at them. Some years passed before they awoke to the fact that they had found a new continent. There may, of course, have been suspicions from the first. Certainly the topical trees and plants were new; the animals, too, all except man. Man was an Indian—that is, an East Indian. Balboa may have had a "wild surmise," but it remained for later Spaniards, as well as the Portuguese, to find in South America a land that could not be Asia. Columbus discovered the New World and thought it was India; the Italian Amerigo Vespucci did not discover the continent named for him, but at least he knew it was not India and gave it a name of its own—*Mundus Novus*.

Then, indeed, our world became a new world, and a world freighted with a problem. The problem was how to put its inhabitants into a proper theological—and ethnological—pigeonhole. As a new and unknown being, the Indian presented a serious issue to the Catholic Church and its clerical and imperial pioneers. Here was a

9

people of whom the Bible made no mention. Shem, Ham, and Japheth had filled three continents very handily, but they had somehow neglected this one. Established authority had no explanation for these new men. Were they, indeed, beings without souls? "While the New World with its gold and other riches was accepted as reality," observes N. C. Nelson, "the truly human nature of its inhabitants was temporarily held in doubt." [1]

Soon, however, the church found an explanation. The Bible mentioned no separate creation in an American Garden of Eden; therefore the forebears of the red man must have come from the Old World. As early as 1512 Pope Julius II declared officially that the Indians were descended from Adam and Eve. For many years thereafter they were considered as children of Babel driven back into the stone age because of their sins.

A Passage from Asia to North America   In 1590—not quite a hundred years after Columbus's discovery—a Spanish cleric, José de Acosta, put on paper an ingenious theory for the populating of the Americas:

It is not likely that there was another Noes Arke, by the which men might be transported into the Indies, and much lesse any Angell to carie the first man to this new world, holding him by the haire of the head, like to the Prophet Abacuc. . . . I conclude then, that it is likely the first that came to the Indies was by shipwracke and tempest of wether.[2]

But Acosta felt the need of a land route to take care of the animals. Noah had let them out of the Ark in western Asia, and they could hardly be expected to sail or even to swim to America. And so Acosta ventured the opinion that somewhere in the north explorers would ultimately find a portion of America that joined with some corner of the Old World, or at any rate was "not altogether severed and disjoined" from it. In this way the animals—and man—had come to the New World.

God-fearing Protestants from England joined clerics of the Roman church in bringing the American aborigine over from Asia. Long before any white man had stared across Bering Strait from the eastern bounds many Tartars there are, both toward the West, and South. And what if the innumerable people of so many Nations,as are known to inhabite & ouerspread the huge continent of America, be also of the same of-spring? Certainly, if I bee not greatly deceiued, they are no other. For first that their originall must be deriued from Asia is apparent,because,(as he that readeth the relations and histories of those countries of America may easily obserue) they haue no rellish nor resemblance at all,ofthe Artes,or learning,or ciuility of Europe: And their colour testifieth,they are not of the Africans progeny (there being not found in all that large continent,any blacke men, except a few about the Riuer of S. Marths, in a small Countrey called Quarequa, which by force and violence of some tempest, are supposed to haue beene transported thither, from the parts of Guinie or Aethiopia.) Therfore it seemeth, that they had their originall from Asia. Which yet, will appeare more credible, if it be obserued, which by the Spaniards discoueries is well knowen to be true,namely,that the West side of America respecting Asia, is exceeding much better peopled then the opposite or East side, that respecteth toward Europe. And, as for these reasons it is very likely, that America receiued her first inhabitants, from the East border of Asia: So is it altogether vnlike, that it receiued them from any other part of all that border, saue from Tartary.Because,in America there is not to be discerned,any token or indication at all, of the arts or industry of China,or India,or Cataia,or any other

other ciuill region, along all that border of Asia: But in their grosse ignorance of letters,and of arts, in their idolatrie, and the specialties of it, in their inciuility,and many barbarous properties,they resemble the old and rude Tartars, aboue all the nations of the earth. Which opinion of mine,touching the Americans descending from the Tartars,rather then from any other nation in that border of Asia,after the neere vicinity of Asia to America,this reason aboue all other, may best establish and perswade: because it is certaine, that that Northeast part of Asia possessed by the Tartars, is if not continent with the VVest side of America, which yet remayneth somewhat doubtfull: yet certainely, and without all doubt, it is the least disioyned by sea, of all that coast of Asia, for that those parts of Asia and America, are continent one with the other, or at most, disioyned but by some narrow channell of the Ocean, the rauenous and harmefull beasts, wherewith America is stored, as Beares, Lions, Tigers,Wolues,Foxes,&c.(which men as is likely, would neuer to their owne harme transport out of the one continent to the other) may import. For from Noahs Ark,which rested after the deluge, in Asia, all those beasts must of necessity fetch their beginning, seeing they could not proceed by the course of nature, as the vnperfect sort of liuing creatures doe, of Putrefaction: or if they might haue Putrefaction for their parentage, or receiue their originall (by any other new sort of generatiō)of the earth without special procreation of their own kind,then I see no necessitie

O

OUT OF NOAH'S ARK AND OVER BERING STRAIT

Two pages from Brerewood's seventeenth century book, *Enquiries Touching the Diversity of Languages, and Religions, Through the Chief Parts of the World,* in which he pictures bears and Tartars crossing to the New World at a point where Asia and America "are continent one with the other, or at most, disioined but by some narrow channell of the Ocean." (Courtesy of the University of California, Los Angeles, Library.)

tip of Asia and discovered Alaska, sixteenth and seventeenth century men were envisioning the neighborliness of the two continents and an easy crossing. It had to be. There was no escaping this solution. Men from Eden could be trusted to force their way across the widest and wildest of oceans, but not animals from Ararat. In 1614 Edward Brerewood worried, like Father de Acosta, over the problem of "the ravenous and harmefull beasts, wherewith *America* is stored, as Beares, Lions, Tigers, Wolves, Foxes, &c. (which men as is likely, would never to their owne harme transport out of the one continent to the other)." He saw that "from *Noahs* Ark, which rested after the

deluge, in *Asia,* all those beasts must of necessity fetch their beginning." He knew men and beasts must have come from Asia because
the Indians were not the color of Africans, and they had "no rellish
nor resemblance at all, of the Artes, or learning, or civility of *Europe.*"
Also, "the West side of *America* respecting *Asia,* is exceeding much
better peopled then the opposite or East side, that respecteth toward
Europe."

Men Out of Asia—and All the Continents   Brerewood moved on
from the questions of how and whence to who. With considerable
hardihood, this learned Englishman picked a single Asiatic race to
supply the Indian with a forebear. Looking askance at the inhabitants
of America, he wrote: "In their grosse ignorance of letters, and of
arts, in their idolatrie, and the specialties of it, in their incivility, and
many barbarous properties, they resemble the old and rude Tartars,
above all the nations of the earth." [3]

Brerewood's reasoning was logic itself and his conclusion inescap-
able compared with much of the theorizing of his day and much more
that went on for three hundred years after the discovery of America.
In 1607 Fray Gregorio Garcia published a book, *The Origin of the
Indians of the New World,* in which appeared these words:

The Indians proceed neither from one nation or people, nor have
they come from one part alone of the Old World, or by the same
road, or at the same time, in the same way, or for the same reasons;
some have probably descended from the Carthaginians, others from
the Ten Lost Tribes and other Israelites, others from the lost Atlantis,
from the Greeks, and Phoenicians, and still others from the Chinese,
Tartars, and other groups. [4]

For good measure, Fray Garcia and his fellow theorists threw in men
of Ophir and Tarsus, old Spaniards, Romans, Japanese, Koreans,
Egyptians, Moors, Canary Islanders, Ethiopians, French, English,
Irish, Germans, Trojans, Danes, Frisians, and Norsemen—a veritable
league of nations.

Iconoclastic Voltaire would have none of this—and none of Eden,
either:

Can it still be asked from whence came the men who people America? The same question might be asked with regard to the Terra Australis. They are much farther distant from the port which Columbus set out from, than the Antilles. Men and beasts have been found in all parts of the earth that are inhabitable; Who placed them there? We have already answered he that caused the grass to grow in the fields; and it is no more surprising to find men in America, than it is to find flies there.[5]

The more or less scientific minds of the nineteenth and twentieth centuries were no less prodigal in theory than the clerics and the philosophers of the seventeenth and eighteenth. Sometime in the 1820's Lord Kingsborough, son of an Irish peer of great wealth, got it into his head that the Lost Tribes of Israel were the ancestors of the Maya and the Aztecs—the same idea that animated Joseph Smith and *The Book of Mormon*; and in 1830—the very year that Smith's American supplement to the Bible appeared—Kingsborough began the publication of the nine monumental and handsomely illustrated volumes, *Antiquities of Mexico,* which cost him £25,000 and ultimately—like Smith—his life. Quite as eccentric theories followed. The otherwise sound and observant George Catlin thought the Mandan Indians the descendants of the Welsh. The "lost continent" of Mu—the Atlantis of the Pacific—reared its ugly head. Elliot Smith left the teaching of anatomy, and W. J. Perry cultural anthropology and comparative religions, to bring from Egypt all the culture of America—together with most of Eurasia's and Africa's—on the backs of those indefatigable travelers of their invention, the Children of the Sun.

In the face of such wild theorizing it is comforting to recall that the great Humboldt recognized as early as 1811 a "striking analogy between the Americans and the Mongol race." We must pardon him for clinging to some vague notion of a primordial American race and declaring that the Indians were "a mixture of Asiatic tribes and the aborigines of this vast continent." [6]

Today science does not have all the answers to the anthropological problem which arose when Balboa discovered the Pacific and Magellan crossed it, thus dropping the world's largest ocean in between the Americas and the Garden of Eden. So far as early man is concerned, we know a good deal about how he came, and whence, and a little about when.

Except for the passionate protagonists of Atlantis and of its "opposite number," the mythical land of Mu lost in the depths of the Pacific, most students agree that early man came across what is now Bering Strait—not by way of the Aleutians, for their inhospitable western tip is separated from Asia by 225 miles of sea with one small island midway between. For a long time, the Bering Strait route was supported only by *a priori* reasoning, but of late years the weapons of early man have been found either alone or with the fossils of extinct mammals in parts of Alaska and northwest Canada.

Bering Strait—Free Way to the New World   Though early man from northern Asia certainly crossed in one area and in one area only, he may have made the crossing by one or all of three methods. That depends on when he came.

If he came rather late—say around 10,000 years ago—he had to negotiate Bering Strait, open water in summer, iced over in winter. If the migrants were a boating and fishing people voyaging north along the Asiatic shore, the 56-mile gap of Bering Strait, broken by the Diomede Islands, was a negligible barrier. If they found the strait frozen over, they would have followed the southern edge of the ice. Men of a more inland type, men less given to water travel, could have crossed to Alaska—as some do now—on the ice of winter.

If early man first came to the New World in the Great Ice Age or in the time when the glaciers were beginning to melt, he could have crossed dry-shod on a land-bridge. Geologists have calculated that the water withdrawn from the ocean to form the masses of ice—which were two miles thick over much of Canada and the northern portion of the United States—would have lowered the water level in the Bering Strait region by as much as 200 to 300 feet toward the end of the Great Ice Age.[7] In addition, the ocean floor of the strait—relieved of so much weight of water—would doubtless have risen to some extent. Since, at present, portions of the strait reaching from shore to shore are not more than 120 feet deep, a land-bridge is a perfectly plausible hypothesis. Of course the bridge would have disappeared with the

THE LAND–BRIDGE TO THE NEW WORLD

A conservative map of shorelines during the last glaciation, based on a drop in sea level of 180 feet. Geologists believe that the ice impounded in the great glaciers and ice fields of the world lowered the ocean 200 to 300 feet. The southern shore of Alaska during the last glaciation may have been much nearer its present position. (After Johnston, 1933.)

end of the glaciers, which means that, if man had to come over dry-shod in the summer, he must have invaded America while the glaciers were still fairly extensive.

Aleš Hrdlička has said that not many men would have frequented northeastern Siberia because of its inhospitable climate, and so only a few would have "trickled over." [8] The opposite seems to have been true in the time of the glaciers. Then northeastern Asia was an excellent jumping-off place for the Old World migrant. In the first place, there was not much glaciation in this area, certainly nothing to interfere with the passage of people along the coast. The last glaciation was "far less extensive than its predecessor," say R. F. Flint and H. G. Dorsey, "and was confined to the higher parts of the higher mountain

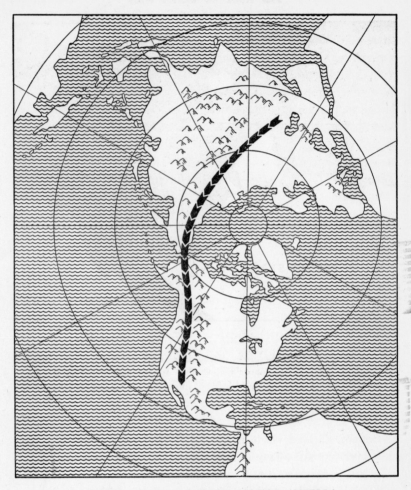

A GREAT-CIRCLE ROUTE TO NORTH AMERICA

On the flat, distorted map of Mercator on page 4 the path of early man across Asia to the New World seems a roundabout curve. On a globe it is very nearly a great circle. This is indicated on a map such as this, projected from a point above the North Pole. From above Bering Strait the route would appear still straighter.

ranges." [9] Secondly, the land-bridge, which made crossing easy, also altered the climate of Siberia south of the bridge.[10] It cut off the arctic currents and therefore to some extent the arctic damp which now makes the Asiatic coast inhospitable. Hrdlička—one of the first and most violent opponents of early man in America—said that the land-bridge was not essential. Even if it had existed, "man would not have used it, but would have followed the much easier route over the water." [11]

Three Roads to the South—with One Detour Once in Alaska, man —early or not so early—had a number of routes to choose from. If he was of maritime habits, and crossed by water, he would have tended to stick to his boats, and sail or paddle southward and southeastward down the coast and on through the inland passages of lower Alaska and Canada which protect boats from ocean storms. When Frank C. Hibben found a certain early kind of spear point in a curio shop in Ketchikan, Alaska, and on the far-away shore of Cook Inlet, he called attention to a route—whether overland or by sea—which hardly anyone had stressed except Hrdlička.[12] Hrdlička stressed it because he brought man over after the glaciers and in boats. But even in the Great Ice Age this route was not impossible for men without boats. Migrants who had crossed by a land-bridge might have turned south along the Pacific shore, climbing and crossing the ice barriers of the glacial rivers that still slide slowly down from the inland mountains. Philip S. Smith points out that "ice surfaces allow fully as easy travel by sled and on foot as do the ordinary land surfaces." [13] But was there game, as well as fish, along the coast to lure the migrant on and to sustain him upon the journey?

Other men seem to have chosen to tramp and hunt eastward and northeastward from the strait. In this direction there were two main routes open to men and game. One route led up the narrow lowlands of the northwest coast to the mouth of the Mackenzie River and then south up its long valley. The other, and much more likely path for early man, was up the ice-free Yukon and its tributaries. These would have taken him eastward to the Mackenzie or southward through the plateau between the northern Rockies and the Coastal Range. Hrdlička thought the Yukon valley a most unpromising route because of the turbulent rivers and the noxious insects; but most students disagree with him and stress the abundance of fish and game. There can be no question that some parts of this route were used by early man—and extinct mammals, too. His ancient spear points have been found in the muck beds of Fairbanks mingled with the fossilized bones of elephant, bison, camel, horse, and an extinct jaguar once called the Alaskan lion.[14] Other early points have been discovered in western Canada in the area of the mountain plateau. In 1944 Frederick Johnson located fifteen camp sites in early soil levels along the route of the plateau corridor and found many varieties of artifacts. Among these were a few points, most of them fragmentary, the butts of which resembled those of an early type.[15] Following Johnson in 1945, Douglas Leechman found other sites and artifacts along this route in soils formed perhaps 9,000 years ago.[16]

The Yukon valley rivers could have taken early man to the Mackenzie and to the northern edge of the plateau; but during a large part of the Great Ice Age he still faced the gigantic fields of snow and ice that covered half of North America. Although ice journeys may not be so very difficult, and early man had learned to live in the chill of northern Siberia (the Eskimo of today proves that human existence is possible in a land of little sun and much cold), I cannot believe that he attempted to cross the icy wastes. A journey on foot across a thousand or two thousand miles of ice becomes a sheer impossibility if there is no provender to be found along the way. There was certainly no food for musk ox or mammoth, and therefore no food for man. Without game to hunt, he would not have felt the impulse to invade the ice fields.

Too many authorities have written as if early man made a free choice of routes through Alaska and Canada. Actually, the animals he hunted chose his route for him—doubtless many routes. Unless he had learned to spear and net fish, the first invader probably pursued a herd of mammoth or musk ox across the land-bridge or over the frozen ice of later winters. You in your armchair are likely to suggest that, once man was in Alaska, he turned south of his own free will and intelligence in order to avoid the cold. The first trouble with that line

MIGRATION ROUTES

The pathways available to early man, as mapped by Carl Sauer—to which have been added a problematical route by sea along the southern coast of Alaska and another down the corridor between the eastern Rockies in Canada and the coastal range. (After Sauer, 1944.)

of thought is that man had gone north in Asia. The second is that primitive man had no conception of where south lay or of the possibility of greater comfort there. At this point, you will probably say that, though he had no ideas about the nature of the south, he had brains enough to follow the sun. Unfortunately this would have spun him round like a slow-motion teetotum; for he entered North America in the neighborhood of the Arctic Circle where the summer sun moves in a great low circle, and sinks out of sight when winter sets in.

If you want to understand early man, and guess with some accuracy at why he came to the New World and how he happened to drift southward and eastward until he filled it, you must think of him as a wanderer looking for food. Game lured him on at random, and vegetation lured both beast and man. Man might eat his way through caribou country, and come upon the bison of another area. As he killed and wandered, he might go south or he might go east. But the animal—and the man who ate berries and roots and wild grains as well as meat—would move as the climate moved. The world has known many changes of climate and shifts of rain belts. Some of these have been extreme—in the Great Ice Age, for example—and some have been less marked. But they have moved the forests and the grasslands, and animals and man have moved with the vegetation.

During the past 100,000 years, glacialists believe that there were three periods when the inland ice melted sufficiently to allow the southward passage of both animals and man. The first was more than 75,000 years ago in the Sangamon Interglacial period before the time when the last, or Wisconsin, glaciation had covered the plains of Canada (see pages 22 and 23). During the Wisconsin, a corridor probably opened about 40,000 years ago along the eastern foothills of the Rockies, and another, perhaps a little later, down the plateau between the northern Rockies and the Coast Range. The third opportunity for man to penetrate from the north came somewhere between 15,000 and 20,000 years ago, when the final retreat of the ice sheets began in those same regions.[17] Perhaps the land-bridge was still usable up to 10,000 years ago, but certainly later migrants had to cross Bering Strait by water or winter ice.

Bering Strait and the great glaciers were not the only obstacles to the peopling of the Americas. The Isthmus of Panama must have presented quite a problem to the pioneers who were to fill Amazonia and the Andean Highlands and to reach Cape Horn. Today nobody sets off blithely by foot through the jungle that separates Costa Rica from Colombia. The beach is the best pathway at low tide; but it is an intermittent one. It is better to hope that the shifts of climate which were involved with the glaciers made Panama a drier country than it is today.

Of course it was not only early man and his prey that used the routes from Siberia across Bering Strait and through Alaska and Canada. The later migrants—ancestors of the Algonquins, the Athapascans, and others—undoubtedly came in the same way.

Problematical Roads to the New World   Other routes from other lands may have brought other migrants. These routes are not so fanciful as the paths from Atlantis and Mu, but they have had few advocates. M. R. Harrington has mentioned the possibility that Magdalenian man of Glacial or Postglacial Europe may have crossed from Europe to Canada by way of Iceland and Greenland and various ice- and land-bridges to father the Eskimo.[18] Ellsworth Huntington adds to the land-bridge over Bering Strait "wind-bridges" across the middle Atlantic.[19] Like Father de Acosta, he believes that storms may have blown occasional vessels to the New World. To suggest that unwilling mariners from the Mediterranean may thus have made one-way trips, he cites from Stansbury Hagar [20] striking resemblances between the zodiacs of Europeans and of the Mayas, Aztecs, and even Peruvians. Whether this matter of the zodiacs is fact or fancy, Huntington's unwilling voyagers could not have come much earlier than the birth of Christ. More fantastic were the claims voiced some years ago that the men who left skulls of Australoid or Melanesian type in the caves of South America reached that continent by a southern route across an Antarctic bridge of land and ice. Of much more serious importance is the possibility that the long-voyaging Polynesians, having negotiated the 5,000 or 6,000 miles that lay between their home on the edge of Asia and the Marquesas or Easter Island, would have tried occasionally to continue their eastward course. If they had done so, they could

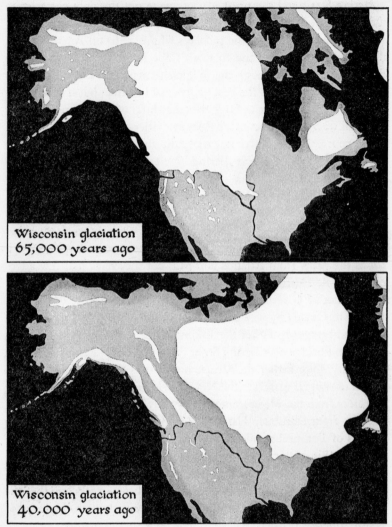

Wisconsin glaciation
65,000 years ago

Wisconsin glaciation
40,000 years ago

GLACIERS AND ICE FIELDS

These maps follow the outlines of the continent today, and so do not show the land-bridge from Alaska to Siberia that existed in varying extent throughout the entire Wisconsin period. The maps indicate tentatively how the great white ice fields may have appeared in different areas at different times, producing an effect

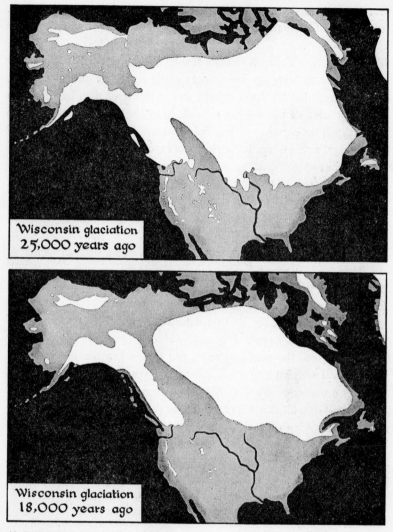

Wisconsin glaciation
25,000 years ago

Wisconsin glaciation
18,000 years ago

AS BARRIERS TO EARLY MAN

of shifting from west to east and then back across the continent. Drawn in 1936,
the first three maps probably show too little ice in arctic Canada and in the Gulf
of St. Lawrence and Newfoundland region. (After Antevs; the first three in Gladwin, 1937, the fourth from data furnished by Antevs.)

23

scarcely have missed South America. But this was in our own era, not in the time of early man.

Ware Dogma! Today we have a few facts about early man and many guesses. Not so long ago there were many reputable anthropologists who believed that the New World was innocent of man before 1000 B.C. Now most of them grant a foothold at least 10,000 years ago to an enterprising savage—called Folsom man—whose taste for travel was as great as his talent for making an exceptionally fine and original type of stone spear point. Some say he came to the New World 25,000 years ago. A few daring students find traces of an earlier Australoid human who may have seen the last glaciers taking shape. Well informed opinion places man's entrance into the New World between 10,000 and 25,000 years ago.

Of course we must not expect early dates to be precise. Whether we stand with Herbert J. Spinden in the corporal's guard that still believes man came to America no earlier than 2500 B.C., or join the far larger group of anthropologists who give man 10,000 more years in America, we must realize that dates become somewhat a matter of guesswork when we are back beyond written history. As we go deeper and deeper into the past and reach the time when the glaciers were waxing and waning, five or ten thousand years one way or another becomes a matter of opinion. To gain a perspective upon such toying with time—as well as upon early man in the Americas—we must next consider the story of early man in the Old World. Incidentally, its contradictions and uncertainties—prefaced by a few in New World prehistory—may help you to look with a charitable as well as critical eye upon certain theories about the peopling of the Americas which may be suspect today yet respectable tomorrow.

3

THE DEAD HAND OF THE AGES

. . . systems into ruin hurl'd.

—Alexander Pope

Conflicts and Confusions   I am afraid that it may be a little hard for you, dear reader, to shake yourself out of the late Victorianism of your schoolbooks and accept the idea that someone discovered America at least 14,092 years before Columbus. It may be still harder for you to believe that he was not that noble yet very vague red man whom you and your teachers called the American Indian. Certainly you will be shocked to hear that two or three anthropologists of note believe he had more than a touch of Negroid or Australoid blood. Your horror will be no greater, however, than that of a few of our archaeologists; such notions give them what might be called Victorian vapors. Others accept ideas like these; and others keep an open mind, for they remember that many a scientific fact of today was sheer nonsense to earlier generations, and *vice versa*.

As late as 1900, the prehistory of Mexico was accounted for very neatly by three successive words, Toltec, Chichimec, and Aztec. Now we know other words, and we know that other peoples and other cultures—Olmec, Zapotec, Mixtec, Totonac, Tarascan, Teotihuacan— also played an important part. We divided the Maya just as neatly into the Old Empire and the New, one south and the other north. Now we know that there were no empires, and that the Maya race grew widely and steadily towards fruition and decay. Once we thought that the Itzá were the Maya that founded Chichén-Itzá in Yucatan. Now we

25

give the name Itzá to the Mexicans or Mexican-influenced invaders that came hundreds of years later. Once scientists disputed whether culture and agriculture began in the highlands of Mexico or in the highlands of Peru. Now certain of them believe that the American became a farmer in the lowlands east of the Andes, while others think he began to till the soil in many spots at the same time. Only a few years ago, we thought that a fairly recent Indian culture—which is called the Woodland Pattern of the eastern United States—had its roots in Middle America. Now its pottery is being traced back through northwestern Canada and northern Asia to the Baltic and even perhaps to Africa.[1] The Mound Builders were once thought an ancient people. Now some of them seem barely to antedate the discovery of America. Bernal Díaz del Castillo—best of the chroniclers of the conquest of Mexico—may have observed that the Mexicans, along with all the Indians of the New World, were ignorant of the principle of the wheel; certainly this has been repeated over and over again for many years. Yet in 1888 Désiré Charnay reported and pictured a Mexican pottery toy with wheels, and since then more of these toys have been found.[2] Throughout his life Roland B. Dixon denied the possibility of productive transpacific migration from Polynesia to South America; yet at the end he accepted the transfer of the sweet potato from South America to Polynesia. From important matters to trivia, the list is long; I have hardly touched it. Obviously, prehistory is not a field where truth is easily and quickly come upon. The student, quite as much as the scientist, must keep an open mind. He must neither cherish dogma nor refuse speculation. Truth still lies afar off.

Doubts about early man in the Americas seem to have been an occupational disease with archaeologists. Geologists have found it much easier to accept him. Men like Ernst Antevs, M. M. Leighton, Kirk Bryan, and Albrecht Penck, perhaps because they are accustomed to dealing generously with time, seem to have little trouble in embracing early man as a Late Glacial interloper anywhere from 15,000 to 100,000 years ago. Physical anthropologists like Earnest A. Hooton and Sir Arthur Keith, and cultural anthropologists and ethnologists like Roland Dixon and A. C. Haddon are not at all afraid to recognize signs of Australoid or Negroid ancestry in the skulls of New World man. Perhaps it is easier for the geologists and the physical anthropologists to accept such ideas because they do not run counter to their own dogmas. Many archaeologists, at any rate, find it extraordinarily hard to adjust themselves to evidence which does not fit accepted theories. They may defend themselves by pointing out that the evidence is not too clear, or at best is merely suggestive; but the theories they cherish arose from no firmer evidence in many cases, and frequently continue quite as unclear or at best merely suggestive. Certainly such reluctance to accept new evidence held back archaeological research when Aleš Hrdlička, W. H. Holmes, and Daniel G. Brinton were in their heyday.

This reluctance to face facts permeated even so great and productive a man as Baron Erland Nordenskiöld. An example of such a Jovian nod may be salutary. Arguing in *The Copper and Bronze Ages in South America* against the theory that the craft of metallurgy may have been brought to the New World by migrants, instead of having been invented here, three times he cites facts that contradict his thesis, and three times he offers a kind of self-conscious apology for blinking them. (The italics are mine.)

If we go through all our material of weapons and tools of bronze and copper from South America, *we must confess* that there is not much that is entirely original, and that to the majority of fundamental types there is something to correspond in the Old World.

It must be confessed that there is considerable similarity between the metal technique of the New World and that of the Old during the Bronze Age.

Bronze is, of course, also a very hard invention, and *I must confess* to finding it most remarkable that the art of alloying tin and copper should have been hit upon independently both in the Old World and the New.[3]

"Admissions," said Charles John Darling, "are mostly made by those who do not know their importance."

Unfortunately there are still a few archaeologists whose attitude resembles Nordenskiöld's. Hooton writes of one of these:

One of our most brilliant and once progressive archaeologists naïvely expressed to me some years ago his sentiments on this question [evidences of early man in America]. He said it would be a pity to have new evidence come to light which would overthrow all the admirable scientific work of the past indicating the recent arrival in the New World of the American Indian.[4]

Of course early man is not a subject that can hope to be free from error and contradiction—even early man in the Old World. Perhaps an account of some of the errors and misconceptions about him that crept into the study of prehistory may be as good a means as any of preparing your mind for new facts or new heresies in the Americas.

The Problem of the Ages   The first confusion that confronts the student of early man is one of nomenclature. It is a by-product of the human animal's inveterate and estimable love of system. Give us some new subject, such as prehistoric relics, and we immediately set up a scheme of classification. The scheme works beautifully for a while, but presently new evidence accumulates which doesn't fit the framework. By that time, unfortunately, it is too late to change the classification. In vulgar parlance, it is our story, and we are stuck with it.

An outstanding example of this tendency to set up a classification system prematurely is the division of the story of man into ages. As far back as A.D. 52 a Chinese with a scientific bent of mind suggested that man had passed through three periods: a stone age, a bronze age, and an iron age. A French magistrate named Goguet wrote a book in 1758 in which he expounded a similar order of ages, inserting copper ahead of bronze. In 1813 a Dutch historian named Vedel-Simonsen argued for stone, bronze, and iron periods in Scandinavian history. A Dane, Christian Jurgensen Thomsen, gave the system permanent and indeed international status in 1836 when he arranged on this basis the exhibits of the institution he directed, the National Museum in Copenhagen.

The scheme is neat but far from scientific. To begin with a small matter, but one that may confuse the layman, the ages overlap. Bronze did not wholly replace stone; neither did iron. The use of chipped flint and polished stone continued into the Iron Age.

The Bronze Age—a Phantasm   "Bronze Age" itself is a misnomer and a phantasm. While "Stone Age" and "Iron Age" do define important culture periods—though not the only periods of man's early activity—the Bronze Age, says T. A. Rickard, "represents a minor phase in the use of copper." [5] This alloy is merely an incident in the much longer history of the first metal used by man. At the start copper seemed to him to be merely a soft stone. He beat it into ornaments. When he began to melt and cast the native metal instead of pounding it, he took the first step in the true use of metals; but when he smelted copper ore—turning a hard rock into a soft metal—he made himself the master of metallurgy. Bronze—at first the accidental mixing of copper and tin—was merely an episode along the way. "The superiority of copper or bronze over flint and stone tools is, I think," says Gordon Childe, "generally overestimated. Not only for tilling the land but also for the execution of monumental carvings and even for shaving, the Egyptians of the Old Kingdom were apparently content with stone." [6]

The Bronze Age was very limited in area. Because of the rarity of tin, the primitive use of the alloy was confined to southern Europe, Asia Minor, and the Inca empire. Most of the world used iron before bronze. Furthermore, the Bronze Age is as delimited in time as it is in space. The earliest bronze is dated 2300 B.C., in the Danube region, and the earliest iron about 1350 B.C. at Gerar in Judea. "Thus," said Rickard, "the so-called Bronze Age shrinks, at most, to a mere millennium . . . the merest fraction of human existence." [7]

The Iron Age is not so significant as it sounds. It was many centuries after the first use of iron and bronze that either played a really important part in the economic life of man. Like the domesticated horse, the trained elephant, and the wheeled vehicle, bronze and iron were first used chiefly in the making of war.

Wood, Bone, and Shell Ages   There is another serious weakness in the Stone Age, Bronze Age, Iron Age sequence. It takes no account of the probability that man used wood, bone, and shell before he used stone. The ape swings a stick much as the first man must have done. The carcass of some bison or stag, picked clean by vultures, must have seemed to our earliest ancestors "a whole potential tool-shop"—as George R. Stewart writes in *Man: An Autobiography*—"thigh bones ready-made for clubs, horns or antlers for awls, shoulder-blades for scrapers." [8] As early as 1864, a British student of anthropology, John Crawfurd, stood out against Thomsen's Stone Age as the beginning of culture. At a meeting of the Ethnological Society, he said: "On man's first appearance, the most obvious materials would consist of wood and bone. . . . This would constitute the wood and bone age, of which, from the perishable nature of the materials, we, of course, possess but slender records." [9] Because the discovery of the stone artifacts of early man in Europe was then creating a scientific furore, Crawfurd's sane observations went unnoticed. Today we have a bone tool from the first half of the Great Ice Age and part of a wooden spear almost as old (see illustration, page 62).

Wood, bone, and shell not only antedated stone; they have continued in use until today. Certain primitive peoples—the Chukchi of Siberia, for example—retained the use of wood and bone after they were given iron.[10] Numerous tribes, when first encountered by explorers and navigators, had not yet begun to use stone; among these were the Aleuts, the Andaman Islanders, Malayans from the hills, and people of the upper Amazon.[11]

Rickard, from whom I have drawn liberally in this discussion, proposes a different scheme of classification for the cultures of man.[12] In the Primordial Age he would include the primary use of wood, bone, and shell. He would accept the Stone Age as the next stage. For the Bronze and Iron ages he would substitute the Metallurgic Age, basing this on the discovery and use of smelting, whatever the metal involved. The dead hand of Thomsen, however, will probably continue to rule. The best we can do will be to take the Stone Age as including all materials except metal, and pay little attention to that illusion the Bronze Age.

Dividing the Stone Age—the Old and the New   Still more conflict and confusion have resulted from attempts to divide the Stone Age into watertight compartments. In 1865 Sir John Lubbock proposed two divisions—the Paleolithic, or Old Stone, Age and the Neolithic, or New Stone, Age.[13] The Paleolithic included objects found in caves and glacial gravels; the Neolithic, on the surface and in tombs. The first period ran from some vague beginning hundreds of thousands of years ago up to the advent of the Neolithic after the glaciers had melted. By definition, paleolithic man made chipped stone implements and no other kind. Neolithic man was supposed to be distinguished by the making of ground, or—as we usually say—polished, stone axes and of other tools shaped by rubbing instead of chipping; agriculture, pottery, and textiles came in as secondary traits.

After a time, however, archaeologists found some disturbing discrepancies. Before neolithic man grew grain and wove textiles, someone of an earlier age seems to have been making axes from antlers, turning out new artifacts called microliths—tiny chips of flint which were set in a row along a wooden or bone handle to make a kind of saw or a sickle—and also producing a partially polished axe with a ground edge, and making crude pots. This was all very upsetting to the old scheme of dividing prehistory into the Paleolithic and the Neolithic. So science inserted the Mesolithic, or Middle Stone Age, between the two, in order to account for the appearance of the new tools.

The trouble with the system that Lubbock launched is that man's behavior toward stone is a very poor basis for classifying him in culture or time. For a while it fitted our knowledge of prehistory of Europe. Now it is out of line on that continent, and completely askew so far as the rest of the world is concerned. The kind of stone available often determines whether a man will chip or grind it. When first discovered, South Sea Islanders were polishing stone, and yet they had no other neolithic trait; the explanation was that they lacked flint.[14] Some Australian natives make chipped stone tools while their neighbors, who control a supply of diorite, go in for polishing; yet none of these Blackfellows can be considered as anything but paleolithic.

Like the Bronze Age, the Neolithic suffers from having shrunk in length. Rickard figures "that 700 years covers what was meant to be a major division of human chronology." [15] To reach this figure he puts the end of the Paleolithic at 3000 B.C., which seems much too late, and the beginning of bronze at 2300. Even though we use the date of N. C. Nelson for the beginning of the Neolithic—5500 B.C.[16]—we have a New Stone Age of only 3,200 years.

Gordon Childe goes so far as to declare that "there is no such thing as a neolithic civilization." [17] Different people, living under different climates and on different soils, have developed different elements of the culture of the New Stone Age and combined them with elements of other cultures.

If we are going to continue using the term Neolithic—as we certainly are—and if we want to limit it in some sensible way that may prove a bit more permanent, let us see what else than polished stone can be used to define it.

Activities of the New Stone Age   Three activities stand out. They are the making of pots, the weaving of textiles, and the planting and harvesting of crops accompanied by the domestication of animals.

There can be no question that pottery is an important factor in neolithic life. It was in the New Stone Age that man fully wrought the miracle of "a sort of magic transubstantiation—the conversion of mud or dust into stone," as Childe puts it. It was, as he says, "the earliest conscious utilization by man of a chemical change." [18] But behind this miracle and this science must have lain many years of almost accidental, adventitious experiment. L. S. B. Leakey claims specimens of partially baked pottery sherds in paleolithic Africa.[19] One of these shows marks of basketry, rather thin support for the theory that the women who daubed the inside of the baskets to make them hold water must have discovered, when the baskets stood too near the fire, a little bit about how to bake clay. It was not until the invention of agriculture tied neolithic man more or less to the soil that true pottery could and did flourish widely. We have added many refinements to the craft of the potter—porcelain, cloisonné, and so forth—but basically it remains unchanged. Incidentally, all agriculturists did not have pottery—the Big Bend and Hueco cave dwellers of Texas, and certain people of the Virú valley in Peru, for example.[20]

The craft of textile weaving almost reached perfection at the hands of neolithic man—or, rather, woman. But it stemmed from basketry, and basketry undoubtedly began in the Paleolithic Age.

The first of two interesting facts suggested by the foregoing is that woman was the only true begetter of the Neolithic Age. She did the weaving—first of baskets and then of textiles—and she invented and practiced pottery making. More than that, she must be credited with the planting and harvesting of grain; for, while her lord and master enjoyed himself on the hunt, she gathered fruits, nuts, and edible seeds, and sooner or later this led her to observe that seeds she carelessly dropped on the midden pile produced new and bigger plants. By so doing woman invented work; for early man was only an idler who gave himself intermittently to the pleasures of the chase. Woman also invented leisure—true, creative leisure—for out of agriculture rose a settled community and a surplus of provender which allowed the few to think and plan and build civilization.

Agriculture—Test of the Neolithic The second fact is that agriculture seems to be the only sound test of the Neolithic. Pottery and weaving preceded agriculture, yet, without agriculture and its fixed communities and its leisure, pottery and weaving could not have reached perfection. As for the polished ax, it was handy enough in in-fighting; but it was of no practical social use until the farmer needed to cut down the trees which began to thrive all over the place when the glaciers disappeared. The Badarians of Egypt were farmers, yet they made no polished axes because there was almost no timber to cut.[21]

Speech was certainly the first great inventive triumph of primitive man. The making of fire ranks second. The third great invention, agriculture, was also the first industrial revolution; without it what we carelessly assume to be *the* industrial revolution would have been impossible.

Science feels sure that agriculture appeared in the Old World before it did in the New, but is not so certain as to where man first tilled the soil and when. James H. Breasted, Sr., put agriculture back to 18,000 B.C.; later writers push it up to 5000 B.C. There has been quite as much disagreement about the area where agriculture began. At first the valley of the Nile seemed to be the right spot, for every fall the flood waters of the river brought not only automatic irrigation but also fresh, fertile soil to enrich the depleted farm lands. Soon, however, the birthplace of agriculture moved to the "fertile crescent" that stretched from Egypt to Mesopotamia. Later it shifted from the Tigris-Euphrates valley to the valley of the Indus. Now it seems to lie somewhere between these two, perhaps in the dry highlands of Iran and Iraq. In northern Iraq, 400 miles north of Ur, the wild ancestors of certain of our cultivated grains still grow, and excavators have come on evidences of farming communities which may be 8,000 years old.[22] There has always been hot argument between the supporters of denuded river valleys and the supporters of dry uplands as the natural site of early agriculture. Lately students have begun to argue for forested or jungle areas, and above all for mountain valleys; and they have plumped for tubers and melons, rather than grains, as the first crops cultivated by early man. These students see man as a gardener before he was a farmer.

Only the beginnings of agriculture are of any importance in a discussion of early man. Early man may invent agriculture, but thereupon he promptly ceases to be early man. With the food, leisure, and fixed abode that farming provides, he is soon inventing writing. He is then no longer even prehistoric.

First a Food Gatherer, Then a Hunter   It is important to realize and remember that early man ate seed grains, tubers, and fruit before he knew how to cultivate them. Probably he began to eat more and more of these natural products just before he became a farmer. Because archaeologists have found evidences that early man was quite a food gatherer at the end of his career, they have been inclined to set up another classification system which is faulty. They see man first as a hunter, then as a food gatherer who was still a hunter, and then as a food producer. This ignores the very important fact that man began as a food gatherer and not as a hunter.

When the first man climbed down out of the trees he was probably still eating the food of a great ape—fruits, nuts, roots, and berries—and perhaps grubs and insects. Occasionally he may have varied his repast with birds' eggs and fledglings. Erect on solid ground, with a broken branch for a weapon, he improved his diet a bit. He knocked over small animals, and he may occasionally have got hold of the carcass of a large one before a saber-toothed tiger arrived on the scene;

but, for thousands upon thousands of years, he was basically a vege-
tarian. His first well developed stone tool—the hand ax shaped rather
like a flattened and pointed egg—was probably more useful for grubbing roots and tubers out of the ground than for killing animals. As
early man learned to make more efficient weapons—first the curved
throwing stick, then the spear and the spear-thrower, and finally the
bow and arrow—hunting became his chief activity, and meat his chief
diet. But his women went right on gathering berries and nuts, tubers
and seeds, and getting ready to invent agriculture. Certainly in the
New World—perhaps in the Old World, too—she invented milling
stones to grind seeds while her man was still a paleolithic. Perhaps
when she watched the wearing away and the smoothing down of
mortar and pestle, milling stone and mano, as she ground her seeds
into flour between them, the idea may have occurred to her—or to her
man who watched her labor—that it was possible to grind and polish
stone into axes and other implements.

I feel that the life-story of prehistoric man can best be divided—
certainly for the purposes of this book—into a Paleolithic, or Old
Stone, Age, which included the making of artifacts out of wood, bone,
shell, and chipped and sometimes polished stone, and a Neolithic, or
New Stone, Age, which was defined by the invention of agriculture
and the perfecting of pottery, of weaving, and of the polishing of
stone. This may reduce a little the confusions that are inevitable in
the study of early man tens of thousands to hundreds of thousands of
years ago. Conflicts of evidence and opinion will remain, of course.
We need not let them deter us from judging early man in the Americas. Indeed, they should free us from paying too much heed to the
dogmas of scientific conservatism.

4

THE GREAT ICE AGE

*Speak to the earth, and
it shall teach thee.*

—JOB 12:8

Our Part of the Geologic Time-Scale The dead hand of another
system of classification lies across a still larger area than the Stone Age
itself or the Age of Man. This area is the entire life of our earth since
it took sufficient shape to support cellular life. As it is so large an area
and much of it is so remote in time, changes in the definition of most
of its various divisions do not much affect the present discussion.

Once upon a time there were four great divisions, neatly numbered
in Latin as the Primary, the Secondary, the Tertiary, and the Quaternary. The first two went by the board when newer scientists found
older ages and stretched the life of the earth a couple of billion years.
The Tertiary is still a respected appellation, but the good name of
the Quaternary—the area of time with which this book is mainly
concerned—is seriously questioned. Defined as the Age of Man, it
was supposed to harbor all evidence of his existence; but hints of his
presence in the Tertiary have rather sullied the scientific standing of
the later period.

In this book we are concerned with two divisions of the Quaternary
which are also growing vaguer in outline, less precise in time. They
are the Pleistocene, or Glacial, Period, or Great Ice Age, and the
Holocene, Recent, or Postglacial, Period in which we now live. (If
your Greek is rusty, you will be amused to discover that those scientific-

36

	PALEONTOLOGICAL DIVISIONS	GEOLOGICAL DIVISIONS	DURATION IN YEARS	CUMULATIVE TOTALS (Round Numbers)
CENOZOIC ("recent life")	Quaternary Age of Man	Holocene ("wholly recent") Pleistocene ("most recent") or Great Ice Age	25,000 1,000,000	1,000,000
	Tertiary Age of Mammals	Pliocene ("more recent") Miocene ("less recent") Oligocene ("little recent") Eocene ("dawn of recent")	14,000,000 20,000,000 15,000,000 20,000,000	70,000,000
MESOZOIC ("middle life")	* Age of Reptiles	Three periods	120,000,000	190,000,000
PALEOZOIC ("ancient life")	* Age of Fishes, Amphibians, and Primitive Marine Invertebrates	Six or seven periods beginning with the Cambrian	310,000,000	500,000,000
PROTEROZOIC ("earlier life")	Age, presumably, of soft-bodied animals	Pre-Cambrian	1,250,000,000	1,750,000,000
ARCHAEOZOIC ("primordial life")				
EOZOIC ("dawn of life")	Problematic signs of life, indicated by presence of carbon			
UNRECORDED INTERVAL SINCE THE ORIGIN OF THE EARTH			Unknown	2,000,000,000 to 10,000,000,000

THE LIFE STORY OF THE EARTH

This summary of the story of the earth is a combination of charts in Arthur Holmes's *Principles of Physical Geology* and Earnest A. Hooton's *Up from the Ape*, with modifications by William C. Putnam and James Gilluly. *The divisions marked with an asterisk used to be called, respectively, Secondary and Primary.

sounding terms are merely translations of "wholly recent" and "most recent.") Most geologists believe that these two areas of time covered about 1,000,000 years; but some give them half a million more, and a few limit them to the 600,000 years of the last four glaciations. Some start the Postglacial 25,000 years ago, when the ice began to shrink toward its present limits; some start it 9,000 years ago, when a relatively modern climate appeared. Some geologists say we are still in the Pleistocene, and merely enjoying a warm spell before another glaciation.

By definition—or lack of it—the Pleistocene is rather vaguely bounded, and quite as much at its beginning as at its end. To the paleontologist, the Pleistocene is the time of certain large and picturesque mammals that are now extinct. To the geologist, it is the time of the waxing and waning of the great glaciers. The beginnings and the ends of these two definitions of the Pleistocene do not correspond too closely. I shall use the term as little as possible, substituting the Great Ice Age.

The Glacial Hypothesis Appears   It is hardly more than a century since science began to realize that large parts of Europe and North America once were covered with glaciers. The discovery came from attempts to explain certain disturbing things called "erratic blocks." These were large masses of stone—sometimes weighing as much as 10,000 tons—which had no business being where they were, because the native rock in their neighborhood was entirely different. Some of the erratic blocks, for example, should have been hundreds of miles up an Alpine valley. The common explanation was that they were water-borne, perhaps by the biblical flood. An American cotton manufacturer accounted for the wearing away and the scratching of such boulders by supposing that they had been embedded in the lower surfaces of icebergs and then swept scraping across the earth by the tumultuous waters on which the Ark had ridden. In 1802 John Playfair, a professor of mathematics at Edinburgh, ventured the theory that the blocks had been transported by glacial ice.[1] This idea had occurred to a mountaineer named Kuhn in 1787, and Saussure echoed it in 1803; they knew and interpreted correctly the moraines of loose stones and boulders which they saw at the foot and the sides of the glaciers. From 1821 to the middle thirties various French, Swiss, and German scientists—Brard, Venetz, Charpentier, and Schimper—discussed and amplified this idea. Though A. Bernhardi, an obscure German professor of forestry, suggested in 1832 that "the polar ice once reached clear to the southernmost edge of the district which is now covered by those rock remnants," [2] it was not until 1837 that the glacial theory took definite shape. Then Louis Agassiz, speaking before a Swiss society, launched the glacial hypothesis that there had been a period of great cold just before the advent of recent life. By 1840, when Agassiz published his *Studies of the Glaciers,* the idea was pretty generally accepted; he had "added the Glacial Epoch to the geological time-table." The theory has been much amplified since then.

Adolphe Morlot, in 1854, discovered fossils of temperate plants between layers of glacial deposits, and advanced the theory that there had been warm periods as well as cold ones during the Great Ice Age. In his "Notice sur le Quaternaire en Suisse" he suggested three separate glaciations with two warm interglacial periods between. In 1874 James Geikie, the geologist of Edinburgh, brought out his *The Great Ice Age and Its Relation to the Antiquity of Man,* building upon Morlot's work; and his *Prehistoric Europe,* in 1881, expanded the glaciations to six. Yet for thirty more years some stubborn scientists still believed in a single glaciation.

It was not until the turn of the century that the work of Albrecht Penck and Eduard Brückner established the history of the Alpine glaciations on a solid scientific foundation that has endured pretty well till today. They found four major glaciations and named them in neat alphabetical order after four Alpine valleys—Günz, Mindel, Riss, and Würm.[3] They divided the Würm glaciation at first into two periods of activity, and later into a number of smaller oscillations toward the end. There has been some controversy over the subdivisions of the Würm, and one to three Danubian glaciers have been suggested hundreds of thousands of years before the Günz; but the general hypothesis brought forward by Agassiz and the amplifications of his successors are now definitely established. With all this goes much knowledge of the ice sheets that covered Scandinavia, northern England, and Germany as far south as Dresden, and North America from ocean to ocean and down to Long Island and the Ohio and Missouri rivers.

The End of the Great Ice Age   Authorities agree that the last melting of the ice sheets and glaciers in the Alpine region began somewhere between 20,000 and 15,500 years ago. After considerable shrinkage and oscillation, the ice increased again for about 5,000 years, and then began to shrink once more. There is some disagreement as to when the Great Ice Age ended; the last and very minor Daun glaciation has been rather rashly dated as late as only 3,500 years ago. These calculations are only for the Alpine region, and we must remember, of course, that the great ice sheets of northern Europe and North America behaved somewhat differently.

We have some fairly exact knowledge about the retreat of the ice across Sweden. This has resulted from the theory of Baron Gerhard de Geer that the varves—layers of alternately coarse and fine clays deposited in lakes in front of the retreating glaciers—represent the summer and winter sediments released by the melting ice. (We have a somewhat similar index in the tree-ring count of wide and narrow rings originated by A. E. Douglass and improved upon by Harold S. Gladwin. Both tree rings and varves may reflect changes in solar radiation.) De Geer counted the varves and determined that the ice sheet began to retreat in southernmost Sweden some 14,000 years ago, and Ragnar Liden determined that it had disappeared by 6840 B.C.

De Geer's Swedish-American pupil, Ernst Antevs, applied the same system in North America, and found the ice beginning to retreat from Long Island 36,500 years ago.[4] A calculation of the time required for the wearing away of the postglacial Niagara Gorge has produced about the same result, but this has been seriously challenged by Richard F. Flint.[5]

The picture of glaciation is more complicated in North America than in the Old World. Europe had two main areas of ice—a small one in the Alps, a much larger one in Scandinavia, the British Isles, north-

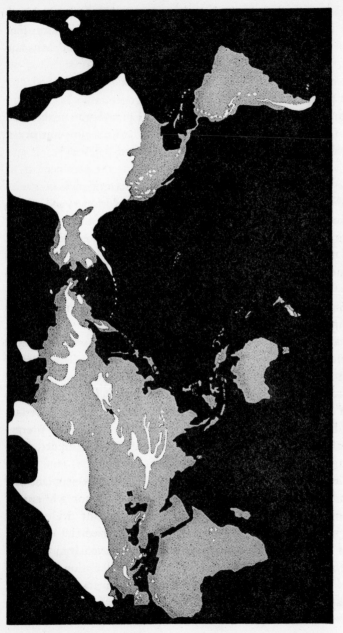

THE ICE FIELDS OF THE LAST GLACIATION

At the height of the last glaciation 5,000,000 square miles of North America were covered with ice, as against 2,500,000 in Eurasia. The volume of ice was three times as great. The shore lines are those of the present rather than glacial time. (Map after Flint, 1947; Antevs, 1928, and Flint and Dorsey, 1945; estimates from Daly, 1934.)

ern Germany, and Poland—but they were self-contained. North America had three ice centers—the Labradoran east of Hudson Bay, the Keewatin west of the bay, and the Cordilleran in the Canadian Rockies; these three sheets of ice did not always grow or shrink at the same time or at the same rate, and they occasionally overlapped (see maps on pages 22 and 23).

Incidentally, most of the ice of the glacial period was in the New World. The area of land covered was almost twice as great as in the Old World, and the bulk of ice three to five times as great.[6]

River Terraces and Beach Lines   There are other evidences of glaciation besides varves, erratic blocks, moraines of stones and mixed debris along the sides and fronts of the ice streams, and scratches and polish on the native rock over which the glaciers passed. Four raised terraces are found along the sides of many river valleys. Four raised beach lines, first found in the Mediterranean region, have now been noted in the Americas and Australia. Submerged beach lines and land-bridges have been found at certain places under the ocean, as well as deep channels prolonging present rivers far out to sea.

Naturally enough the Great Ice Age was a time of notable changes of climate. Vegetation advanced and retreated widely. The level of the sea rose and fell some hundreds of feet. Whether or not there was more rain and snow—a moot point with science—the many rivers of the world grew in volume, and often in speed, at certain times and became low and sluggish at others. These profound alternations created the river terraces which have aided so much in determining the age of man and his various cultures. As the ocean sank, while the glaciers grew, the slopes of river beds became steeper, and the rivers themselves grew swifter. Because vegetation was widespread and vigorous, the turbulent rivers could not greatly widen their courses, but, instead, cut deeper channels and carried the displaced materials far down their valleys and ultimately even into the sea. During the cold, dry period at the climax of each glaciation, the dying trees and brush and grasses released their grip on gravels and silts, the intermittent flood waters of the melting glaciers carried away the debris and—because the rivers lost in slope and grew sluggish as the

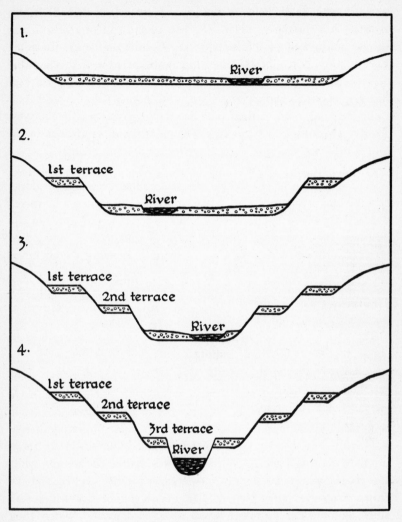

THE AGE OF RIVER TERRACES

These simplified sections of a river valley show how successive channels were cut deeper and deeper, leaving the older deposits of gravels and silts in the higher terraces at the sides. The discovery of this habit of nature was of the greatest value in determining the age and the succession of the cultures of early man in Europe. The oldest flint tools were found in the gravels of the highest terraces, and the newest in the lowest.

sea level rose—they deposited the gravels and silts in their beds. As the glaciers grew again and the oceans sank, the rivers once more became swifter and more turbulent, cut deeper channels, carried away part of the gravels and silts, and left the rest as terraces. Thus the passing of each glaciation meant the adding of a new and a lower terrace to the river valleys. Four such sets of river terraces are found just outside the areas where the glaciers have been active—in the valleys of the Rhine, the Thames, the Somme, the Isar, and other rivers.

Farther to the south, periods of great rainfall produced similar river terraces in valleys like the Nile. The concentration of masses of ice in central and northern Europe upset the zones of climate of Africa and other parts of the earth and caused great climatic disturbance. Rainfall belts moved far south, and the rain increased in violence. Such periods of rain are called pluvials. There is still a good deal of argument about whether pluvials occurred principally in glacial or interglacial periods. This affects the dating of early man, and it is particularly important to us in the New World.

The raised beaches and the submerged beaches were obviously caused by the lowering and raising of the sea level and not of the land. There were land movements, of course—as there are even now— but they were either too small or too irregular to account entirely for the systematic arrangement of old beaches in many parts of the world.

There has been much controversy about other glacial matters, but there can be no question that the submerged beaches and the land-bridges were a by-product of glaciation. The great masses of ice— estimated to have averaged 9,000 feet thick in North America and 5,000 in northern Europe—depressed somewhat the parts of the earth on which they lay; the rest of the land tended consequently to rise a bit, though not enough to account for sunken beaches and the land-bridges that united Africa and Europe, England and the Continent, England and Iceland, Alaska and Siberia. It was the immense amount of sea water drawn up and locked in the glaciers that reduced the area of the ocean and created new shore lines and the land-bridges.

Estimates of how much the seas were lowered range from 70 to 1,800 feet; the best are 200 to 300 feet.

The raised beaches belong to a later discussion of the cause of the Great Ice Age as a whole.

The Cause of Glaciation   Most geologists believe that a comparatively slight drop in temperature would bring back the glaciers and the ice fields. The German geologist Brückner calculated that summers in the last glaciation were only 4° centigrade, or about 7° Fahrenheit, colder than they are today.[7]

What could have caused this slight drop in temperature in the Great Ice Age? Most of the explanations are not satisfactory. One is that the earth happened to pass through a dust laden nebula that reduced solar radiation. Another is a hypothetical decrease in the amount of carbon dioxide in the atmosphere. Other explanations have to do with changes in the altitude of land, shifts in air currents and ocean currents, volcanic eruptions filling the air with dust that screened the rays of the sun. All these adventitious causes would have had to be repeated with the curious and complex rhythm which is characteristic of the waxing and waning of the ice sheets.

One theory seems to have a good deal of cogency. It depends on three known alterations in the relation of the earth to the sun. The first is a slow, regular change in the shape of the earth's orbit through a cycle of 92,000 years. The second is a shift in the inclination of the earth's axis through 40,000 years. The third is what a layman would call the wobble of this axis through 21,000 years. The first change increases or decreases the distance of the earth from the sun. The other two alter the angle of the sun's rays and thus also increase or decrease the warmth given a particular area of the earth at certain seasons. No single unfavorable position would have had a great deal of effect in lowering summer temperature in the northern hemisphere, but two occurring at the same time—let alone three—would have appreciably diminished the sun's heat.

This astronomical theory of the cause of glaciation goes back a hundred years. As long ago as 1842 the French mathematician and astronomer J. Adhémar suggested that changes in the earth's axis increased rainfall and provided the floods which he thought had moved the erratic blocks. Between 1864 and 1875 James Croll com· bined the wobble of the earth's axis and the change in the earth's orbit. A number of other men worked unsatisfactorily on the problem. The Serbian astronomer and physicist Milutin Milankovitch combined all three, and, between his first publication in 1913 and his latest in 1938, calculated the variations of solar radiation for the past 650,000 years.[8] In 1924 W. Köppen and A. Wegener applied Milankovitch's early figures to the glaciation question, and Frederick E. Zeuner has lately used the revised figures of Milankovitch. Zeuner's results, somewhat simplified, appear on page 47. They are fairly close to the geological estimates of B. Eberl and W. Soergel; his last two glaciations extend further back than those of Penck and Brückner.[9] Zeuner's dates do not agree, of course, with those of an extremist like the geologist Kirtley F. Mather, who dates the first, or Günz glaciation, as ranging from 2,000,000 to 1,500,000 years ago.[10] Zeuner's findings work out well enough for the American glaciations, except that there is no New World equivalent for his first Würm maximum of 115,000 years ago. Many authorities refuse to accept any such condition in the Old World. Because of this glaciation Zeuner moves back the appearance of *Homo sapiens* a good 50,000 or even 75,000 years.

There is one serious objection to Zeuner's theory. Two of the three movements of the earth on which it is based would have reduced the warmth of summer in the northern hemisphere, but they would at the same time have increased the temperature of the southern hemisphere, thus alternating glaciation in the two hemispheres. Unfortunately, it is fairly well established that glaciers north and south of the equator have waxed and waned at the same time over a considerable number of years.

It is not enough, of course, to find the cause of the individual glaciations. There must be a cause for the glacial period as a whole. The Great Ice Age was an almost unique event in the history of the earth. We have to go back 200,000,000 years, to the time of the reptiles that preceded the dinosaurs, before we come again on major glaciations.

Zeuner states frankly that the astronomic theory "does not provide

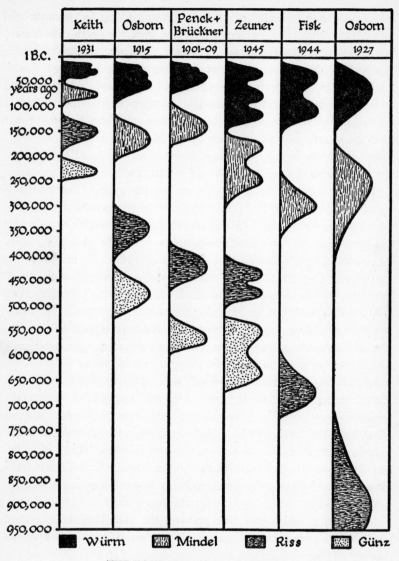

Keith	Osborn	Penck + Brückner	Zeuner	Fisk	Osborn
1931	1915	1901-09	1945	1944	1927

1 B.C.

50,000 years ago
100,000
150,000
200,000
250,000
300,000
350,000
400,000
450,000
500,000
550,000
600,000
650,000
700,000
750,000
800,000
850,000
900,000
950,000

■ Würm   ▨ Mindel   ▧ Riss   ▦ Günz

THE FOUR GREAT GLACIATIONS

Six varying estimates of their duration made by five authorities. Fisk's are
of the New World glaciers, which are generally equated with those of Europe.

the cause of the Ice Age" as a whole.[11] Some added factor must be found. One which he considers is a migration of the north pole from the direction of the Pacific to its present location; but Zeuner and others think the movement occurred before the Great Ice Age. Certainly the former position of the pole would have prevented glaciation in Europe, but not in North America. Another theory—that of continental drift, the movement of America westward from Europe—has been suggested; but it does not bring North America or Europe nearer the polar regions. Another explanation is a general decrease in solar energy; Zeuner holds this in reserve for lack of evidence.

A theory accepted by some present-day geologists seizes on the possibility that the heat of the sun may have changed from time to time, and uses it in a curious, almost paradoxical way. The author of this hypothesis, Sir George Simpson, believes that the great masses of ice resulted from an increase instead of a decrease in temperature.[12] As the weather grew slightly warmer, cloudiness and rain and snow increased, the snow-line fell, and glaciation resulted. As the weather grew still warmer, the ice melted. (Simpson demonstrated the basic principle of this through an ingenious laboratory experiment.) His glacial theory, which is explained in more detail on the opposite page, postulates two increases in solar energy, and draws from them a meteorological pattern that provides the four glacial and three interglacial periods. The first and last interglacials would be warm and wet, the second cold and dry. Zeuner objects to this theory on the ground that the last interglacial—which, according to Simpson, should have been warm and wet—was mainly cool and dry.[13] But, while it may have been cool and dry in the German area which Zeuner has most closely studied, other areas probably had other climates. Simpson's hypothesis would account for the heavy rains, or pluvials, of Nilotic Africa, which may link up with the glaciations of Europe; but he provides only two pluvials, and there are evidences of three or more in Africa.

Zeuner has an explanation of why the periodic decrease in the heat from the sun produced glaciation during the last million years and not for 200,000,000 years before. He introduces the geological factor called Eustatism,[14] meaning by it simply a progressive drop in sea

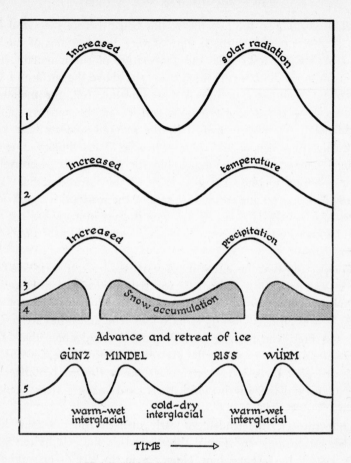

GLACIATION THROUGH WARMTH

A somewhat modified graph of Simpson's theory of the cause of the Great Ice Age. The following summary by Carl Sauer includes quotations from Simpson: "(1) Increased solar radiation received by the earth leads to increase in the general circulation of the atmosphere, which forms a great cloud blanket and causes increased precipitation in appropriate areas. In particular, in high latitudes and altitudes there is increased snowfall, which gives rise to glaciers. Bitter weather does not produce great snowfall or glaciers. (2) 'As the radiation increases still further, the ice melts away and we have overcast skies and much precipitation but no ice accumulation.' (3) 'When the solar radiation decreases, conditions are reversed and the whole sequence is gone through in reverse order.'" (After Simpson, 1938. Quotation from Sauer, 1944.)

level. According to the hypothesis, this began before the Great Ice Age, and was caused by the sinking of very deep portions of the sea floor. As the sea level sank, the temperature of the mountains and plains dropped also, for the higher we rise above the surface of the ocean the cooler the air grows. The snowline fell, the mountain glaciers grew larger, and the snow and ice on the northern plains could not be completely melted by the reduced summer heat, and gradually grew deeper and more extensive. Thus the lowering of general temperature made it possible for the periodic decrease in solar radiation to cause the glaciations of the Great Ice Age. The theory of a general and steady lowering of the sea level is based on a series of four raised beaches occurring uniformly in many parts of the world. Other students believe these terraces were products of a regional rise of land.

Considering that the Great Ice Age ranges back at least 600,000 years—and probably 1,000,000, if we credit evidence of three earlier Danubian glaciations—it is small wonder that scientists are not entirely agreed on many factors in its story. "The difficulties are such," says the French archaeologist A. Vayson de Pradenne, "that after fifty years of study to which the greatest geologists have devoted all their energies, there is no certainty yet as to the exact number of glaciations and the way in which the faunal changes are related to them." [15]

Unfortunately, the student of early man in America must lean heavily on geologic and faunal theory, and do the best he can with what knowledge is given him. However, in the face of uncertainties and of conflict of opinion, he may at least weigh the evidence and make his choices without too much reverence for established theory in his own field.

5

EARLY MAN IN THE OLD WORLD

Bone of our bone, and flesh of our flesh,
are these half-brutish prehistoric brothers.

—WILLIAM JAMES

Archaeology, a New Science Archaeology—digging up the ancient past—is a fairly young science. It is not so young, of course, as electronics or aerodynamics or radiology. It is not so old as astronomy or mathematics or metallurgy. Excavation began in 1748 with the uncovering of Pompeii; but it was hardly scientific, and it reached only a short distance into the past. The deciphering of the Egyptian hieroglyphics in 1819 and of cuneiform writing in 1837 pushed back history two or three thousand years. But deep explorations of man's prehistoric past won no serious status until the middle of the nineteenth century. "In 1859 prehistoric archaeology," says Gordon Childe, "may be deemed to have become a science." [1]

There were discoveries before that, but they were neglected and misinterpreted or despised and disputed. As early as 1690 a man named Conyers discovered "opposite Black Mary's, near Gray's Inn Lane," London, a fossilized tooth which, we now know, belonged to an extinct elephant, and a crude hand ax of stone which, we now admit, was made by man fairly early in the Great Ice Age; but it was long before they won an honored place in the British Museum. A friend of Conyers named Bagford thought that the elephant belonged to the Roman army of the Emperor Claudius, and that the flint was a weapon used by a Briton to slay it (see illustration, page 52).

In 1797 John Frere reported to the Society of Antiquaries on the finding near Hoxne in Suffolk of "weapons of war . . . in great numbers" together with "some extraordinary bones, particularly a jawbone of enormous size." His discovery has been called as important, in its way, as the geographical discovery of a New World; by emphasizing "the situation in which these weapons were found," he became the first man to apply modern archaeological methods to a prehistoric find. Frere boldly declared that the hand axes belonged to a "very remote period indeed; even beyond that of the present world." ² (See Illustration page 60.)

The first hand ax found and recognized, probably an Acheulean implement, discovered in London in 1690 together with the tooth of an extinct elephant. The tool is about six inches in length. Like almost all hand axes, it is thinner than it looks from this angle. (After Sollas, 1911.)

Frere's reasoning had little effect, however, on a certain type of mind. When in 1823 William Buckland, a teacher of geology who was to become Dean of Westminster, dug out of a cave near Paviland a female skeleton which was painted with red ocher—a peculiar habit of early man and of man not so early—and which lay beside some ivory rods and bracelets and the skull of a mammoth, Protestant prejudice got the better of science. Buckland wrote that the skeleton was "*clearly* not coeval with the antediluvian bones of the extinct species" with which it had been found. Like Bagford, he turned to the time of the Roman invasion. His "Red Lady of Paviland" became a camp follower, and thus he missed his chance to recognize the first Cro-Magnon skeleton of man from the last glaciation.³ Yet religious dogma —which held back Victorian science for so many years—did not prevent Father John MacEnery from seeing the true significance of a flint tool and the tooth of a rhinoceros which he found under a layer of stalagmite in Kent's Cavern, England, in 1825. Around 1830 Tournal, a French scientist, and Schmerling, a Belgian, saw the truth as clearly, and published their discoveries of man-made flints with the fossils of extinct animals.

The most important find, and the one that ultimately established Glacial man as a reality, was announced in 1838 at a meeting of the Société d'Emulation of Abbeville in northern France; but twenty years passed before it received scientific sanction. The discoverer was an inconspicuous tax collector, Jacques Boucher de Crèvecœur de Perthes, who matched his diversified name by writing tragedies, novels, and books on travel, economics, and philanthropy. He had explored caves as early as 1805 and had found fossils and man-made tools of flint, but no hand axes. The hand axes that he found in the river terraces were hardly as important as his theory that these terraces dated the tools, and that the terraces were formed far in the past when the rivers were swollen with water. His only mistake was that he went to the biblical flood to find the water instead of to the great glaciers. In 1849, after making other finds, Boucher published *De l'Industrie primitive, ou Les Arts et leurs origines,* dated 1847; more finds and other books followed. His hand axes and other discoveries were almost completely ignored until 1858 when the English geologist Hugh Falconer "happened to be passing through Abbeville and saw the collection." [4] He brought British colleagues back to Abbeville, and in 1859 Falconer, Sir Joseph Prestwich, and Sir John Evans declared officially for the reality of glacial man. The finds of Boucher, they asserted, proved that human beings had existed at the same time as Pleistocene mammals now extinct. Significantly, it was the same year that Darwin published *On the Origin of Species by the Means of Natural Selection.*

Mortillet's Cramping Classification   Progress thereafter was rapid, perhaps too rapid. Notable finds were soon followed by attempts to freeze knowledge into chronologic classifications. R. Rigollot, Gabriel de Mortillet, Edouard Lartet, Milne-Edwards, and Henry Christy found in the river terraces and the caves of France innumerable and varied evidences of man's activity in the Great Ice Age. Mortillet named various cultures from the places where stone tools were found, and then, in 1869, he set them up in a chronological series.[5] Modified by later discoveries, the series runs as follows, beginning with the oldest: Chellean, Acheulean, Mousterian, Aurignacian, Solutrean, and Magdalenian. (Many prehistorians use the word Abbevillian instead of Chellean because later research proved that the tools found originally at Chelles were Acheulean in type, while those found at Abbeville were earlier.) In the light of present knowledge, the list is much too simplified. It is based only on European finds, yet it is supposed to fit the world picture. For more than fifty years it has served as a scientific straitjacket, patched with new material here and there, but still gaping at the seams as the husky young giant of archaeological science grows in stature.

Enter the Eolith   One of the early difficulties that Mortillet's list of cultures encountered was the discovery of implements that preceded his first culture, the Chellean—or Abbevillian—in time and type. Cruder axes from older levels had to be called Pre-Chellean (see illustration, page 60). In England scrapers and other crude tools cropped up in formations that go back more than 500,000 years.

Then eoliths—"dawn stones"—appeared. They were irregular-shaped pieces of flint with chips knocked off here and there. Often the chipping looked purposeful; the flakes made an edge or a point that could be used to scrape or drill.

Time scale of early man in a limited area of Europe, as estimated by Robert J. Braidwood.

These rudely shaped flints were first championed by Abbé Louis Bourgeois in 1863;

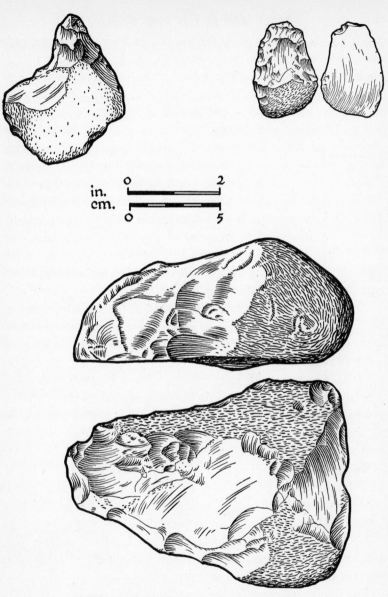

in. ⊢0———————2⊣

cm. ⊢0———————5⊣

THE "DAWN STONES" OF EARLY MAN

Upper left, a borer. Right, two sides of a scraper. Below, side view and bottom of a rostrocarinate. (After Peake and Fleure, 1927, Moir, 1927, and Lankester, 1912.)

but his finds were in strata far too old to win scientific recognition. This was not the case with the Englishman Benjamin Harrison, who recognized eoliths in later formations some eighty years ago. Harrison was one of that variegated and comradely group of country "antiquaries"—noblemen and shopkeepers, vicars and village laborers—who founded and developed the study of the prehistory of England. Harrison left his old-fashioned general store and its cakes, fruits, and draperies, to walk the High Downs of Suffolk, searching with utter conviction for traces of early man in the glacial gravels. He began as a youth, when Boucher de Crèvecœur de Perthes had only just won his battle, and in 1865 he recognized his first eoliths. In 1889 the distinguished scientist Sir Joseph Prestwich gave them his backing. It took twenty more years, however, for the eolith to win anything like respectable recognition, and some still deny that these flints were worked by men.

The fact that some eoliths were found in geological formations much older than man—so far as we know his history—was an argument against all of them, particularly because the most recent were quite as artificial-looking. Another cogent objection was that eoliths could have been made by natural forces, such as a landslide, the pressure of heavy strata, or one stone knocking against another. A heavy cart can make an eolith when it rolls over a smooth flint. But in spite of arguments and antagonisms, which still persist, there were two things that seemed to establish the eolith as the work of man.

To begin with, some kind of tool, some form of experiment, had to lie behind even the crudest hand ax. At first man must have picked up a natural eolith and used its cutting edge. A little later he must have improved the edge. In any case he threw the stone away when he had finished the job, and later looked for and improved another one. Gradually he developed his dawn-stone technique and made tools that he would use until he lost them.

The second argument for the dawn stone was impressive. In 1910, after years of search, J. Reid Moir found eoliths near Ipswich, England, under unusual conditions. They came in two layers, which seemed to indicate that early man had camped twice in this neighborhood at different times. They were bedded in soft sand and therefore could not have been chipped by geologic pressure. The sand dated from the Pliocene Period which preceded the Great Ice Age. Later, in the same district, he found eoliths in a layer of delicate shells— again a sign that the eoliths had not been chipped by natural forces.[6] Moreover, many of Moir's eoliths had a new and peculiar shape; they were keeled like an upturned boat or beaked like an eagle. Sir Ray Lankester called them rostrocarinates. In 1900 Mortillet had to admit man—or pre-man—to an Eolithic Age.

Flake vs. Core Industries   More difficulties beset Mortillet and his system of names and cultures as time passed and as fellow scientists dug new caves and terraces, and turned up stone tools of other patterns and other periods. Implements appeared that did not fit into the Frenchman's classic system. A supplementary scheme had to be devised, and soon it, too,.failed to fit the facts.

The new system divided all paleolithic tools into two types—which was sound enough—and assigned each type to certain peoples and to those peoples only—which proved not so sound. The division lay between cores and flakes. It lay between tools that had been made out of the heart of a lump of flint, and tools that had been made from chips flaked off the lump. The fact that there were core tools and flake tools was plain enough, but the fondness of scientists for strict classification led the prehistorians into theories that time disproved.

First of all, they had to set up a time sequence. They decided, not unnaturally, that man must have begun by hammering things with a handy rock until his rude tool began to chip away into something approaching an edge and eventually a point. Thus the hand ax, or *coup de poing,* came into being (see illustration, page 60). In the course of time man began to notice the chips, and to use the larger ones to cut and scrape with. Soon—that is, after a couple of hundred thousand years—he was deliberately knocking flakes off a stone core, and using them for spear points as well as scrapers. The prehistorians called hand axes the products of a "core industry," and chips the products of a "flake industry." They believed that one industry had preceded the other by hundreds of thousands of years, and that the Chellean and Acheulean had stuck to cores and left flakes to the Mousterian. And they believed that certain cultures had devoted themselves exclusively to the core, and certain others to the flake.

The theory that the early stone workers had a core industry and the later ones worked flakes was rudely upset by the discovery of flaked tools—called Cromerian—in an English stratum as old as the French sources of the first hand axes, and possibly older. Some say they lie at the beginning of the Great Ice Age or at the end of the earlier period, the Pliocene. This demonstration of a very early flake industry was reenforced by the discovery of a special type of flaked tool—the Clactonian—which runs from late Chellean into Acheulean times. Another type—the Levalloisian—laps over from the Acheulean into the Mousterian. Moreover, core tools and flake tools are found side by side in most European cultures.

Furthermore, the core industries and the flake industries would not stay nicely separated. The first excavators had found only hand axes because these tools were so much more interesting than scrapers; later students found flake tools in the same ancient levels. No hand axes turned up in Clactonian culture-sites, but they appeared at the end of the Levallois, and the flake-loving Mousterians made them for a time. "Flake and core run parallel to one another in time," says W. B. Wright, "and even intermix." [7]

If we do not try to apply the core-versus-flake theory too broadly and too strictly, it suggests a fascinating picture of two kinds of men and two kinds of life through the first two-thirds of the Great Ice Age. One kind dominated during the cold of the glaciations; the other, during the warmth of the interglacials. For the flake tools of the Clactonian and Levalloisian peoples are found mainly with the fossils of cold-loving animals in the north and east of Europe, and the core tools of the Chellean and Acheulean peoples with warmer-blooded animals in the west and south. Two kinds of man seem to have advanced and retreated in time with the ice.

Science accepted Mortillet's system of orderly cultures and the theory of successive core and flake industries, and for fifty years tried to apply it to new discoveries both in Europe and elsewhere. Though

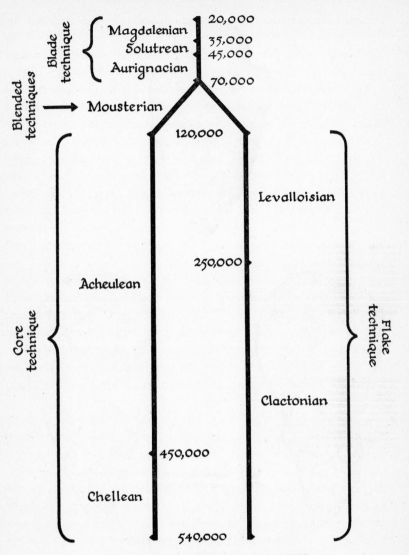

THE MAJOR PALEOLITHIC CULTURES

A chart of the core, flake, and blade-making peoples, devised and dated by Robert J. Braidwood. The heavy lines have to do only with dates, and their junction does not indicate a fusion of cultures. The Solutrean was distinguished for double-faced, leaf-shaped projectile points, rather than blades.

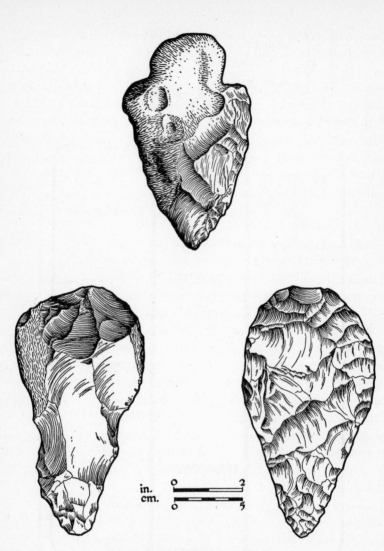

MAN'S FIRST PERFECTED TOOL

Three European hand axes that may bridge 300,000 years. They are, top, Pre-Chellean, left, Chellean, and, right, Acheulean. The last is one of the tools found by John Frere at Hoxne in 1715. Most hand axes are not so well formed. Some-what similar tools have been found in neolithic American cultures hafted at the top of a wooden handle or in the middle as a sort of spokeshave. (After Osborn, 1915, Leakey, 1935, and Burkitt, 1933.)

the system has had to be modified in parts, and in parts abandoned, its terms are still used, and used in a way that is confusing because the terms are no longer exact. In Africa the various types of tools resemble only approximately those of Europe, though they do not seem to correspond in time. The hand ax spreads south from Spain into almost all Africa, and eastward into southern India, but there are plenty of flaked tools, too, in these regions. Central and northern Asia seem to be devoted to the flake, and to eschew the hand ax in favor of a kind of chopping tool made out of a core. Asia, like Africa, has tools made out of large, smooth pebbles.

Dating Early Man in Europe One good thing can be said for Mortillet's sequence of Chellean, Acheulean, Mousterian, Aurignacian, Solutrean, and Magdalenian. It may not be complete enough, and it may not apply too well to the world outside Europe; but it is chronologically sound in that area. It is a succession of cultures along a time scale. If an archaeologist finds two or more varieties of paleolithic tools in a new site, he finds, for example, Acheulean beneath Mousterian, or Mousterian beneath Aurignacian. Similarly, when he comes upon Chellean and Acheulean in separate terraces of the same river, he always finds the Chellean in a higher terrace than the Acheulean, and, as I have explained on pages 43 and 44, the higher terrace is always the older.

Dating these cultures in terms of our years is another matter. The first step is fairly simple. If the tools are found with the fossils of a warmth-loving animal like the hippopotamus, they belong to an interglacial period; if they are found with the fossils of an animal like the hairy mammoth, which could survive a harsh climate, they belong to a glacial time. The species of animal may determine which glacial or which interglacial. If the tools are found in the

Magdalenian
Solutrean
Aurignacian

Mousterian

Acheulean

Chellean

20,000
35,000
45,000
70,000

120,000

450,000

540,000

gravel of a certain river terrace, then they belong to the geological period when the material of the terrace was being laid down. The terraces often contain fossils, and this may cross-date the terrace materials
with cave deposits. But scientists are often faced with the problem of
picking the right glacial or interglacial period on scanty evidence, and
the still more difficult problem of setting the period in the terms of our
years. There is room here for much disagreement. Glaciologists do not
agree as to the age or the length of the various glacials and interglacials (see illustration, page 47). Some prehistorians accept and use
the dates of one glacialist; some choose another's. They do not all
concur as to which culture came in which glacial period.

Chellean and Acheulean Man   Chellean man had some flaked tools—
which may have been used for scraping—but his chief output was the
hand ax. It was rather thin and not too well formed. Undoubtedly
he also used wood and bone; but the only evidence we have today is

Ancient implements of bone and wood.
Left, part of the thigh bone of a mammoth, shaped by Chellean man, and found
at Piltdown, England, in the same deposit
as the famous skull. Right, part of a
wooden spear, its point hardened by fire,
found at Clacton-on-Sea, England, and
probably made by Acheulean or Mousterian man. (Left, after Dawson and Woodward, 1917; right, after Crawford, 1921.)

part of a femur of an elephant which has been rather crudely shaped
to a point. Some put Chellean man in the first interglacial about
500,000 years ago. Some move him up 200,000 years into the second
interglacial. Some even place him in the third. Perhaps he lived
through all three. At any rate he liked a fairly warm climate.

So did Acheulean man, who followed him. Perhaps they both re-
tired to Africa during the glaciations.

The Acheulean made a better hand ax, and various kinds of scrapers,
gravers, and cleavers. It was probably he who left us part of a very
crude wooden spear at Clacton-on-sea, though some date it a little
later. The particular interglacial in which Acheulean man lived depends on which one is assigned to the Chellean.

We are not too sure about the physical appearance of the men we
call Chellean and Acheulean. There are no dependable skeletons to
help us, and not even complete skulls. All we know of the shape and
size of these early Europeans must be guessed from parts of five or six
craniums, a jaw that may have belonged to one of them, and a jaw
that certainly did not. The first of the skulls and the questionable jaw
were found at different times near Piltdown, England. Except for
three fragments of another Piltdowner, they are all we have of *Homo
eoanthropus dawsoni* (Dawson's Dawn Man). The
skull is closer to man than to ape, and the jaw is
nearer ape than man. Some say they belong together;
some say not. A few think the skull is relatively recent. The partisans of Piltdown Man think he may
have been pre-Chellean or Chellean, the time- and
culture-area now covered by Abbevillian. Another
piece of skull is also English, from Swanscombe,
and it is Acheulean rather than Chellean. The
second jaw is the jaw of Heidelberg man, found under 80 feet of sand. Some put him in the first interglacial as a Chellean; many think he may have been
ancestral to the Neanderthal man who belongs in the
third interglacial. The Swanscombe skull, a similar
but questionable one—the Galley Hill from England—and parts of a cranium found at Charente,
France, in 1947 seem to a number of scientists to
have the cranial characteristics of *Homo sapiens.*
This is the modern type of "thinking man," identified much later as Cro-Magnon, who inhabited Europe during the last glaciation. In spite of the

Swanscombe, Galley Hill, and Charente evidence, we cannot be sure how much Chellean and Acheulean men differed from the men with low foreheads and heavy brow ridges who have turned up in Java and China as representatives of an earlier time—or, for that matter, from the Mousterians who came into Europe just before the last glaciation.

Ancient Man in Java and China   In the 1880's a Dutch army surgeon named Eugène Dubois decided to go to Java to find a kind of ape-man that the great German scientist Ernst Haeckel had envisioned fifteen years before. In 1891, beneath ancient deposits of the Solo River, Dubois discovered what he was looking for—or perhaps a slight improvement on it. What he found was the skull top, two molar teeth, and a thigh bone of a thing which was much more man than ape, but which received the name *Pithecanthropus erectus* (erect ape-man). For some years the skullcap of this Java man—a handier name—stood alone as the only fossil of really ancient man. Now it has been joined by portions of three other adults from the same geological level and the cranium of a child from a still older level, the discoveries of G. H. R. von Koenigswald. Reconstructions of Java man give us a fellow with a low sloping forehead, no chin, not much room for brains, and a very prominent ridge of bone above his eyes. This human of 300,000 or more years ago probably looked a good deal like the most primitive of modern men, the native Australians, who seem to have miraculously and uniquely survived without much change from the beginnings of *Homo*.

Java man—who is either pre-Chellean or early Chellean—has a slightly younger relative in Peking man, also beetle-browed. The first finds were made in 1929 about forty miles southwest of Peking in the Choukoutien Cave on Dragon Bone Hill. Since then parts of about forty men and women have been dug out. We now have four skulls that are more complete than those of Java man. We also have 148 teeth and thirteen jaws, and some odd pieces of other skulls. We have fire hearths and a large number of implements, ranging from eoliths to hammerstones and crude choppers and scrapers. We also

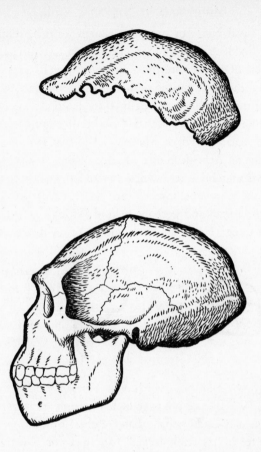

JAVA MAN—Pithecanthropus erectus

Except for two molars and a thigh bone, the skullcap above was all that Dubois first found of Java man. The reconstruction, actually the right side of the skull, has been reversed for comparison. (The skullcap after Osborn, 1915; the reconstruction after Weinert, 1928.)

have some fossil bones of monkey, baboon, ostrich, rhinoceros, and mammoth, besides animals common to China today. The most interesting bones, of course, are those of man himself, and our concern with them is increased by the odd and disturbing fact that the thigh bones had been cracked for their marrow as only a man could crack them, and the skulls had suffered violence. If Peking man was not a cannibal, he had a neighbor who was. And that is probably true for the Chellean and Acheulean men of Europe. But, at least, Peking man, like Java man, stood erect, which is more than can be said of the Neanderthal.

Behind Java man and perhaps behind Peking man, too, may lurk a giant ancestor. There are four pieces of evidence. The first is

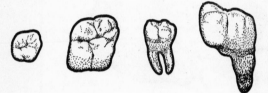

Gigantopithecus—giant ancestor of man? A normal human molar contrasted with one of a number of teeth found in a Hong Kong store. (After Koenigswald, 1947.)

Pithecanthropus robustus, which von Koenigswald found in Java about 1939 (see illustration, page 68); the teeth are larger than man's and the bone is unusually thick. Later, Robert Broom found in Africa a jaw with teeth "relatively huge." [8] In 1941 von Koenigswald came across teeth and a part of a jaw that were even larger. And between 1935 and 1939 he discovered in a Hong Kong apothecary's shop three molars that had six times the cubic capacity of our teeth. All these teeth had definitely human characteristics. Of course height is not necessarily equated with the size of teeth; the orangutan has larger teeth than man.

The Progressive Neanderthal   In Africa there is evidence of man— and of manlike ape—as old as the Chellean and the Acheulean and perhaps older; Australia provides two skulls from the last interglacial. But let us get back to Europe and the next culture in Mortillet's scale.

This is the Mousterian; we know it better by the name of the place in Germany—Neanderthal—where, in 1856, the first Mousterian skeleton was found. It took thirty years for this skeleton to win scientific recognition, but now we have about a hundred admitted specimens.

The Neanderthal was not a pretty spectacle. He had the low forehead and heavy brow ridges of Java and Peking man, and the same lack of chin; his jaw stuck out, and, unlike those Asiatic men, he seems not to have been able to walk quite erect. And yet he was the cleverest fellow that had ever lived, and the most sensitive, which may seem rather odd, since some of the earlier skulls found in England, Africa, Java, and Australia come nearer the modern type of what we call thinking man, *Homo sapiens*.

On the evidence we have, the Neanderthal seems to have been the inventor of religion. In his caves we find burials for the first time, and burials accompanied by tools for the dead man to use in the other world. We also find shrines made of the skulls of cave bears.

As a chipper of flint, he was much more skillful than those that had gone before. He soon gave up making tools which, like the hand ax, would serve a number of purposes, but none very well. He invented the spear point. There is still considerable argument about his flint work, or at least about the technique which he may or may not have developed.

When man began to make tools he pounded one rock with another. He hoped he would knock off just the right chip in the right spot. This is called the percussion method of flaking (see illustration, page 70). Some say the Neanderthal was not content with this. They think that he must have discovered how to place a piece of bone or very hard wood against a flint at the point where he wanted to knock off a flake, and then strike it with a hammerstone (see illustration, page 71). This might account for the small chips, or "retouches," taken off the edge of some of his spear points as in

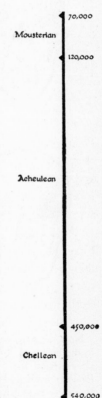

70,000

Mousterian

120,000

Acheulean

450,000

Chellean

540,000

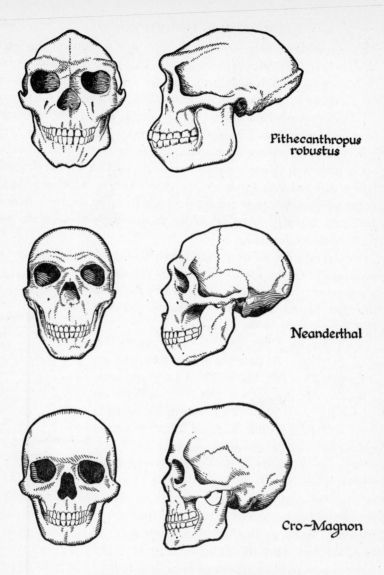

THREE TYPES OF OLD WORLD MAN

Note the progressive lessening of brow ridge and jutting jaw and the increase in the height of forehead and vault. *Pithecanthropus robustus* was found in the same general area as *Pithecanthropus erectus,* or Java man, and was probably a forebear leading down from still larger forms. (*Robustus,* after Weidenreich, 1946; Neanderthal, after McGregor, 1926; Cro-Magnon after Verneau, 1906.)

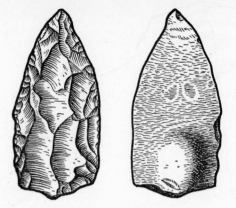

MAN'S FIRST SPEAR POINTS

Two views of a flake of flint which has been chipped on one face and retouched along the edges by a Neanderthal man. To remove the tiny lateral chips he probably held it with the smoother side against a chunk of wood, and struck small and careful blows with a hammerstone (as shown at the bottom of page 70). Acheulean man may have used this technique in making the best of his hand axes. (After Mortillet, 1881).

the illustration above. Even the Acheuleans are occasionally credited with this invention because many of their hand axes are so symmetrical. There are those who say that the Neanderthal had progressed so far in flint work that he knew the art of pressure flaking—the third step in flint knapping—which involved the pressing off of small chips with the bit of wood or bone held in the hand (see illustration, page 72). It seems more likely that Neanderthal and Acheulean men used the anvil method of percussion flaking (lower drawing, page 70), not an inaccurate way of knocking off small chips.

The Neanderthal—or Mousterian—seems to have invaded Europe from Asia toward the end of the third and last interglacial, anywhere from 80,000 to 125,000 years ago, and to have left from 15,000 to 100,000 years ago, depending on what authority you choose, and how that authority dates the last interglacial. Unlike his predecessors, the Neanderthal lived in caves; but that was probably because he was

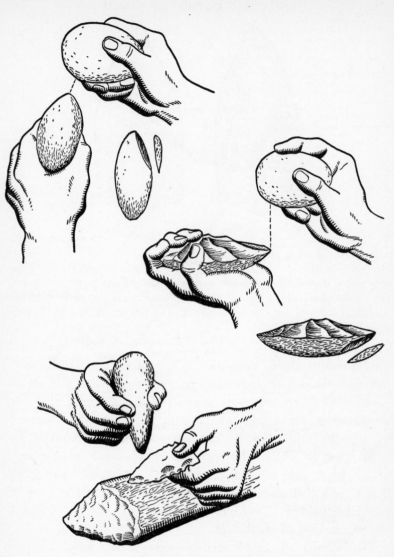

PERCUSSION FLAKING

The first method by which early man shaped his tools. (After Holmes, 1919.)

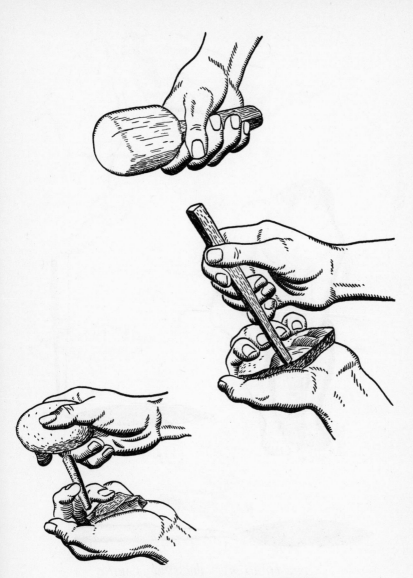

THE SECOND STEP IN FLINT KNAPPING

For more accurate work, early man applied a small stick of hard wood or a piece of bone at the proper spot and hit the interposed tool with a mallet of heavy wood or a rock. No one knows who invented this technique—Acheulean, Neanderthal, or later man. (After Holmes, 1919.)

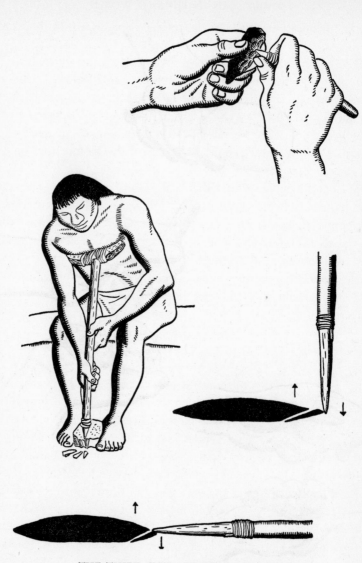

THE THIRD STEP—PRESSURE FLAKING

The discovery which gave early man complete control over the shaping of flints was that a slow and continued pressure would dislodge just the flake he desired. Above, we see how he worked on a small point, and, below to the left, how he chipped thin slivers from a core. (After Holmes, 1919.)

the first man in Europe to survive a glacial winter—tens of thousands of them.

The Neanderthal seems to have disappeared quite suddenly from Europe, taking his Australoid features with him. There are traces of him in Africa, and also in Palestine where he is thought to have produced a hybrid among the Mount Carmel people. Sir Arthur Keith said, in 1915, that the Neanderthal never left Europe, but was merely absorbed into the next peoples. We can see the Neanderthal profile on an occasional passer-by.

Most anthropologists are rather cool to the Neanderthal. They cast him quite outside the sacred ranks of our ancestors. They say he was not *Homo sapiens*—merely *Homo neanderthalensis*. This means that he was a sort of dead end, a blind alley, up which one sort of ape-man ran, while another was taking a turn that ended in his being master of the atom but not of the atomic bomb. Other anthropologists do not agree. Like Keith, they take the Neanderthal into the sacred circle— at least at stud.

Homo Sapiens—New or Old?   The relationship of all these forms of early man is much disputed. For many, many years they were all supposed to be barren offshoots of our ancestral tree. Nobody could find the particular breed of ape-man from which we were descended. Now science is inclined to lump most of them together in one way or another. There are many theories and many genealogies. Piltdown man, descending through Swanscombe man, plays grandfather to *Homo sapiens*. Java man and Peking man become the forebears of the Mongoloid. Other men from Java father the Australian, and even the Neanderthal. The Neanderthals breed out their stooped stance in some sort of union with *Homo sapiens*. Or all of them are admitted to the ranks of Homo, with poor, stooped Neanderthal a degenerate offshoot without issue.

The earlier picture was simpler and more dramatic. From *Pithecanthropus erectus* to *Homo neanderthalensis*—Java man to the Neanderthal—these creatures bore no relation to our own happy breed. Then, quite suddenly, came *Homo sapiens* in the person of the Cro-

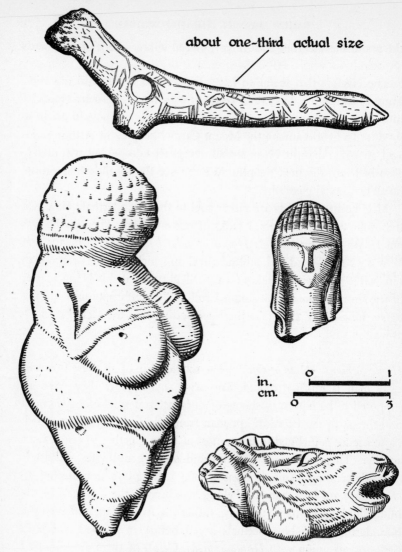

about one-third actual size

in.
cm.

0   1
0   3

SCULPTURE OF THE OLD STONE AGE

Above, one of the carved and perforated reindeer antlers of the Magdalenians that are sometimes described as *bâtons de commandement;* the Eskimos used a similar tool. Left, the Venus of Willendorf, an Aurignacian carving in stone, found near Spitz, Austria. The woman's head from the Grotte du Pape, Brassempouy, France, may be either Aurignacian or Magdalenian. The horse's head, made of reindeer antler, from Mas d'Azil, France, is Magdalenian. (After Osborn, 1915.)

74

Magnon. He was the kind of tall fellow with a well domed, narrow Nordic head whom Hitler identified with the better class of human beings. Except for the "Red Lady of Paviland," the first specimens were found at Aurignac, France, in 1852, though nobody recognized the outstanding quality of the skulls until the find at Cro-Magnon, France, in 1868 (see illustration, page 68).

For many years the French clung to what Hooton calls the rather chauvinistic myth that here, in the waning years of the Great Ice Age, we find a superior kind of man that was predominantly a product of the French area. Certainly he was a remarkable person in many ways. For one thing, he discovered art. He painted on the walls of his caves and carved on pieces of bone and elephant ivory pictures of mammoths, bison, and boars, and he made sculptures of fat women in stone. Also, he began to fish in the swift streams that ran off from the glaciers. He hunted reindeer and made use of their antlers as tools. For quite a time he was supposed to represent the peak of achievement by early man.

Aurignacian   45,000

Mousterian   70,000

                 120,000

Acheulean

                 430,000

Chellean

                 540,000

Before long, however, the Cro-Magnon became only a factor in a broader culture, described as the Aurignacian, and soon the Aurignacian suffered from scientific fission. Through this whole period and, indeed, until the end of the Old Stone Age, new tools in the form of blades, chisellike burins, and implements of reindeer bone make their appearance; but they vary in shape and in the time of their emergence. Some of these tools divide what was formerly called the Aurignacian into three parts: the Châtelperron, the Middle Aurignacian, and the Gravettian. The Châtelperron people developed a narrow, curved blade out of a tool vaguely Mousterian. The Middle Aurignacians appeared as invaders with thin blades and scrapers notched or narrowed halfway along each side. Finally, a people who had hunted mammoths in southern Russia—the Gravettians—turned up in France as the inventors of a thin, narrow, and straight blade made by carefully detaching sliver after sliver from a well shaped core of flint. Sometimes one edge was blunted to make it handier to use; occasionally the point of a blade or other tool was chipped off diagonally to produce a chisellike engraving tool. Another type of tool, the Font Robert point with a stem, also appeared (see illustration, page 80).

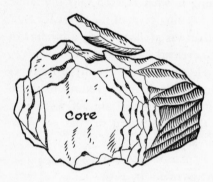

How blades were split off a core. The technique was perfected by the Gravettians, an Aurignacian people, and was practiced by the Aztecs of Mexico. (After Evans, 1872.)

Just as I have used the older term Chellean instead of Abbevillian, in this rather brief and generalized account of the Old Stone Age, I shall use the term Aurignacian in a general sense to include the bulk of European culture between the Acheulean and the culture that followed the Gravettian.

Henry Fairfield Osborn once dated the European advent of the Aurignacians at about 27,000 years ago, Nelson at 20,000, Mather at 15,000.[9] Zeuner, however, believes they flourished from about 100,000 until 75,000 years ago.[10] Dating the last of the glaciers is the key to this dispute.

The Aurignacians are a variegated lot, which argues further for subdividing them. One specimen, the tall, high-domed Cro-Magnon, is variously credited with producing the modern European man, the Eskimo, and even the Indian of America. Another specimen, the Grimaldi from the Riviera, is distinctly Negroid. Another—from hints in several places—seems to be Mongoloid. Apparently, the Aurignacians were almost variegated enough to have peopled the modern world. But almost as much could be said for the inhabitants of

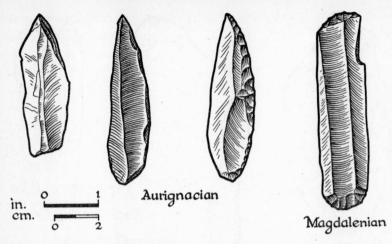

in.
cm.
Aurignacian

Magdalenian

Upper Paleolithic tools from long flakes taken off cores after the manner shown on page 76. The burin, or graver, at the left is probably Upper Aurignacian, though commoner in the Magdalenian culture. The others are usually called blades. (The burin, after Burkitt, 1933; the blades, after MacCurdy, 1924.)

an upper level in the Choukoutien Cave near Peking. There, in one spot, they divide nicely into Negroid, Eskimoid, and Melanesoid.

Solutrean Flint Workers Invade Europe   After the Aurignacians comes a remarkable people called the Solutreans. They appear quite suddenly as invading hunters, and they disappear as suddenly. Their

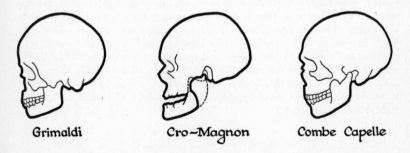

Grimaldi   Cro-Magnon   Combe Capelle

Three Aurignacian types that suggest the Negroid, the Caucasoid, and the Mongoloid. (After Peake and Fleure, 1927.)

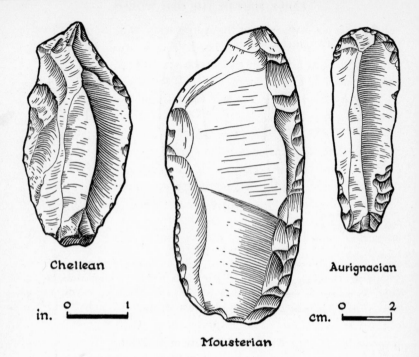

Chellean

Aurignacian

in. ⊢━━━━┥ 1

cm. ⊢━━━━┥ 2

Mousterian

THE MEANING OF SCRAPERS

"A primitive thing called a scraper is crude and not at all eloquent until you realize that it points to much else. It means not only a scraper, but a thing to be scraped, most likely a hide; therefore it means a growing ability to kill, to take off the hide and cure it. That is just the beginning, for a scraper also shows a knowledge of how to scrape, and a desire for scraping, and enough leisure (beyond the struggle to get food) to allow time for scraping. All this means self-restraint and thought for the future, and it implies a certain confidence in the ways of life, because no one would be liable to go to all the trouble of scraping if he did not have reasonable hope of enjoying the results of the work."—George R. Stewart in *Man: An Autobiography.* (Left and center, after MacCurdy, 1924; right, after Leakey, 1935.)

78

culture does not evolve out of the Aurignacian, and it does not evolve
into the next culture, the Magdalenian. The Solutreans stayed a relatively short time in Europe; Braidwood gives them 10,000 years, but
Mather and Peake and Fleure only 500.[11] Guesses as to when they
arrived vary as widely. Peake and Fleure think it was about 12,000
years ago, while Zeuner puts them back to 67,000 years before our
time.[12]

Where the Solutreans came from is another of the unsolved riddles
of archaeology. Until recently, they were generally supposed to have
come out of western Asia, because the most primitive of their remarkable tools were found plentifully in Hungary and sparsely in western
Europe. For sixty years Solutrean points were found
no farther south than northern and eastern Spain.
Now, however, points of Solutrean type have begun
to appear in North Africa, Egypt, and Kenya Colony. Here they are jumbled together in the same
strata with Mousterian points and the tanged points
of the Aterians, a purely African people. Hence certain archaeologists are inclined to believe that the
Solutreans may have originated in Africa as an offshoot of the Mousterians (see illustration, page 80).

In spite of their fondness for the chase, the Solutreans of Europe continued the interest that the
Aurignacians had shown in art—or so at least certain authorities who admire the relief carvings of Le
Roc in France tell us. But their chief distinction is
that they knew the craft of pressure flaking called
Folsom and Yuma in the New World. The Solutreans are represented mainly by thin, willow- or
laurel-shaped tools. By pressing—not pounding—a
piece of bone or wood against the surface of the flint
they flaked off slivers across the tool in a way that
no one equaled in the Old World until the Egyptian
had entered the neolithic and agricultural age many
thousands of years later. The Solutreans also made
small points with a tang at one side (see illustra-

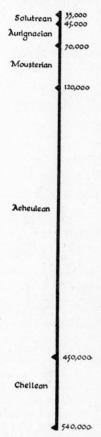

Solutrean   35,000
             45,000
Aurignacian
             70,000
Mousterian
             120,000

Acheulean

             450,000
Chellean
             540,000

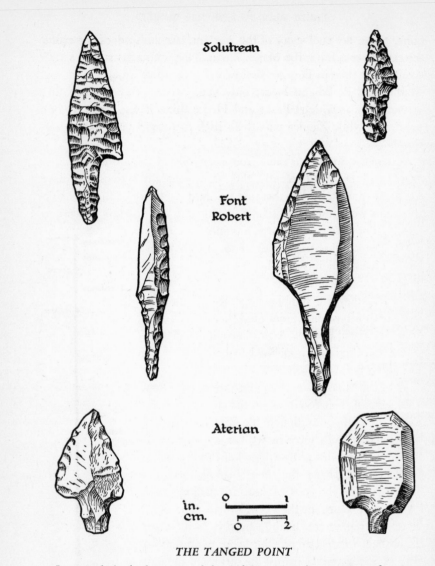

Solutrean

Font
Robert

Aterian

in. $\overline{0 \quad\quad\quad 1}$
cm. $\overline{0 \quad\quad\quad 2}$

THE TANGED POINT

It was only in the late years of the Old Stone Age that man learned to put a tang on a point and so make it easier to fasten to a shaft. This advance may have been made in connection with the spear-thrower, but it seems more likely that the arrow brought forth this technological refinement. Only Solutrean man and the American paleolithic made truly efficient points. (The Solutrean, after Burkitt, 1933; the Font Robert at right, after Burkitt, 1933, at left, after MacCurdy, 1924; the Aterian, after Plant, 1942.)

tions, pages 80 and 125). This was for the purpose of fastening the flint to a shaft; but whether it was used with a bow or a spear-

A laurel-leaf Solutrean point from France, ⅓ natural size. (After MacCurdy, 1924).

thrower is not clear. (Incidentally, points of somewhat this shape appear in the New World.) At about the same time, the Aterians of North Africa used a very crude tanged arrowhead; and in the late Aurignacian the Font Robert point with its rude tang appeared. The superior spear point of the Solutreans seems the natural product of a people who were particularly active and energetic in the chase. In a single camping place they left 35,000 tools of flint.

Following these Asiatics, a people very similar to the Aurignacians appeared in Europe. They were the Magdalenians, and they carried on the general traits of the men of Aurignac and added to them (see illustration, page 77). They made better blades and burins. (Long, slim blades of the Aurignacian-Magdalenian type have been found in Mexico, but there are no burins in northern Asia or the New World.) The burins helped the Magdalenians to make new implements of bone such as needles, fishhooks, harpoons, and spear-throwers. Besides all this, they brought to perfection the arts of painting and sculpture which used to be too much credited to the Aurignacians (see illustrations, pages 84 and 87). The magnificent poly-

Magdalenian 20,000
Solutrean 35,000 / 45,000
Aurignacian
70,000
Mousterian
120,000
Acheulean
450,000
Chellean
540,000

chromes of the Magdalenians in the Font-de-Gaume cave in France and the Altamira cave in Spain testify to the genius of this people. The customary dispute exists about their time of activity. One authority

A tool to make a tool. Such burins, with a transverse edge at the top rather like that of a chisel, were used by the Magdalenians to shape bone implements and engrave designs upon them. (After Wilson, 1898.)

A Magdalenian harpoon, 4¾ inches long, made from an antler and discovered in the rock shelter of La Madeleine, where engraved art of early man—a picture of a mammoth—was first found, by Lartet in 1864. (After Lartet and Christy, 1875.)

The first illustration of a blade, probably Magdalenian. (After Mercati, 1717.)

puts it from 11,500 to 8,500 years ago, and another from 70,000 to 25,000.[13]

Weapons and Tools—from Hand Ax to Arrowhead   One of the many mysteries of prehistory is who invented the bow and arrow. The smaller Solutrean points argue that their makers used a bow and invented this primitive but effective machine. But since the bow was made of wood, it has not been preserved in the caves and terraces

Our first machine, the spear-thrower, as used by early man and certain later
peoples in the New World as well as the Old. An invention difficult to conceive
and effect, it marked an important step forward in man's use of his brain and
his body. In effect, it extended the length of the human arm by at least two
feet and therefore its power by perhaps 50 per cent. (After Harrington, 1933.)

that spared the bone spear-throwers of the Magdalenians and the
flint projectiles; so for evidence we must fall back on the paintings of
primitive man. We find the spear-thrower portrayed in South Africa
but not in Europe. The newer weapon, the bow, is on the walls of
rock shelters in southern and eastern Spain. At first these paintings
were thought to be neolithic. Later they were credited to the Magdalenians, in spite of the fact that the use of the human form and the
bizarre and almost humorous caricature contrast with the subjects
and the style of Magdalenian art. Now they are generally credited to
the Capsians, a people from northern Africa. The paintings resemble
prehistoric work from Rhodesia and also the historic and protohistoric
designs of the Bushmen (see illustrations, pages 85 and 86).

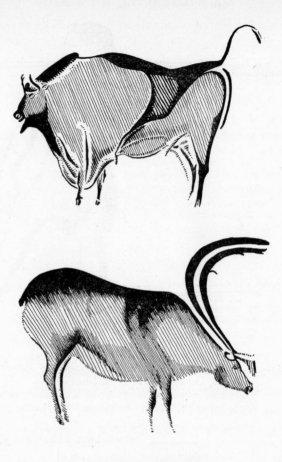

THE FIRST PAINTINGS

Although prehistoric engravings of animal figures on bone had been discovered in European caves as early as about 1840, and engravings on cave walls in the sixties, it was not till 1878 that paintings were found. The discoverer was a child. While Marcelino de Sautuola was searching among the debris on the floor of the cave of Altamira, near Santander in Spain, he heard his little daughter cry, "Toros! toros!" and saw her point to polychrome paintings of bison and other animals on the roof of the cave. One of them appears at the top of this page. The other painting shown is from the French cave of Font-de-Gaume. These two caverns contain the finest lineal art of early man, chiefly Magdalenian. (The bison after Cartailhac and Breuil, 1906; the deer after Capitan, Breuil, and Peyroni, 1910.)

The history of even the simplest of man's tools from the hand ax to the arrowhead is long, interesting, and puzzling. It is hard to say what many of the tools were used for, or indeed what they were *not* used for. The hand ax would obviously be best for grubbing out roots and tubers, yet, like most of the implements of early man, it must

Aurignacian and Magdalenian men of France drew and painted animals, almost never the human form. The artists who worked in the caves and rock shelters of eastern Spain drew figures of hunters and women, as well as of animals. These artists may have been Capsians who lived in North Africa in the Aurignacian period and spread into Europe at some time between then and the Neolithic. The style resembles that of the African Bushmen. The two archers on the left are from the cave of Saltadora; the two at the right, from the Cueva del Mas d'en Josep. (After Obermaier and Weinert, 1919.)

have served a variety of other purposes also. Until the Mousterians began to make spear points, 90,000 to 150,000 years ago, all man's implements—even what we call his scrapers—were pretty generalized. Later, with the Aurignacians and the Magdalenians, came artifacts that were obviously blades or knives or chisels or harpoons. The tool to make other tools appeared, and this we must add to the list of man's prehistoric achievements: speech, fire making, stone chipping, pressure flaking, and carving and painting.

The attempt of science to record and interpret the story of early man in the Old World has been an extraordinary triumph over the obstacles of half a million years of prehistoric darkness. Hundreds of men and women, laboring long and ingeniously, have won to an almost miraculous success, and the end is not yet in sight.

The work has suffered, of course, from many a human limitation. Not the least of these has been the desire to interpret knowledge too quickly, to freeze it into forms and classifications, and to stand doggedly by those forms and classifications when they have become weakened by new knowledge. The student and the intelligent layman have been confused by all this. They have been particularly confused—as I think I can show—when it comes to early man in the New World.

An archer drawn in the cave of Saltadora, Spain (after Obermaier and Weinert, 1919).

An archer from Alpera, Spain (after Obermaier and Weinert, 1919).

The Danger in Universal Time-Scales   When we apply to the paleolithic cultures of the rest of the world the names of the European culture sequence—Chellean, Acheulean, Mousterian, Aurignacian, Solutrean, and Magdalenian—we produce acrimonious argument and not much more. These terms are of no use in the rest of the world except as a description of types of tools. In parts of Africa, for example, Mousterian and Aurignacian objects are found together; in other parts, Mousterian and Solutrean. In the first case, the Aurignacian includes primitive pottery; in the second, Aurignacian is missing altogether.

Tied in with the mistake of setting up prehistory in Europe as a frame for prehistory elsewhere, lies the worse mistake of trying to read general time in terms of things and ideas which are purely local. The Paleolithic, Neolithic, Bronze, and Stone ages mean less than nothing as a dating machine for more than a single locality. "The

MAGDALENIAN ENGRAVINGS

These extraordinary drawings of horses and a mammoth are a transcript of the art of primitive man found upon the walls of the cave of Font-de-Gaume (after Capitan, Breuil and Peyroni, 1910).

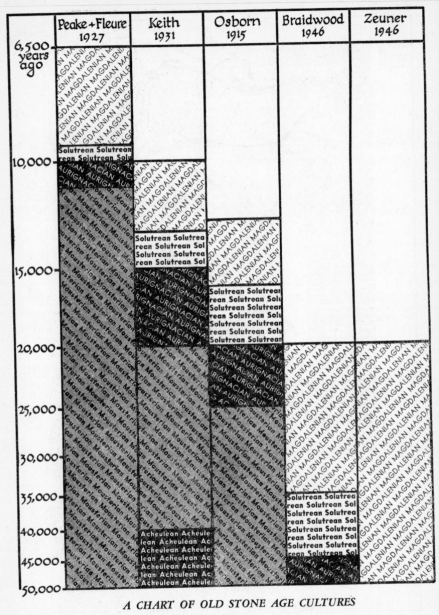

	Peake + Fleure 1927	Keith 1931	Osborn 1915	Braidwood 1946	Zeuner 1946

A CHART OF OLD STONE AGE CULTURES

The section on this page covers 50,000 years; that on the next page, almost 500,000. Both are based on a logarithmic time scale in which the years nearest the present are exaggerated in length.

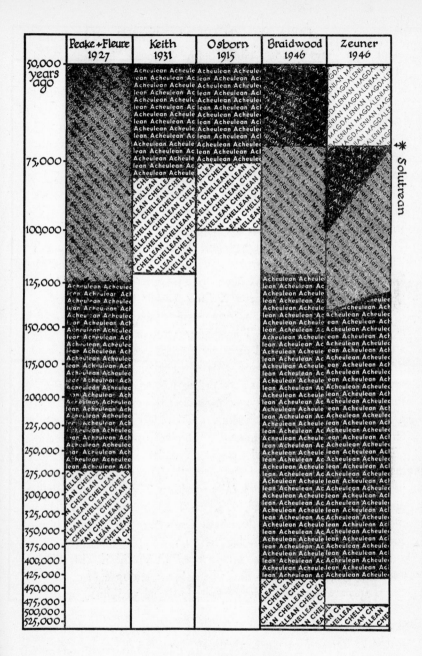

	Peake+Fleure 1927	Keith 1931	Osborn 1915	Braidwood 1946	Zeuner 1946

* Solutrean

50,000 years ago
75,000
100,000
125,000
150,000
175,000
200,000
225,000
250,000
275,000
300,000
325,000
350,000
375,000
400,000
425,000
450,000
475,000
500,000
525,000

89

Stone Age," says Childe, "ended before 3500 B.C. in Mesopotamia, about 1600 B.C. in Denmark, and A.D. 1800 in New Zealand." [14] Post-glacial means one thing in Germany and another in Sweden, one thing in Buffalo and another in Winnipeg.

The impossibility of measuring time and space together should be clear enough if you consider merely the matter of when the invention of writing in the Near East began to give us written records in other parts of the world. Again I quote Childe: "In England they take us back to A.D. 40, in France to 60 B.C., in Italy a little beyond 500 B.C., in Greece before 700, but nowhere in our continent before 1000. In China written records are available as early as 1400 B.C., in Asia Minor to 1800, only in Egypt and Mesopotamia to 3000 B.C." [15] Thus the use of writing would give us no time scale for the Old World. Fortunately, we have never tried to date the history of nations in terms of an Illiterate Age, a Writing Age, and a Printing Age.

There is similar difficulty over the fossils of extinct mammals which help to date man in Europe. They do fairly well as an index to whether a tool was used in a glacial or an interglacial period. But they some-times create scientific disagreements when they are used to place the tool in one glacial period or another. And when we reach the crucial time of the end of the last glaciation, and the extinction of the last great beasts, we are in most serious trouble. Here we are dealing with tens of thousands of years instead of hundreds of thousands, and the evidence is simply not that sharp. We do not know when Magdalenian man saw and painted his last mammoth. The mammoths died by inches—or by miles, geographically speaking. They were still alive in one area when they had died out in another. And when we reach the New World, we have still less basis for setting our watches by the fossils—as will be seen in a later chapter.

Our knowledge of early man in the Old World is still shifting and developing. There has never been too much agreement—as the charts on pages 88 and 89 demonstrate in the area of time—and there probably never will be. I have risked this brief and oversimplified sketch of a much disputed and complex subject only to provide some sort of background for the facts, the theories, and the dogmas that are involved in the story of early man in the New World.

6

WHAT THE BONES HAVE TO SAY

Prophesy upon these bones.

—EZEKIEL 37:4

Early Man As Adam's Progeny   Early man is only a century old—in the New World as well as the Old. The same year that a Frenchman theorized about hand axes and the river terraces of the Somme a German discovered in Missouri the bones of an extinct sloth which had been stoned and burned by man. That was 1838. Within twenty years early man had won his title to glacial antiquity in Europe. It took ninety, however, for him to get a really sound and solid claim to even 10,000 years in our hemisphere. The study of early man in the Americas has suffered from blindness and prejudice and also from ardor and infatuation. It has run afoul of the dogmatism of science quite as much as the dogmatism of religion.

Before nineteenth century science began to talk of glacial man as a possible and provable fact, there was little or no churchly antagonism. The religious had long shown a fondness for what they called antiquarianism. To find ancient things did no violence to the Bible. Adam was still the first man, and any descendant of his who left stone tools about or who carved mysterious signs on rocks was merely "antediluvian": he had simply missed the boat. In 1690 the Reverend Cotton Mather called the carvings on Dighton Rock in Massachusetts "the wonderful works of God," and, before those signs were proved to be of sixteenth century origin, more than 600 books and articles had been written about them. To Mather the fossils of extinct mammals proved the validity of the Bible. "There were giants in the earth in those days." In 1712 he described the "17-foot thighbone" and the four-pound tooth of a mastodon.[1]

In this spirit of sweet reasonableness the pursuit of early man went forward for one hundred and fifty years. When the Dutch traveler Peter Kalm wrote in 1772 of certain curious discoveries in New Jersey, he had no idea that he had come on something which, N. C. Nelson was to declare, "hinted strongly of 'Quaternary age.' "[2] Though the Mound Builders seemed much more ancient to General Rufus Putnam than they now seem to us, they were still post-Adamites when he mapped the prehistoric earthworks of Marietta, Ohio, in 1788. I doubt that Thomas Jefferson worried one way or the other about biblical sanction when he assumed the role of first archaeologist of America by excavating a Virginia mound in 1784, and reporting on it in his Notes on Virginia. Like another deist, Voltaire, he suggested that the origins of the American Indians might be determined by comparing their various languages with the languages of Asiatic peoples.

There was still no conflict between religion and the science of man when word came from Missouri in 1838 of the first linking of the fossils of extinct animals with signs of human activity. "Dr." A. K. Koch, a German who collected fossils and sold them to museums, dug up a sloth, which he mistook for a mastodon. The significant point was that Koch found evidence of fire among the bones, and also numerous stones which seemed to have been carried to the spot and thrown at the unhappy animal as it stood bogged in a swamp. Two years later, in the same state, Koch came upon a genuine mastodon as well as a spear point lying beneath it. From a chain of descriptions of the weapon it may be that Koch found the first of those unique Folsom spear points which were to turn up ninety years later among the fossils of extinct bison and mammoths.[3]

While Koch was circusing his mammoth up and down the country as the "Missourium," the first scientific paper appeared on a New World find of human skulls and the fossils of extinct animals. This was the 1842 report of the Danish naturalist P. W. Lund on the Lagoa Santa Caves of Brazil.[4] Four years later M. W. Dickeson re-

ported a petrified human pelvis from Natchez, Mississippi; in 1849
the British scientist Sir Charles Lyell described his visit to the spot,
and in 1863 he pointed out that the pelvis was quite as fossilized as
some mammoth bones that had been found near it.[5]

Neither of these finds aroused any more enthusiasm or controversy
than Koch's. It was all very curious and interesting but perfectly
natural. There was no question of the men and the mammoths being
particularly ancient—just antediluvian. Agassiz's glacial hypothesis
was hardly known, and Darwin had not yet turned back time past the
Garden of Eden. Adam and the Bible were safe enough.

Science and Religion Embattled   But by the time the next few finds
began to be discussed, the spiritual and intellectual climate had
changed. A wind off the glaciers chilled the enthusiasm of the
churchly and banished bland talk of "antediluvian antiquities."
Agassiz and Darwin and early man had to go down together or
triumph at the expense of Genesis. The issue was joined. The church-
man grew bitter and blind; the scientist, ardent and uncritical.

Of the many conflicts and controversies, the most celebrated raged
around the Calaveras skull. Except for the fact that in this case the
churchmen seem to have been right and the scientists wrong, it was
characteristic of most of the disputes over early man. Fittingly enough,
the skull was found in the California county which Mark Twain made
famous about the same time by his own discovery of the celebrated
jumping frog. There is no question that a mine operator with a reputa-
tion for veracity far superior to Truthful James's found the thing in a
shaft 130 feet below the surface. There is also no question that the
bone was fossilized and encrusted with the kind of gravel that distinguishes California mines. Unfortunately, the skull proved too much—
or seemed to. It lay under four strata of lava and three of gold-bearing
gravels, and therefore belonged at the very least to the Pliocene period
which ended some million years ago—unless, of course, a practical
joker had salted the mine. Some scientists accepted the skull. Some
felt that despite its heavy brow ridges this cranium looked far too
much like *Homo sapiens* to be older than Java man. Some preachers
and religious editors were content with evidence from Holy Writ,

but most of them preferred the practical joke argument. Various wits and various victims were involved, but the most popular explanation held that the mine operator was known as an agnostic, and that certain miners thought it would be amusing to plant faked evidence for him to embrace—which presumes a considerable amount of churchly enthusiasm in the miners of Calaveras County. Science asked where the miners could have got so ancient and fossilized a skull, and a few scientists and a good many Protestants replied that the name of the county had come from the Spanish word for skulls *calaveras* because whole skeletons and "uneasy crania" were constantly turning up in its soil and its river beds.

The controversy raged through the 1870's and gained new vigor in 1880, when J. D. Whitney, a leading geologist of his day and director of the California Geological Survey, brought out *Auriferous Gravels of the Sierra Nevada of California.* In the fourteen years since the discovery of the skull, Whitney had studied the region thoroughly and gathered data from everyone who remembered the circumstances of the find. He concluded that the skull had been discovered *in situ,* and had not been planted. Some twenty-five years later, when the religious fury of the attacks had subsided, Hrdlička produced craniums from the caves of California that were quite as fossilized as the Calaveras skull and showed the same heavy brow ridges. He had to admit, however, that the ridges of the Calaveras skull extended clear across the eyes and nose—"a much less common form." [6]

In the days of Queen Victoria scientists were sometimes as extravagant in their claims for early man in the Americas as the fundamentalists were absurd in their attacks upon him. Fiorino Ameghino, a museum director of Buenos Aires, got a hearing for what he called evidences of Argentine man in an age when the mammals had only just reached ascendancy. He made his initial discovery at nineteen; that was in 1873. For forty or fifty years he went on making find after find and raising controversy after controversy. The fossilized bones of man and mammal that he discovered at nineteen he placed in the Pliocene Period, prior to the Great Ice Age; geologists claimed that the stratum where he made his finds is of the Ice Age or later. Much the same criticism applied to most of Ameghino's discoveries.

He set up four primitive types of early man, based on the discovery of various bones, and placed the first in the Miocene Period more than fifteen million years ago. The geologists again put his strata in the Glacial Period. Anthropologists and paleontologists were quite as annoyed as the geologists when Ameghino made Argentina the center from which all human and mammalian forms spread over the world.

Yet, in spite of Ameghino's extravagant claims and others that were somewhat less extravagant, belief in early man persisted and grew. There was considerable stir when, between 1872 and 1899, C. C. Abbott and others discovered some primitive stone implements [7] (see illustration, page 109), parts of a human thigh-bone, jaw, and skull, in glacial gravels near Trenton, New Jersey. There were more finds at other sites, and by 1890 it was generally conceded by scientists that man had invaded the Americas during or close to the time of the last glaciers. The Protestant church subsided into a quietude which was not to be broken until the Scopes "monkey trial" of 1925.

Reaction, Led by Science   In the nineties—which was roughly the beginning of more intense and thorough scientific study in the whole field of American prehistory—a reaction set in. Early man and his sponsors were violently attacked—not by the church but by certain scientists. Thomas Wilson, Curator of the National Museum in Washington, and F. W. Putnam of the Peabody Museum at Harvard, who had long championed early man, were furiously set upon by W. H. Holmes, then of the Field Museum of Chicago, and Aleš Hrdlička of the National Museum. Taking advantage of every error, every failure to weigh evidence with the utmost conservative care, and using new knowledge in physical anthropology, Holmes and Hrdlička routed their opponents completely. How completely may be judged from the fact that when it became proper to issue the Putnam Anniversary Volume at Putnam's seventieth birthday, not one of the twenty-five essays in anthropology dedicated to him dealt with the thesis of which he had been one of the chief champions—early man in America.

Men discovered new sites, but, if they had the temerity to announce their finds, their work was ignored or scouted. For twenty-five or thirty years, as Frank H. H. Roberts, Jr., writes, the subject of early man in the New World became virtually taboo, and no scientist desirous of a successful career dared intimate that "he had discovered indications of a respectable antiquity for the Indian." Opponents of early man had definitely retarded progress in this field.[8]

From close to the turn of the century Hrdlička was the leader among these opponents just as he was the leader among the physical anthropologists of his day and a man of the greatest ability. For about forty years he wrote much, and he wrote effectively. His long series of papers were studded with denials of the antiquity of man on this continent. Beginning in 1907 with his *Skeletal Remains Suggesting or Attributed to Early Man in North America,* he demolished one American skull after another. He tore to shreds the evidence by which Ameghino pushed man back millions of years in Argentina.[9] His most effective argument against North American claims was to produce the craniums of Mound Builders or even Indians of historic times which duplicated finds of early man. He stigmatized skull after skull as "not in the least primitive," "essentially modern," "not to be distinguished from the modern Indian." Unfortunately, as he grew older, his attacks on spurious evidence developed into violent opposition to practically *all* evidence. As late as 1942, he saw his opponents as men characterized by "wishful thinking, imagination, opinionated amateurism, and desire for self-manifestation." [10] He recognized no prejudice on his own side.

Yet, against the harm that Hrdlička did science by intimidating its students, we must set a practical value which Earnest A. Hooton— himself as great a physical anthropologist as Hrdlička, but a more receptive one on the subject of early man—has well expressed:

It is to the everlasting credit of professional American anthropology that it has not succumbed to the itch for ancestors by giving recognition to the many dubious and spurious finds whose claims have too often received a facile acceptance abroad. No one can deny that this salutary state of affairs is due almost entirely to the righteous scientific iconoclasm of one formidable veteran, Dr. Hrdlička.[11]

The Red Herring of the "Primitive Skull"   It was Hrdlička's misfortune—and the misfortune of science—that until almost the end of his life he refused to meet his opponents on common ground. He was right enough in challenging early man as an inhabitant of America 200,000 years ago, but he challenged him in terms that applied or seemed to apply to any man earlier than the Indian of three or four thousand years ago. Hrdlička failed to define properly the thing he was attacking. He merely prated of the lack of "primitive skulls."

That was not the issue. Except for Ameghino, scientists of the twentieth century were not claiming to have found Chellean or even Neanderthal man in the New World. They were merely saying that certain skulls and certain tools might go back to the end of glacial times or perhaps a little earlier. This was no earlier than the Cro-Magnon of Europe, and the Cro-Magnon was modern enough in physical type. So were the skulls found with glacial animals and paleolithic tools in the upper Choukoutien Cave near Peiping. As Hooton puts it, the glacial antiquity of a New World skeleton cannot be disproved by "the modernity of its anatomical characters alone. *Homo sapiens* was full-fledged in the Old World before the end of the Glacial Period. Late Glacial entrants into the Americas need not prove their age by an array of archaic and simian physical features. The acid test of their antiquity must be geological." [12] Roberts points out that opponents of early man in America "demand a more primitive physical type as evidence for some antiquity in the New World than was living in the Old at a comparable time." [13]

As pressure of evidence and opinion piled up in favor of early man, Hrdlička began to weaken a bit. In 1937 he admitted that, compared with Europe, the situation in America "is not so simple. It is complicated by the fact . . . that individual skulls of recent and even present-day American aborigines not seldom show features that are more primitive than the average in the white races. There are American skulls of recent date that are practically replicas of the Magdalenian and even of some of the upper Aurignacian skulls of the Old World and there are occasional skulls that in some of their characteristics remind one even of the Neanderthals." [14] In other words, a skull of an early American man which resembles a skull of a historic Indian may also resemble the skull of a glacial man of the Old World.

By 1923—after the harm had been done—Hrdlička was willing to concede that migration to the Americas began "somewhere between possibly 10,000 or at most 15,000 years ago and the dawn of the proto-historic period in the Old World." [15] Yet he still clung to his Indian skull, and wrote in one of his last papers: "There is as yet not a specimen of a skull or bone that could be accepted as that of any earlier or different being than the American natives of proto-historic or historic times." [16] Even when a skull had the heavy brow ridges and the long narrow shape of the Australoid—and the Neanderthal— Hrdlička gave no ground. Such notable examples as the skulls from the Lagoa Santa Caves of Brazil—which I shall describe later—were merely "a peculiarly American variant." [17] He got only so far as grant- ing that American man had a relationship with the Cro-Magnon and the Magdalenian, but he hinted at this relationship merely in the man's "early Old World ancestry." [18]

The Mystery of the Missing Bones   So far as skeletal relics are con- cerned, the friends of early man in the New World would have been at something of a disadvantage even if Hrdlička had been less vocal and less violent. Until the edge of the Christian era, physical evidence is scanty in the Americas. The bones of early man are few and far between. The mastodons, elephants, sloths, camels, bison, and horses that once thronged the plains and plateaus south of the glaciers have left us a great sufficiency of skulls and teeth, vertebrae and ribs, leg bones and toe bones, and even some skin, hair, and feces. We have uncountable skeletons of small animals that live on today. But the fossil beds are very short indeed on man, and even the dry caves help us only a little. In the two continents there are not more than twenty- five finds of the bones of early man which must be considered seriously, and some of these are not a little dubious.

It may seem strange that thousands of spear points, scrapers, and arrowheads can be identified as the products of early man while we find so few of the skulls that held the brains which conceived them. It may seem stranger still—unbelievably strange—that, while the five- and six-foot skeletons of man have disappeared, there remain to us in excellent shape the delicate bones of fox and gopher, even the pack rat. We may believe, however, that, though the Americas thronged with animals that had been there for millions of years, there were relatively few men. Northwest Asia, from which they had come, was not a place to nurture great tribes, and to send forth migrants by the hundreds of thousands. The first men in America had to live by hunting and gathering, and hunters and gatherers do not multiply like agricultural peoples. Against hundreds of thousands of large animals—millions upon millions of small fry—we can place only some tens of thousands of men. To find a human skeleton among such a welter of animal bones would be like finding a single needle in the combined haystacks of all the Middle West. Further, did early man leave his body where we should be likely to find it? If he did not cremate his dead, then he literally exposed them to the elements—whether they lay on a scaffold like the dead of the Plains Indians or were buried in the earth—and the elements did a good job in scattering or hiding them. A great deal of water has flowed over land-bridges since the glaciers began to melt, and a great deal of silt and gravel and loess has spread deep over river bottoms and even high plateaus, burying the bones of early man beneath it.

What do we find in the way of human bones? Not too much, compared with the many skulls and skeletons of the Neanderthal and Cro-Magnon in Europe. They range from the top of a cranium or part of a pelvis to a few complete skeletons, some properly buried. They are not all of equal value. The best, however, tell us something about how certain early Americans may have looked. By that, at least, they contribute more than the thousands of stone tools which early man left behind him.

South America Provides the First Skulls So far as anthropology is concerned, it was a busy and important decade that ended in 1850. Prescott's histories of the conquest of Mexico and Peru, and John L. Stephens's two books of travel and study in the Maya area had become best-sellers. Lord Kingsborough was publishing his nine-volume *Antiquities of Mexico*. Boucher de Perthes was finding additional hand axes, and beginning to write upon them. More important for our purposes is the report of the Danish naturalist Lund that he found the skulls of men mingled with the bones of extinct mammals in the Lagoa Santa caves of Brazil.

It would be pleasant to think that Lund left Europe in 1835 imbued with enthusiasm for the discoveries of Boucher de Perthes, but this is highly unlikely. The Frenchman and his theories were pretty generally ignored by science until the late fifties. I don't know why Lund chose to explore caves in the state of Minas Geraes, north of Rio de Janeiro, but in the end it was a fortunate choice. He examined eight hundred caves, and in six of them he found human remains. For eight or nine years he was dubious about his finds, but he was convinced in 1844 when he found human bones mingled with the bones of extinct animals, all equally fossilized.

Though it was the bones of the mammals that convinced Lund of the antiquity of the Lagoa Santa craniums, it is certain peculiarities of the skulls themselves that have given them a very special importance in the whole argument for early man in the New World. These skulls were long and narrow, while those of most Indians and other Mongoloid peoples are relatively short and broad. Again in contrast to the men of northern Asia, the Lagoa Santa had very heavy brow ridges; their skulls were straight-sided and had keeled vaults. The total effect was archaic. This was to prove a basic type to which all the later finds of the bones of early man could be related.

Dr. Lund's bones were not received with too much enthusiasm. If they had belonged to any animal other than man, says Sir Arthur Keith, "their antiquity would never have been questioned, but being human all sorts of doubts were raised as to how and when they became mixed with the remains of extinct animals." [19] Many years passed before the Lagoa Santa skulls began to win respectful attention and final acceptance as other long and narrow skulls with even stronger brow ridges turned up under similar conditions.

No one worked in the Lagoa Santa regions for almost a century. In 1933 members of the Academy of Science of Minas Geraes excavated a neighboring cave called Confins. They found the molars of a young mastodon under a few feet of dirt inside the entrance. Deeper down and farther back, they discovered fossils of horse, giant sloth, mastodon, and other extinct mammals. Finally they came on a nearly complete human skeleton. They had cut through a layer of stalagmitic material and more than six feet of alluvial soil to reach the bones of

Confins man, and so they knew that he had died during or just before a period of great moisture. They write of this time as the Post-Pleistocene, or Pluvial. Post-Pleistocene means, of course, Postglacial, and Pluvial means a time of much rain. Some scientists push the Pluvial back into the Glacial, but the finders of Confins man prefer to date him at "a few thousands of years ago." The discoverers of the Confins skull write of it as "one of the most primitive types of *Homo sapiens* . . . yet discovered in South America." [20] But this statement seems based more on the conditions under which it was found than on its shape. The skull is long and narrow, with heavy brow ridges and a low forehead; but it is not straight-sided, and its vault is not keeled. It is somewhat less archaic than the Lagoa Santa craniums.

Certain skulls from Ecuador seem much more archaic than any of those found in Brazil. These are the Punin specimen found in 1923, and the group discovered at Paltacalo almost twenty years before.[21] Associated with the fossils of extinct horse, camel, and mastodon, they have all the peculiarities of the Lagoa Santa specimens, and in addition they have retreating foreheads, lower vaults, and unusually large teeth.

Far down in Chile long-headed skulls have been found in association with fossils of extinct horse and ground sloth. They are not so extreme in appearance as the Lagoa Santa skulls, though they resemble them. As for their age, Junius Bird, who made the discovery in caves just north of the Straits of Magellan, reckons—in what he calls "a few degrees better than an outright guess"—that they belonged to men who were given cremation burials not more than 5,400 years ago. He does not venture to guess how many years it took these people to travel the 11,000 miles from the strait of Vitus Jonasson Bering to the strait of Ferdinand Magellan.[22]

North American Skulls and Bones   Since the discovery of human bones in glacial gravels near Trenton, New Jersey, three skeletons of some importance and a number of skulls that resemble those of Lagoa Santa and Punin have been found in North America.

The three finds of complete skeletons made in Minnesota between 1931 and 1935 have aroused much debate. All three were encountered in road-making or the digging of gravel, and scientists were not present at their discovery. A. E. Jenks's study of these skeletons has done much to clarify them. "Minnesota man"—really a girl—was found in a geological stratum marked by varves, or thin layers of clay, laid down in successive years by a glacial lake about 20,000 years ago.[23] Antevs believes her body was thrust into this stratum at a later time; but other geological authorities, including Kirk Bryan, Paul Mac-Clintock, G. F. Kay, and M. M. Leighton, deny it and present rather convincing evidence.[24] Hooton unhesitatingly expresses the opinion that "this discovery establishes a very strong probability, though not an absolute certainty, of the existence of *Homo sapiens* in the New World in Late Glacial times." [25] Artifacts found with the skeleton—a pierced conch shell and a knife made from an antler—do nothing to aid in dating the find. In the gravel of Browns Valley where the second skeleton was found there were also spear points (see illustration, page 120). From geological evidence connected with this find—the most generally accepted of the three in Minnesota—a date between 8,000 and 12,000 years ago seems plausible. The third skeleton, Sauk Valley man, has been the center of much dispute. Some geologists believe that the depth of the occurrence and the presence of a certain sand within the skull argue a considerable antiquity. Like the owner of the Punin skull, "Minnesota man" had a primitive type of teeth, larger even than those of some paleolithic specimens. Jenks and L. A. Wilford find twenty-six archaic traits in the Sauk Valley skull.[26]

Some ten or twenty thousand years before the elephants and the men of our three-ring circuses took up winter quarters in Florida a different kind of elephant and a different kind of man seem to have come into contact there along the Indian River. It was a very firm contact indeed; for, if evidence dug up at Melbourne in 1925 means anything, it means that a mammoth or a mastodon stepped on the skull of some variety of early man and left it flat as a pancake. Other elephants and a goodly array of mammals that are now extinct left some of their bones in the same geologic formation with the skull. Ten years before, other such fossils and an even more mutilated skull had been found in the same kind of stratum forty miles away at Vero.

The history of these finds is typical of the disrepute in which early man was held from 1900 to 1930. A few men—E. H. Sellards, who made the Vero find, J. W. Gidley and F. B. Loomis, who published on both sites, and some others—believed the evidence, but "that doughty doubter" Hrdlička bore down upon it and left it as flattened as the Melbourne skull.[27] It was only in 1946 through a study by T. D. Stewart, curator of physical anthropology in the National Museum, that the finds received a fair estimate as proof of early man in Florida during glacial or near-glacial time. Besides upholding the geologic evidence of Sellards, Gidley, and Loomis, Stewart announced that Hrdlička had left the reconstruction of the Melbourne skull to a minor technician, and showed by a more careful fitting together of the broken pieces of bone that the Melbourne man had the long, narrow, flat-sided head, the low forehead, and the strong brow ridges typical of most craniums found under conditions that suggest antiquity.[28]

Other skulls with the peculiarities of the Melbourne and South American specimens have been found in the United States and Mexico. Most of them were fairly close to the surface in soils of recent types. Only a few were found in geological formations old enough to be worth discussion—the Lansing, Kansas, skull, for instance, which was buried under twenty feet of loess, and certain skulls found below hardpan in California—and none of these won general acceptance as anywhere near glacial. Yet in a number of skulls discovered in Texas, Lower California, the California coastal area, and the Sacramento Valley there remains a case for early man in North America.

Early Man Not Solely Mongoloid or Indian Broadly speaking, these western craniums, like the other skulls I have mentioned, are not typically Mongoloid, and they do not resemble too closely the less Mongoloid skulls of the long-headed Indians of the Plains and the Northeast. Even the freshest and least fossilized specimens—three groups from coastal and central Texas—have "no affinity," according to the physical anthropologists George and Edna Woodbury, "among the tribes of North America." Instead—although the brow ridges are "not a conspicuous feature"—they resemble certain skulls from Lower California called Pericú, which in turn belong to the archaic type found in the Lagoa Santa caves and were discovered in 1883 by the Danish anthropologist, C. F. ten Kate.[29]

Along the coast of California to the north, other narrow skulls with heavy brow ridges have been found in the neighborhood of Santa Barbara and the Channel Islands and from just east of San Francisco to Sacramento. Some consider the Oak Grove specimens from Santa Barbara the oldest, but until 1946 most anthropologists were not inclined to give any of them more than 4,000 years. Now, however, nine skeletons have been found near Concord which will probably move all the California skulls of this type a few thousand years farther back. These skulls, from what is called the Monument Site, were under four feet of earth which the soil experts of the neighboring University of California believe took anywhere from 4,000 to 8,000 years to accumulate and weather.[30] Through shell ornaments in the burials, Robert F. Heizer identifies the Monument skulls with what is called the Middle Central California culture found near the capital of the state.[31] This culture lay above Early Central California, and the skulls of the latter were found in and beneath four feet of cementlike hardpan.[32] Heizer estimates the age of these early men "in the neighborhood of 4,000 to 5,000 years," but he states that "a number of soil chemists, geomorphologists, and geologists who have seen our Early horizon sites have suggested an antiquity in the neighborhood of 10,000 years." [33] The Monument Site seems to argue that the latter figure is not impossible. Even this date gives us no glacial age for early man in California, but here again we have skulls that are older and more archaic in type than those of the Mongoloid Indian. They have some features of the skulls from Florida and South America that have been found with the fossils of extinct mammals.

In 1949 Heizer unearthed, not a skull, but the record of a skull that had been found in 1922 embedded in four or five feet of gravel now considered "early recent," a product of the melting of the last glaciers. The gravel and sixteen or twenty feet of silt above it formed the bank of a creek near Stanford University. The skull is long and narrow.[34]

The year 1947 presented us, at last, with an early skull that seemed as if it could be dated pretty accurately without the aid of elephants. Yet without their aid it might never have been found.

Travelers have long reported bones of mammoths and mastodons in Mexico. The first to do this was Cortés's young lieutenant, Bernal Díaz. To be sure, he thought that the bone the Tlascalans showed him belonged to one of their gigantic ancestors, as they said it did. In his book, *The True History of the Conquest of New Spain,* he wrote: "So that we could see how huge and tall these people had been they brought a leg bone of one of them which was very thick and the height of a man of ordinary stature, and that was the bone from the hip to the knee." If we try to visualize Cortés and Díaz inspecting this mammoth bone, the scene adds, if possible, to the extraordinary picture that the conquest presents. "I measured myself against it and it was as tall as I am although I am of fair size." [35] Since the days of Cortés more and more fossils of elephants have been found south of the border. Indeed they crop out of eroded arroyos, drainage ditches, and old lake beds only a few miles from Mexico City itself.

Until November, 1945, little had been done to place early man in Mexico or to link him with its many fossils. Then Helmut de Terra— who had worked long in eastern and southeastern Asia—went to the Valley of Mexico to study the glacial moraines on neighboring mountains, and to link them with the soils of the old lake beds in which fossils had long been found. Expanding the work of A. R. Arellano and Kirk Bryan, he established the fact that a certain layer of caliche, or soft, earthy limestone, had been laid down upon the shrunken shores of Lake Texcoco after the glacial ice had retreated up Popocatepetl and other mountains. Under the caliche—which he dates as beginning to form between 9,000 and 11,000 years ago—he found a wet, silty clay which contained, here and there, the bones of elephants and a few rudimentary tools of stone and bone. Then in February, 1947, he decided to hunt for larger objects in an area near Tepexpan with an electrical device used for detecting valuable metals and military mines but never previously used for archaeological purposes. The resistance of a certain section of the clay to the passage of an electrical current between two metal stakes driven into the ground told him that a foreign body lay a little below the surface. He dug, and unearthed a skull and a considerable part of the skeleton of a man who was probably hunting an elephant or running from one when he became mired in the bog of the lake shore.

Because of the lake sediment in which de Terra found the bones, he dates Tepexpan man between 11,000 and 12,000 years ago.[36] Another anthropologist, Glenn H. Black—basing his opinion on published photographs of the excavation—has suggested the "possibility, even probability" that Tepexpan man got into old lake sediment through "intrusive burial," which means that he was interred by his fellows at a much later date.[37]

The skull of this very meaningful man is not so long and narrow as the other early craniums but not so round as most Indians'. Weidenreich, an outstanding authority on Java man and his Peking cousin-once-removed, has found eight features of the skull and bones "which are more primitive than those usually found in modern human skulls." The brow ridges are very heavy and form a well marked torus, or bulge, above the nose, "such as occurs in the Australian bushman of today and in other 'primitive races.' " A torus on the back of the head "resembles even the condition found in Neanderthal skulls." [38]

Javier Romero and T. D. Stewart, however, do not agree with Weidenreich's analysis. Romero finds the brow ridge "not very markedly developed." Stewart calls it "predominantly Indian in character." [39]

The old skulls of the New World may not be entirely satisfactory proofs of the antiquity of early man in this hemisphere; for Tepexpan man and Minnesota man both have been challenged as intruders in an older soil. On the other hand, all the skulls except the Mexican specimen suggest to the partisans of glacial man in the Americas that the first immigrants were *not* "predominantly Indian in character." They make an interesting and significant point. Can it be a mere coincidence that when we find a head which has been stepped on by an elephant, it is not round like most Indians', but longer or narrower, and it has very heavy brow ridges? Can it be a coincidence that when we find a skull in a cave with the bones of extinct mammals, it has those same peculiarities? Can it be a coincidence that when we find a skull under rocklike hardpan or a distinctly ancient layer of soil, it has those unusual stigmata? It does no good to hunt up the skull of a Sioux or a Mound Builder or an Algonquin which looks like one from Punin or Florida or Lower California. That is not much better than finding the skull of a modern New Yorker that looks like one of early man's—which you could do without too much trouble. If *all* Sioux skulls or Mound Builder skulls or Algonquin skulls were as archaic as *all* the Punin and Florida and Pericú skulls, or if some early skulls were short and broad, then the case for the Mongoloid Indian as the earliest man in America would be incontestable. But until we find a round-headed, thoroughly modern Mongoloid skull that has been stepped on by an elephant or got itself interred with a mammoth or buried under earth that ought not to be on top of it, we shall have to believe that the simon-pure Indian of Hrdlička's idolatry was not the first American. We shall have to think that the archaic fellow from Punin or Florida or Lower California or the Lagoa Santa Caves was our earliest man—and quite early at that. Just how early, the bones do not yet say.

The bones may give their answer, however, before this book appears; for science has discovered in radioactive carbon 14 a time-clock that may be fairly accurate up to 20,000 or 25,000 years ago. Carbon 14, absorbed from the atmosphere by organic bodies, disintegrates at a fixed rate. Tests on two samples of wood from ancient Egypt have come out very close to the known age of the tombs in which the wood was found. Analyses of any charcoal that may be found with the bones of early man should date him in the New World.

7

THE ARTIFACTS OF EARLY MAN

Artifact, oh, artifact!
Spear point or scraper or hand-axe—
First tool of man,
Ancestor of steam shovel and power lathe,
Dynamo and bomb.

—EMIL SPIELMANN

Artifacts from Heaven "Thunderbolts of God"—from England to Japan and from Norway to Africa, that was how men once explained the stone axes and arrowheads which they found buried in the earth. The philosophers and scientists of the Renaissance dug a little deeper, and one of them came up with the verbose and remarkable suggestion that these stones were made "by an admixture of a certain exhalation of thunder and lightning with metallic matter, chiefly in dark clouds, which is coagulated by the circumfused moisture and conglutinated into a mass (like flour with water), and subsequently indurated by heat, like a brick." [1] Some found a simpler explanation: these artifacts were iron tools petrified by time. Toward the end of the sixteenth century, Michele Mercati, physician to Pope Clement VIII, saw the truth: "They have been broken off from hard flints by a violent blow, in the days before iron was employed for the follies of war; for the earliest men had only splinters of flint for knives." [2] The English historian William Dugdale said much the same thing in *Antiquities of Warwickshire*. The theory was not generally accepted, however, until the Spaniards found American Indians making arrowheads and stone axes without the aid of thunder, lightning, or God.

The Folsom Point—Unique and Potent Quite a different thunder-bolt—and a potent one—was the spear point that J. D. Figgins, of the Denver Museum of Natural History, found in 1927 between the ribs of an extinct bison near Folsom, New Mexico. It was a thunder-bolt that destroyed, startlingly and for all time, thirty years of opposition to the presence of early man in the Americas.

This was not the first discovery of a Folsom point. Koch may have found one under a mastodon in 1839. Certainly the Smithsonian Institution possesses a Folsom that was picked up in New Hampshire in 1888, and other specimens have been discovered in old collections. But, in spite of the fact that these points were very odd in shape and had never been found in the Old World, scientists had paid little attention to them until 1927.

Figgins was not the first to discover spear points—of whatever shape—with the fossils of extinct animals or with other evidence of considerable age. In at least eight localities during the second half of the nineteenth century men had made such finds; and there had been five more finds in the first quarter of the twentieth.

Some of the first group won easy, if uncritical, acceptance; but antagonism to the flint tools that C. C. Abbott found near Trenton, New Jersey, was so great that he wrote: "Had the Delaware River been a European stream, the implements found in its valley would have

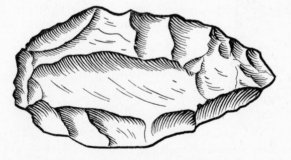

A spear point, or possibly a scraper, found near Trenton, New Jersey, in 1872. Except for lack of retouching on the edges, it resembles the Mousterian point on page 69; but it is a little longer—5¾ inches. This implement was found on the surface, but it was said to be identical with some discovered with human bones in the glacial gravel beds below. (After Abbott, 1872.)

been accepted at once as evidence of the so-called *Paleolithic man*." [3]
By 1925 almost everyone seemed to have forgotten the obsidian blade
that a museum director named W J McGee had pulled out of the
unmistakably glacial deposits of extinct Lake Lahontan, Nevada, in
1882,[4] and the spear point that had been found in 1895 under the
shoulder blade of an extinct type of bison at Russell Springs, Kansas.[5]

Discoveries after 1900 were, in a sense, more important because
better authenticated; but unfortunately they had to encounter the
general hostility to early man which had been bred by a more scientific
approach to American prehistory and nurtured by Hrdlička at Vero
and Melbourne. In 1924 the finding of a point under a bison at Lone
Wolf Creek, Texas, by men from the Denver Museum of Natural
History went relatively unnoticed.[6] Only harsh controversy welcomed
the discovery, at Frederick, Oklahoma, in 1926, of artifacts and a
variegated array of fossilized fauna in what the geologist E. H. Sellards
believed was a glacial formation.[7]

The Folsom discovery changed the hostile attitude of almost all
anthropologists toward early man. This was
partly because the evidence was so striking
and unmistakable, but largely because of the
fierce white light of scientific publicity that
was made to beat about a New Mexico arroyo.

The Denver Museum had found its first
Folsom point in 1926.[8] It had been embedded
in the clay surrounding a large bone; but when
Figgins spoke or wrote of this discovery his
fellow scientists suggested that the point was
"intrusive," that it had dropped down through
a hole made by some rodent. So the next year,
when Figgins came upon a Folsom point between two ribs of a bison, he stopped all work

The Lake Lahontan point, found in the glacial clays of Nevada associated with the fossils of extinct mammals. (After Russell, 1885.)

and wired to a number of institutions in the
East to send witnesses. Barnum Brown of the
American Museum of Natural History, Frank
H. H. Roberts, Jr., of the Smithsonian In-
stitution, and Alfred V. Kidder of the Pea-

body Foundation at Andover arrived to view the point *in situ.* Their testimony and the collaboration of Brown in work at Folsom established beyond doubt that man in America had trafficked with animals which were supposed to have been dead by the end of the Glacial Period. Once this was proved, other anthropologists and institutions were off on the trail of more such finds.

Americans Hunted Animals Now Extinct   The Folsom find was arresting, even dramatic. Not only was one of the nineteen points from the first three field seasons actually lodged between the ribs of an ex-

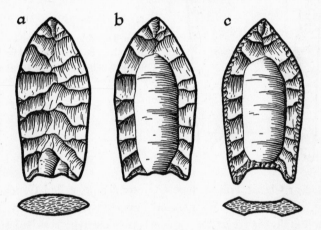

The making of a Folsom point. The flint was first flaked to the general shape desired. (This sketch is perhaps a little too schematic.) Next the maker removed a long flake on each face. Then he retouched the edges, and usually ground the base and the sides of the ears. (After Clarke, 1940.)

tinct bison. More, the skeletons of twenty-three of these animals testified that here was the scene of a prehistoric kill. Man had indeed had something to do with these beasts before they had grown cold; for the tail bones of each bison were missing, and hunters will tell you that, in skinning, "the tail goes with the hide." [9]

Another arresting feature was the shape of the point—unique in all the history of primitive man—and the fact that it was better made than any other point of equal antiquity. It was rather broad, with a

deep concave base that terminated at each side in a jutting point, or
"ear." The edges were most skillfully chipped, and the base and ears
were often ground smooth. It was particularly distinguished by the
fact that a long flake of stone had been chipped away on each face
from the base almost to the tip. The flute, or channel, left by the flake,
made the point look a little like the end of a grooved bayonet. This is

The minute, ribbonlike flaking of a
Folsom. This drawing, one and one-half
actual size, is from a broken point
found at Lindenmeier. (Courtesy of the
Denver Museum of Natural History.)

the True or Classic Folsom type. A second type, called Generalized
Folsom, is larger, without ears, and imperfectly grooved. Though a
terminology has been set up by which the first type is called simply
Folsom, and the second Clovis Fluted, Ohio Fluted, etc., depending
on where found, I shall, for convenience, adhere to the older names.

Since 1926 more than sixty points of the Classic Folsom type have
been found, many on the surface, some in association with the bones
of extinct bison, mammoths, camels, and horses. Most of them were
found in the general area of the High Plains, but some in southern
Texas, on the west slope of the Rockies, in Massachusetts, and even in
Alaska and Ontario and New Brunswick. Hundreds of the Generalized
type have been recognized in collections or found in the field; they
came from forty-two states, and possibly Alaska, and Canada.[10]
While Generalized Folsoms have usually appeared as surface finds, a
few have been found in pre-pottery sites in Illinois and Kentucky

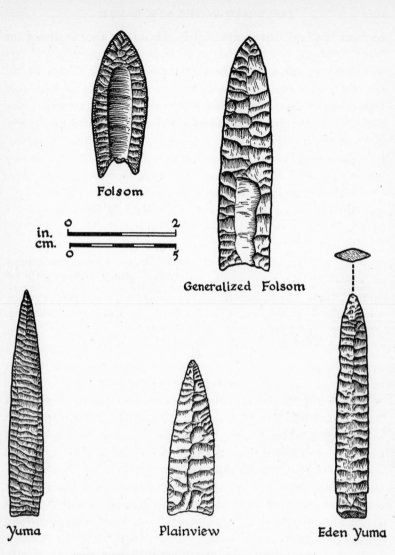

Folsom

Generalized Folsom

in.
cm.

Yuma

Plainview

Eden Yuma

THE FINEST FLINT WORK OF EARLY MAN

Two varieties of Folsom and Yuma points and the Plainview type, which has been called unfluted Folsom or Yuma-like. The Plainview was found in Texas. (Upper left, after a cast from the Laboratory of Anthropology, Santa Fe, N.M.; upper right, after Wormington, 1944; the Yuma point after Howard, 1935; the Plainview after Krieger, 1947; the Eden Yuma after Wormington, 1944.)

together with a Classic point.[11] It is only in the far corners of the Southeast that they have not been discovered.

There has been some argument over whether the Classic or the Generalized Folsom is the older. John L. Cotter reports the finding of Generalized Folsom points and elephant fossils near Clovis, New Mexico, in a stratigraphic level lower than one containing Classic Folsom and bison.[12] Harrington points out that Generalized Folsom has been found four times in association with mammoth, as well as once with the bison, but that, when the Classic type is partnered with fossils, these are almost invariably the bison's.[13] The wholly extinct mammoth is usually presumed to be older than the bison, one species of which still lives. Furthermore, in Burnet Cave, New Mexico, a Generalized Folsom has been found with bones of an animal of the musk-ox type.[14] Within fifty miles of the Mexican border, the musk ox, says Roberts, is "generally considered good evidence of an ice-age fauna." [15] The Classic may be a localized expression of the basic pattern, reaching perfection in the High Plains while the Generalized spread more widely.

Two Other Folsom Sites—Clovis and Lindenmeier   The second site of Classic Folsom was that near Clovis, discovered by Howard in 1932, and dated by the glacialist Ernst Antevs and the geologist Kirk Bryan. It was notable on two counts. The finds were in the dried beds of lakes which had apparently been formed in the pluvial, or very wet, period which occurred at least as early as the end of the last glaciation —12,000 to 13,000 years ago—and probably still earlier. This time there were fossils of other extinct mammals besides bison—mammoths, horses, camels, and peccaries. In addition to classic Folsom points, Howard found an unfluted artifact which he considered to be a Folsom knife.[16]

The third major discovery of Classic Folsom artifacts came officially in 1934 when Roberts dug a site called Lindenmeier in Colorado; but as far back as 1924—two years before the first discovery of a Folsom point in New Mexico—Judge C. C. Coffin and his son, A. L. Coffin, had begun to pick up such points in this area without recognizing their importance. Lindenmeier is particularly significant because it was an

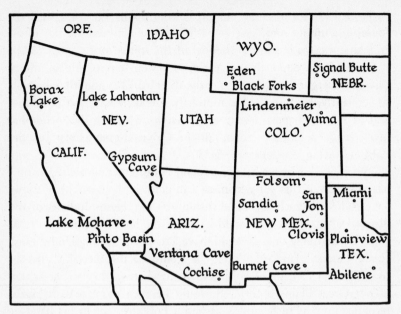

ORE.

IDAHO

WYO.

Eden
° Black Forks

Signal Butte
°
NEBR.

Borax
Lake

Lake Lahontan
°

NEV.

UTAH

Lindenmeier
°
Yuma
°
COLO.

CALIF.

Gypsum
Cave
°

Folsom°

Sandia
°

San
Jon
°

Miami
°

Lake Mohave •
Pinto Basin

ARIZ.

NEW MEX. °
Clovis

Plainview
•

Ventana Cave
°

Burnet Cave °

TEX.

Cochise
°

Abilene°

This map shows the chief sites where artifacts of early man have been found
in the Southwest. (After Hurst, 1945, with some additions.)

occupational site, a camp of some duration. It was also a factory, for
Roberts found spear points, scrapers, and other tools in various stages
of manufacture. Again there were bison bones.[17] There were also
traces of camel, as well as an elephant tusk not too closely associated
with the artifacts. A skillful geological study of the old and elevated
river terrace on which the site is located linked it with glacial moraines
which indicate a readvance of the glacial ice.[18] The date of Folsom
man is uncertain. Some believe he lived during the last years of the
Great Ice Age. Some place him a little later than the melting of the
glaciers. The date may lie between 25,000 and 13,000 years ago, depending on whether you accept the estimate of Bryan or of Antevs.[19]

One thing is certain, however: the Folsom point won the battle for
early man in the Americas because it proved that he had hunted extinct
bison, camels, mammoths, peccaries, and horses. Hitherto every find
of human artifacts with fossils had been thrown out of court on the
argument that the artifacts might be intrusive. That charge could not

be leveled at two of these unique Folsom points because they were found in a unique and decisive position—one between the ribs of an animal and the other in the channel of the spinal cord.

Some of the opponents of early man were not convinced. They shifted the argument. Man was early, the Hrdličkas admitted, but not so very early, because the bison and the elephant were late. More of that in a later chapter. Meantime, it is worth noting that a humble invertebrate, a mollusk, found in the Clovis dig, suggests that the Folsom-bearing deposits were glacial.[20]

You may ask why we have not found Folsom man himself. Howard has pointed out that early man, as a migrant hunter, would probably have followed much the same customs as our Plains Indians in the disposal of his dead. He would have left the bodies exposed on scaffolds or in trees, or he would have cremated them. "Under such circumstances," Howard writes, "it would be the merest chance to come across a skeleton of Folsom man anywhere in the enormous area of our Great Plains country. It would be even more remarkable to recognize him as such, unless he had a Folsom point in his hand or was holding an elephant by the tail." [21]

Another Fine and Ancient Point—the Yuma   Folsom man and his spear point had only just begun to worry conservative anthropologists when A. E. Jenks—who was to champion skeletons of early man in Minnesota—noted, in 1928, a still finer type of flint in the collection of Perry and Harold Anderson, of Yuma County, Colorado. It was long and narrow, with parallel sides and a triangular point, and looked rather like a half-bayonet without its Folsom flute. It was consummately chipped by pressure over its whole surface. The Yuma point is easily the finest job of flint knapping in the New World, and it is equaled only by the later neolithic daggers of Egypt and Scandinavia (see illustrations, page 118). This might be a good argument for Yuma points' being neolithic if artifacts with Yuma chipping had not been discovered in association with Folsom tools and also with the fossils of extinct mammals. Evidence from a site near Eden, Wyoming, indicates that the Yuma industry as a whole is younger than the Folsom. The Yuma points found there are nearer 7000 than 25,000 years old,

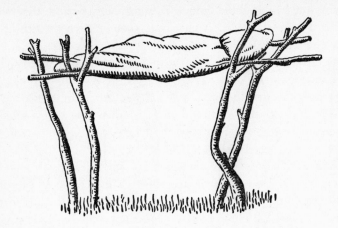

Australia

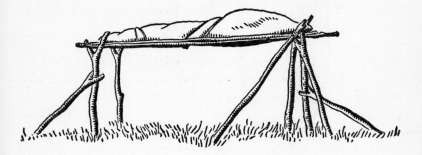

Sioux

BURIALS IN THE OLD WORLD AND THE NEW

Disposal of the dead by exposure as practiced among hunting tribes. (After Sollas, 1911.)

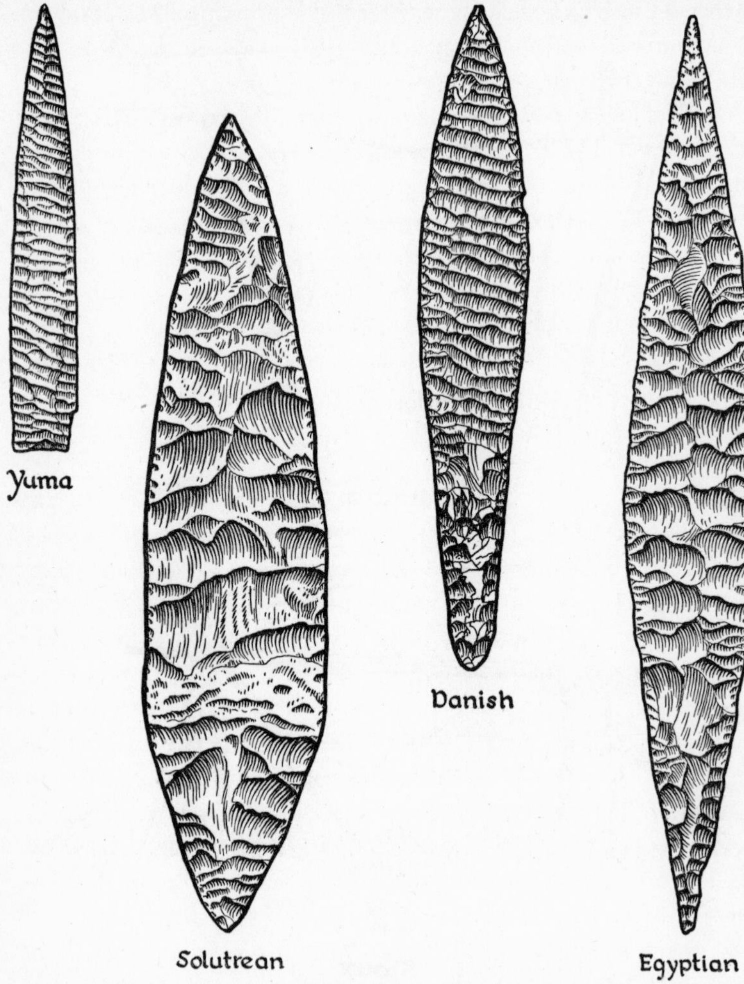

Yuma

Solutrean

Danish

Egyptian

FLINT KNAPPING OF THE OLD AND NEW STONE AGES

From 10,000 to 60,000 years separate the Solutrean artifact of the Paleolithic period from the Neolithic work of Denmark and Egypt, depending on whose time scale you accept. The Yuma point may have been made 10,000 years ago or even nearer the Neolithic. (The Yuma after Howard, 1935; the Solutrean after Sollas, 1911; the Danish after Plant, 1942; the Egyptian after De Morgan, 1925.)

for the soil in which they lay was formed during a moist period late in that interval of time. Yumas are fairly widespread; some have been found in Canada and in Alaska.[22]

Anthropologists now recognize two chief varieties of Yuma points. One of these is beautifully patterned by long, parallel pressure flakes that cross the blade obliquely on a low diagonal. In the other, parallel flakes meet on a center line. The first was originally called Oblique Yuma; the second, Collateral Yuma. Now the first is generally labeled merely Yuma, and the second, Eden Yuma (see illustration, page 113). The base and lower edges are usually ground. There is often a single or a double shoulder for hafting. Many anthropologists list another type of Yuma, the Scottsbluff; it is flaked like the Eden, but shorter and wider, and it has a definite stem with right-angle notches.

The Plainview Point   Another type of early point has given students a good deal of trouble. It is shaped somewhat like a Folsom but it has no long chip, or flute, removed from its two faces. The lower edges are often ground. Its surface is sometimes chipped like a Collateral, or Eden, Yuma, and sometimes patterned with larger, and less regular flakes. When such points were found with Folsoms, they were often called Folsom-like. At other sites, they were called Indeterminate Yuma, or Yuma-like. As the result of the discovery in 1945 by Glen L. Evans and Grayson E. Meade of eighteen whole or broken points of this sort near Plainview, Texas, in association with numerous fossils of extinct bison, there is a tendency to give these "Unfluted Folsoms" and "Indeterminate Yumas" the label Plainview.[23] Like the Folsoms, Plainview points can now be recognized among artifacts collected before their recognition as a distinct type. F. G. Rainey and Frank Hibben have found them in the frozen muck of central Alaska, identifying them by the older names of Yuma-like or Generalized Folsom.[24] This muck is an extraordinary formation four to one hundred feet deep. Packed into it are masses of dismembered skeletons of the mammoth, a jaguar, and other extinct mammals, accompanied here and there by ligaments of flesh and hair. Hibben picked up a point in a curio store at Ketchikan on the southern coast of Alaska, and another from Chinitna Bay on the shore of Cook Inlet, both of which he called Yuma-like, but which may now be regarded as very much like Plainviews. Alex Krieger lists as Plainviews a considerable number of points which have been hitherto identified as Generalized Folsoms or Indeterminate Yumas at sixteen different sites [25] (see illustration, page 113).

Two points that resemble somewhat the Plainview type, and may indeed be merely deviations from it. The one at the left was found by a fisherman at Chinitna Bay, Alaska, and called by Hibben Yuma-like. The other was discovered by Jenks at Browns Valley, Minn., associated with a human skeleton. (Left, measurements not available, after Hibben, 1943; right, about natural size, after Roberts, 1940.)

Krieger suggests that Plainview lies between Folsom and Yuma, in its type of flint work. Later excavations may prove that the three points have a similar historical relationship, and may throw more light on some nine or ten other types of points that early man seems to have made.[26]

Besides generalized Folsom, Yuma and Plainview, Alaska has provided cores which Nelson finds "identical in several respects with thousands of specimens found in the Gobi Desert." He recognizes them as evidence of migration from Asia 9,000 to 12,000 years ago.[27]

A New Point—and Sloths—in Gypsum Cave   After the discovery of the Yuma point, the next important development came in 1930 with M. R. Harrington's excavation of Gypsum Cave, Nevada. Here he found the dung, hair, skin, and bones of the ground sloth in clear association with a wide variety of artifacts. Besides the sloth, there were fossils of camel and perhaps horse. Among the artifacts was a new type of diamond-shaped point, and—quite as remarkable—there were parts of painted dart shafts with the butts pitted for use with a spear-thrower. In addition to knives and oval scrapers, there were fire hearths. Gypsum man burned sloth dung as well as wood, and used torches. Harrington dates the culture at about 10,500 years ago; Gypsum appears to follow Folsom.[28]

A Gypsum Cave point. (After Roberts, 1940.)

Such discoveries of the traces of early man in the United States and Canada spurred anthropologists to new work in the field, with the result that we now have between eighty and one hundred sites where a few of man's bones or a host of his artifacts have been found with the fossils of bison, elephant, camel, horse, or sloth or in geological strata that date him close to the Great Ice Age and probably in it. Seven North American sites, and two in Middle America remain to be discussed. Some are outstanding in evidence of age.

Old Lake and River Sites   In 1934 and 1935 Mr. and Mrs. W. H. Campbell found traces of man along the beaches of vanished lakes in the southern California desert. At first Antevs believed that the lakes formed when the glaciers were melting away 20,000 to 25,000 years ago, but now he dates the artifacts and camp sites as less than 10,000 years old. At Lake Mohave, in the Campbells' first year of work, they found only stone tools—Mohave and Silver Lake points, as well as Folsom—but in the Pinto Basin they came upon the bones of extinct mammals as well as artifacts.[29] Malcolm J. Rogers challenges the dating of Mohave and Pinto as "largely a matter of opinion," and believes that "even approximate dates . . . cannot be set." In his own opinion, Pinto points—mixed with Gypsum in the same area—range only from 1,800 to 2,800 years ago. The Lake Mohave industry cannot begin, he maintains, earlier than 3,000 to 4,000 years ago.[30] In 1946, Robert F. Heizer and Edwin M. Lemert and later A. E. Treganza discovered in Topanga Canyon, north of Los

Pinto Basin   Lake Mohave   Silver Lake

Three early points from the borders of extinct lakes in the desert area of southern California. (The Pinto after Wormington, 1944; the other two after Campbell, 1937.)

Angeles, points and crude scrapers and choppers very like those at Lake Mohave and Gypsum Cave and also milling stones.[31] Lake Mohave artifacts have been found in northwestern Canada.[32]

A number of sites in the West and Southwest are particularly notable for their age or for the character of their artifacts, or for both. Some push the record of man in America back beyond Folsom, possibly far, far beyond; and some bring into the picture a type of artifact—the milling stone—which does not seem to have appeared in Europe until later. The publications upon these sites from 1935 to 1941 aroused much controversy even while broadening and deepening our knowledge of early man.

Confusion, as well as controversy, distinguishes the area which might prove the most significant of the four if more extended work were done there by geologists as well as archaeologists. This area is in the neighborhood of Abilene, Texas, and includes the banks of the Elm Creek branch of the Brazos River. Cyrus N. Ray, a local physician, has studied the Abilene sites assiduously for twenty years. In 1931 Gila Pueblo—Harold S. Gladwin's research institution—sent E. B. Sayles to work there. Later Gila arranged to have Antevs, Howard, and M. M. Leighton, Chief of the Illinois State Geo-
logical Survey, study the finds and the sites. It is unfortunate that the men who worked in this area have not agreed on a consistent set of names for the various cultures and geological formations. As H. M. Wormington has observed, "the only way to approach publications dealing with the archaeology of this region is with a large bottle of aspirin in either hand."

The artifacts occurred in two strata. The upper contained Generalized Folsom and a type of long, narrow point called Abilene. Leighton placed these tools from what he called the Elm Creek Silts in the latter portion of our last Glacial

An Abilene point. (After Wormington, 1944.)

period.[33] To reach Abilene at this time, early man may have passed through the gap that is thought to have appeared in the ice sheet east of the Rockies 40,000 years ago, or else when the Wisconsin ice of the last glaciers was in retreat 20,000 years later (see illustrations, pages 22 and 23).

Still greater age is claimed for certain other objects of the Abilene area. Below the Elm Creek Silts lie the Durst Silts, which were laid down, Leighton thinks, prior to the last glaciation.[34] In connection with these silts Sayles found what may be very crude artifacts.[35] They are the "eoliths" that, wherever found in the Old World, are accepted or attacked as problematical evidences of man's first attempts at roughly chipped artifacts. If these are indeed the work of man, and if Leighton is right, the men who made them must have come to Texas during the Sangamon Interglacial period preceding the last, or Wisconsin, glaciation—a matter of 70,000 years ago.

Some authorities attack Leighton's dating and therefore Sayles's eoliths. The reported discovery later of Abilene and Folsom points in the Durst Silts suggested to Kirk Bryan that the silts would have to be moved up in time.[36] He might have argued that the artifacts should be moved back, which would have been in line with his championing of very early man elsewhere. Agreeing with Bryan and C. C. Albritton, Frank C. Hibben redated the Durst Silts by connecting them with a late glacier in the Rocky Mountains rather than with the Wisconsin ice field of the north.[37] Leighton, on the other hand, maintained—and he has had some good support—that the soil at various depths had been radically changed by chemical action which would take tens of thousands of years. This "soil profile" theory as a test of geological age is gaining in importance.[38]

Sandia—Older Than Folsom   However problematical these evidences of pre-Folsom man near Abilene may be, there can be no doubt about the meaning of Frank C. Hibben's discoveries in Sandia Cave, New Mexico, in 1936. He began by finding the remains of Pueblo Indians. Under the Pueblo he came upon a layer of stalagmitic travertine one-half inch to six inches thick, laid down during a moist period. Sealed off beneath this were Folsom points together with scrapers and evidence of extinct mammals. Next he found another sterile seal, two inches to two feet thick. This time it was of yellow ocher—a substance induced by fir and spruce under moist conditions, Kirk Bryan points out. Fir and spruce require more cold and more moisture than the neighborhood of Sandia provides at present—which argues that the ocher was manufactured during the last pulsation of the fourth and final glaciation more than 25,000 years ago.[39] Beneath this stratum Hibben found a new type of point.[40] New to the New World, that is, but not to the Old; for it resembles in a crude way a point of the Solutrean culture of Europe which has a notch at the bottom to aid in hafting. Since this discovery, points of the same type have turned up sporadically throughout the Mississippi Valley and along the eastern seaboard. In every case, Hibben writes, there were indications of "considerable antiquity." In fourteen instances out of thirty-eight, "the points were found with extinct bones, although in each case by amateurs." [41]

The Sandia point is, of course, definitely older than the Folsom. The two periods of moisture indicate that the cave was inhabited by

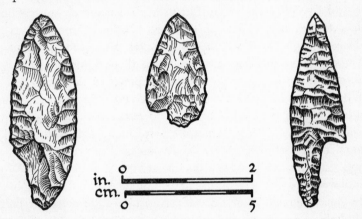

in.
cm.

A Sandia point, left, compared with two Solutreans. The first of the Solutreans was found with Mousterian artifacts in a cave in Tangier; the second, in France. (The Sandia point after Hibben, 1941; the Solutreans after Howe and Movius, 1947, and Plant, 1942.)

Folsom man toward the end of the last glaciation, or 15,000 to 25,000 years ago, and by Sandia man still earlier. Unless, of course, you wish to believe, as some do, that both pluvial periods were Postglacial.

A site discovered at Lime Creek, Nebraska, in 1947 may prove to be older than Sandia. In the sharp bank of the stream C. Bertrand Schultz found crude points, bone awls, scrapers, and tools made out of antlers. Together with fossils of mammals they lay as deep as forty-seven and one-half feet below the surface, in a silt containing the remains of decayed vegetation. Above this soil were seventeen feet of loess, another layer of soil, another layer of loess, and finally a "mature," or well developed, and therefore fairly old top soil. Schultz and W. D. Frankfurter write that the seventeen feet of loess covering the earth in which the artifacts were found appears to have been deposited before or at the beginning of the last expansion of the Wisconsin, or final, glaciation. If this is true, it means that the men of Lime Creek lived 25,000 or 35,000 years ago, and that their forebears may have come through the corridor in the ice fields of Canada 5,000 to 18,000 years earlier (see page 23). Antevs and Wormington doubt it.[42]

The Milling Stone Appears   In the early thirties archaeologists began to find a peculiar kind of artifact that broadened their conception of the activities of early man in the New World. Anthropologists had always thought of him as merely a hunter. He needed spear points, scrapers, knives, hammerstones to shape these things, and fire-drills to make it possible for him to cook his prey; but that was all. Then milling stones began to appear, and it became clear that early man— at least in some areas—had been a food gatherer and food grinder, as well as a hunter. These stones are very simple slabs with a hollow worn in the surface by round handstones used in grinding seeds and nuts. Such milling stones, or querns, are not seen in the Old World until we approach the Neolithic, or New Stone Age, and the people who developed agriculture and textiles. Agriculture did not enter Europe until about 2500 B.C., and milling stones are not found in its caves until after the Magdalenians of the Old Stone Age. The reason for the precipitate outcropping of milling stones in the Americas—they occur in Chile as well as North America—is not that our early man practiced agriculture. He did not do that, and he did not make polished stone axes until close to the birth of Christ. He was merely a food gatherer. Was he also a food grinder because he was an Australoid who brought the habit to America just as he brought it to Australia? Or, if not, was he another sort of man who happened to be smart enough to recognize that North America provided him with many tempting grains and seeds to grind, foods that were not so available in the Old World? [43] In Chile he used milling stones to grind paint and perhaps vegetal products.

The first site to provide milling stones was at White Water Creek in Arizona. Byron Cummings had found artifacts and fossils there in 1926. When Gladwin heard of this at an anthropological meeting five years later, he again set Gila Pueblo in motion. Sayles and Emil W.

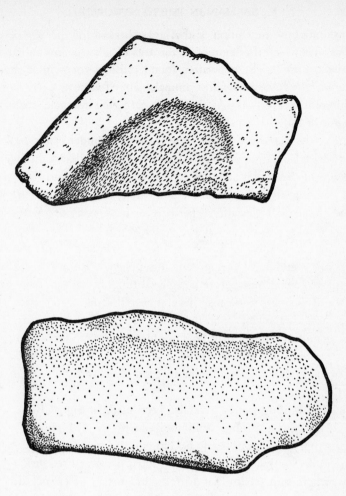

COCHISE MILLING STONES

The lower comes from the oldest horizon, the Sulphur Springs; the upper fragment, from a later one, probably the Chiricahua. (The Sulphur Springs stone after Martin, Quimby, and Collier, 1947; the other, courtesy of the Southwest Museum.)

Haury undertook excavation, and Antevs checked the geology of the various sites which they studied in the area of what is now called the Cochise culture.[44] The excavators found milling stones in the same stratum as the fossils of extinct animals. They found no spear points in this oldest level—a sign that food gathering was the dominant economy of the early Cochise.

The artifacts and the fossils were lying in or under clays left by a lake that has now disappeared. If Lake Cochise was, like Lake Bonneville, one of the bodies of water created while the last great ice sheets were growing, then the Cochise culture must date from the last wet period of the final glaciation—perhaps as much as 35,000 years ago. Antevs thinks, however, that the water which laid down the clays belonged to a number of ponds, not to a single large lake, and that the ponds could have formed and disappeared, formed again and disappeared again, just before postglacial times brought a much drier climate. Any single pond may have appeared as late as 10,000 years ago to provide the clay—and the date—for the Cochise culture. The Cochise milling stones may be far older, however, for among the extinct animals was the dire wolf, and the dire wolf became extinct earlier than other departed animals, certainly before the end of the Great Ice Age.

Finds of milling stones have also been made at Signal Butte, Nebraska, by W. D. Strong, at Pinto Basin by the Campbells [45]—the first site probably about as early as Gypsum, the other 10,000 years old —and under hardpan at that much disputed site near Frederick, Oklahoma, where some claim that artifacts and fossils of extinct animals appear together in an interglacial formation. Milling stones have also been found at sites of later cultures such as the Edwards Plateau in Texas and Santa Barbara in California. There are indications of an ancient horizon of milling stones, as well as Pinto and older points and scrapers, in Sonora and Lower California. The fact that they were found with the bones of elk and bison and along the shores of dry lakes in Mexico argues that this culture is as old as Cochise, perhaps older. Carl Sauer, who found the materials, believes that only during the last glaciation could the climate of these two desert areas have been moist enough to produce lakes and support so much animal life.[46]

At Borax Lake in California, in several years of work following 1938, Harrington found more milling stones. There were also quite a variety of points—Generalized Folsom, Gypsum, Pinto, Mohave, and Silver Lake—scattered through an alluvial fan of dirt carried down by some early stream that flowed when the country was well watered and verdant, instead of arid like so much of California today.[47]

In 1948 Harrington and Willy Stahl found milling stones and a great wealth of Pinto, Mohave, and Silver Lake points in another part of California that is now desert. This is near Little Lake, which is fed by underground waters and small intermittent streams from the Sierras. Near by, in glacial times, a small river cut a channel through a great lava flow, producing a falls that has now moved up half a mile from the edge of the lava. Here, where the blow sands of the Mohave Desert meet the lava, and under about ten feet of old, consolidated sand, Harrington and Stahl found milling stones and points in two feet of soil. This soil was dark with the remains of vegetation that must have been trees and bushes when the intermittent stream was still a steady torrent. Underneath the dark soil there was clay deposited by the stream at some period of great flow. Across about two-thirds of the camp site a similar coating of clay indicated that after the user of the milling stones and Pinto points had departed, the stream had overflowed again during a time of great rains. This time may have been the "Little Pluvial" of some 3,000 years ago, or the "Great Pluvial" that some say occurred 10,000 years ago when the glaciers had finally retreated, with the former the more likely date. In this camp site Harrington and Stahl found the post holes of some sort of hut or shelter, the oldest evidence of housebuilding in the New World.[48]

A Paucity of Art Objects Advanced as early man in America may have been in his stone industry, he seems to have been singularly backward in making the kind of spiritualized artifact which we call art. In the caves of France and Spain men of the Old Stone Age left remarkable paintings and sculptures of animals. There is nothing like this of corresponding age in the Americas. Early man in Europe and in northern Asia turned out many little figures of women—undoubtedly symbols of fecundity, since the female characteristics are

An animal head carved from the vertebra of a variety of llama, or camel, and reputedly found with fossils of other extinct mammals in the Valley of Mexico in 1870. About eight inches wide. (After Barcena, 1882.)

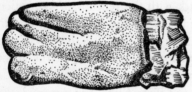

A sculptured foot carved from a mammoth's tooth. The little toe, which was at the top and to the back, has been broken off. About one and a half inches long. (After de Terra, 1948.)

highly exaggerated; but in the New World female figurines are to be found only in later levels such as those of the Eskimo, Southwestern, and Middle American cultures, all of which date from close to the birth of Christ. Of all the forms of art, we have only three examples that may have been made by early man. In the United States there are the dubious trio of crude, round heads which Sellards reports from a gravel pit in Henderson County, Texas.[49] During the digging of a canal in the Valley of Mexico in 1870, a workman picked out of a fossil-bearing stratum a vertebra of what was described as an extinct llama carved in the shape of a coyote's head. It was about forty feet below the surface of the ground in the same layer of earth with fossils

of elephant, horse, giant armadillo, and camel.[50] In 1948 Helmut
de Terra, while working in the same valley, obtained a small bit of
sculpture whose incisings held the same fine sand that he found in
a glacial beach from which he had extracted ivory tools and the
bones of mammoth and horse. It was a human foot carved from
the tooth of an elephant. He dates these artifacts at "several thousand years prior to the Tepexpan
Man," which means at least 14,000
or 15,000 years ago. He calls the
sculpture Upper Pleistocene.[51]

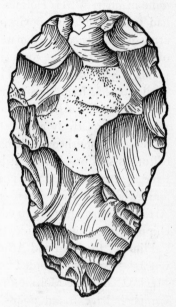

Hand Axes in the Americas Of
all the bits of stone that bear on the
existence of early man in America,
perhaps the most puzzling—and
certainly the most neglected—are
the artifacts which E. B. Renaud
has found in countless numbers in
southwestern Wyoming. Here at
105 sites on the arid surface of.
Black's Fork Valley he had picked.
up by 1940 some 7,000 chipped
stones—many of them like rude
hand axes—which suggest a parallel with the industries of paleolithic
man in the Old World.[52] European
authorities such as J. Reid Moir,

A hand ax of the Black's Fork culture. (Courtesy of the Denver Museum
of Natural History.)

champion of English eoliths, Reginald A. Smith, of the British Museum, and D. Peyroni, of the Musée des Eyzies, have stated that Renaud's finds agree in type with the hand axes, choppers, and blades of
the Chellean, Acheulean, Mousterian, and Clactonian cultures of Europe and Africa. While emphasizing the resemblances, Renaud is careful to claim no parallel in time.

Renaud's artifacts recall a gathering of hand axes under most unscientific circumstances more than sixty years ago. In the late 1880's
Thomas Wilson of the National Museum became convinced that the

collections under his care contained numerous hand axes of paleolithic type and age. He listed 950 in the Museum and appealed through a printed circular for more examples. He got them. His correspondents in thirty-five states donated 789 and described enough more to bring the total up to 8,501.[53]

Wilson's hand axes and Renaud's artifacts were attacked in the same manner. W. H. Holmes of the Bureau of American Ethnology had little trouble in convincing the scientific public that Wilson's array of casually collected material came from quarries and workshops of the Indian and were cores from which he had struck flakes to make points or scrapers. The critics of Renaud's artifacts pointed to certain similar objects found less plentifully in late camp sites on the Plains, and suggested that Renaud's artifacts might be merely the blanks and rejects of a relatively recent stone industry.[54] Many of the finds are certainly not finished implements, and the date of the Black's Fork culture is still problematical; but among Renaud's material there are hand axes and scrapers that bear comparison with the cruder Chellean and Acheulean work. There are also chopping tools of Asiatic and African pattern, made from edged pebbles that have been deliberately chipped, first from one side, then from the other.

Flints of Chellean and Acheulean types—whether true artifacts or rejects—have been recorded by Kirk Bryan at Cerro Pedernal in New Mexico.[55] At Lake Mohave in the Pinto Basin, Mr. and Mrs. W. H. Campbell have found points of a Mousterian shape and scrapers suggestive of the Aurignacian. They are so crude, however, that they seem more like the "elementary ideas" which, as Bastian claimed, could be the product of primitive man anywhere. In Texas, there are many tools so well developed and so close to Acheulean forms that they cannot be turned aside as either "elementary ideas" or blanks and rejects. These are the hand axes which Sayles and other archaeologists have found.[56]

Early Man in Mexico   Besides the skull which de Terra found with the fossils of elephants in Mexico there are artifacts south of the border which reinforce the argument for early man. They are more important than the chance resemblance to a Folsom point which

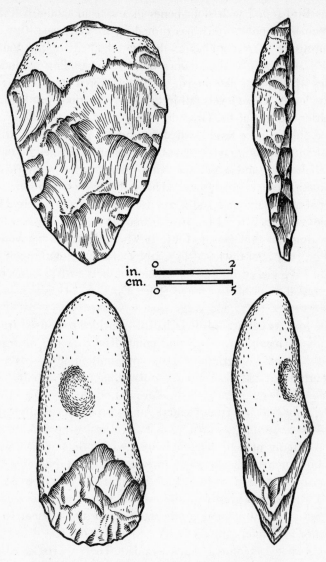

in. 0 2

cm. 0 5

A HAND AX AND A CHOPPING TOOL FROM TEXAS

The dating of these tools is uncertain, but the upper resembles early paleolithic specimens from Europe despite its more flakelike quality. The other is somewhat like chopping tools made from pebbles in Asia and Africa. (Courtesy of Gila Pueblo.)

Junius Bird found with sloth bones in a cave in southern Chile, or the Yuma-like point which has turned up in Venezuela.[57]

During de Terra's studies of the dry lake beds of the Valley of Mexico and the glacial moraines on the surrounding mountains— studies which began late in 1945—he discovered stone tools in two culture levels. These levels fall in two pluvial periods just before and just after the end of the Great Ice Age.

The older culture level—called San Juan—contained ten artifacts, including scrapers, gravers, flakes, and chipped pebbles of obsidian and chalcedony and a pointed bone tool, together with fossils of mammoth, sloth, camel, bison, and horse. De Terra found some of this material at Tequixquiac and some near Teotihuacán, where Manuel Gamio came upon fossil bones of mammoth and bison when he was excavating that famous site. Close to where de Terra discovered the skull of early man discussed in Chapter 6, another anthropologist is said to have picked up part of a point of Folsom type—the first to be recorded south of the United States. De Terra places the San Juan culture 12,000 to 20,000 years ago.

The younger culture—called Chalco—provided sixty-five variegated artifacts of basalt, including one point. The presence of manos— roundish stones for grinding seeds on a milling stone—as well as other artifacts, causes de Terra to compare this culture with the Cochise in Arizona. He dates the Chalco culture at 4,000 to 10,000 years ago.[58]

The only evidence from Central America—neither skulls nor arti-facts—is extraordinary in nature, but as yet makes no definite contri-bution in terms of years. The finds are the footprints of men, women, and children in a lava bed at El Cauce near Managua, Nicaragua. They are buried beneath many feet of ash and lava and four separate layers of soil. At a time of great rainfall—which suggests a pluvial connected with either the formation or the melting of the glaciers—a river excavated a channel sixty feet wide and almost ten feet deep. Geolo-gists have not yet ventured to give us a date. There are tracks, however, of a bison—an animal long extinct so far south.[59]

The story of early man in the Americas, so far as it is interpreted by the finding of his artifacts, did not begin with Folsom and will not end with the most recent discoveries in Middle America. As far back as 1869 a geologist named C. J. King found a pestle—ordinarily a product of the Neolithic, or New Stone, Age of polished artifacts—so firmly cemented into the gold-bearing gravels under Table Mountain near Tuttleton, California, that he "forced it out of its place with considerable difficulty." [60] (Other neolithic implements had been reported from mine shafts in the 1860's, but none had been found by a geologist imbedded in gravels.) As late as 1919, W. H. Holmes, ever critical of evidence for early man, called King's pestle "the most important observation yet made by a geologist bearing upon the problem of man's antiquity in America." [61] If the gravels in which the pestle was found and the lava which lay just above it were indeed products of the Pliocene period which preceded the Great Ice Age, then we have to face a staggering idea. We have to believe that a strain of *Homo sapiens* originated in the New World long before Java man. We have to believe that he acquired the skills of the New Stone Age far ahead of man in the Old World, and that he then dis-

The broken pestle found by C. J. King in gold-bearing gravels in California. (After Becker, 1891.)

appeared. It is easier—but not too easy—to think that the lava flowed in recent times, after glacial waters had worked a pestle of early man into the gold-bearing gravels, which would push the seed-grinders of California far, far back in time. It is still easier to believe that King was out of his head.

The excavations and studies of the next few years may not provide evidence as startling as King's, but carbon 14, the new time clock, promises to date any site of early man where a few ounces of charcoal can be found. Already W. F. Libby has provided a date between about 6,300 and 6,900 years ago for trees charred by the eruption of pumice from Mt. Mazama, Oregon, and beneath this pumice lie four or five sites where L. S. Cressman has found artifacts of early man and the fossils of horse and camel.[62] Similar tests are going forward on almost a dozen prehistoric sites.

THE MORE IMPORTANT SITES OF EARLY MAN

The listing on the three next pages is not exhaustive. There is room for argument over a number of the finds; but the arrangement of the materials in columns provides a rough perspective. The sites are listed in order of discovery. The symbols indicate one or more occurrences: 🕱, skull; ◢, part of skull; ✕, a considerable number of bones; ◥, a few bones; 💀 and ✕, a skeleton or the major parts; ◗, Folsom; ✖, Plainview; |, Yuma; ▲, other types of point; ✋, charcoal; ▬, milling stone; ♣, pottery; ◉, rocks thrown by man; ✵, horn and shell objects; +, bone and flake tools; △, bone tools and a human foot carved from a mammoth's tooth; 🐘, mammoth or mastodon; 🐃, extinct bison; 🐏, sloth; 🐪, extinct camel; 🐎, extinct horse. Occurrence of the saber-toothed tiger, tapir, giant beaver, or extinct armadillo is not indicated. The Plainview symbol does not suggest the shape of the point, but rather the fact that in type it lies between Folsom and Yuma. Finds that seem problematical or not definitely associated with other finds are shaded. Sandia points were found with the five extinct mammals indicated in the Sandia cave and below the Folsom. Finds at Little Lake, Calif., Lime Creek, Nebr., Bat Cave, N. M., and in Lower California were too late for inclusion.

Date	Place	Human Bones	Artifacts, Fires	Extinct Mammals
1835-1844	Lagoa Santa, Brazil	🕱 (skull)		○
1838	Gasconade County, Mo.		(disk) (fire)	(sloth)
1839	Benton County, Mo.		(arrowhead)	(mammoth)
1846	Natchez, Miss.	(bone)		(mammoth) (sloth) (horse)
1872-1879	Trenton, N.J.	(bone)	(spear point)	(mammoth) (bison)
1872	Omaha, Nebr.		(spear point)	(mammoth)
1882	Lake Lahontan, Nev.		(spear point)	(mammoth) (bison) (camel) (horse)
1895	Russell Springs, Kans.		(spear point)	(bison)
1902	Lansing, Kans.	(skull) (crossbones)		
190?	Paltacalo, Ecuador	(skull)		
1915-1916	Vero, Fla.	(skull) (bone)		(mammoth) (sloth) (horse)
1920	Sacramento, Calif.	(skull) (crossbones)	(spear point) (bar)	
1923-1927	Santa Barbara, Calif.	(skull) (crossbones)	(spear point) (bar)	
1923	Melbourne, Fla.	(skull) (bone)	(spear point) (fire)	(mammoth) (sloth) (horse)
1923 & 1931	Grand Island, Nebr.		(artifact)	(bison)
1923	Punin, Ecuador	(skull)		(mammoth) (sloth) (horse)
1924	Lone Wolf Creek, Tex.		(artifact) (spear point)	(bison)

137

Date	Place	Human Bones	Artifacts, Fires	Extinct Mammals
1926	Folsom, N.M.		(point)	(bison)
1926 & 1935–1940	Lake Cochise, White Water Creek, Ariz.	(point, bone)	(log, fire)	(mammoths, camels, horse)
1926	Frederick, Okla.		(point)	(mammoth, sloth, camels, horse)
1928	Alangasi, Ecuador		(pot, fire)	(mammoth)
1929	Abilene, Tex.		(point, crossed tools, point, fire)	(mammoth, horse)
1929	Conkling Cavern, N.M.	(skull, bone)		(sloth, camels, horse)
1930	Burnet Cave, N.M.		(point)	(bison, camel, horse)
1930	Gypsum Cave, Nev.		(point)	(sloth, camel, horse)
1931	Pelican Rapids, Minn.	(skull, crossed bones)	(wheel)	
1931	Angus, Nebr.		(point)	(mammoths)
1931	Yuma, Colo.		(point)	(mammoth, bison)
1932	Signal Butte, Nebr.		(crossed tools, point, log, fire)	
1932	Clovis, N.M.		(point, crossed tools, fire)	(mammoth, bison, camel, horse)
1932	Scottsbluff, Nebr.		(point, point)	(bison)
1932	Dent, Colo.		(point)	(mammoth)
1933	Browns Valley, Minn.	(skull, crossed bones)	(crossed tools, point)	
1934	Lindenmeier, Colo.		(point, crossed tools, point, fire)	(mammoth, bison, camel)
1934	Miami, Tex.		(point)	(mammoth)
1934	Pinto Basin, Calif.		(point, log)	(camels, horse)
1935	Confins, Brazil	(skull, bone)		(mammoth, sloth, horse)
1935	Sauk Valley, Minn.	(skull, bone)		

Date	Place	Human Bones	Artifacts, Fires	Extinct Mammals
1936	Lake Mohave, Calif.		(point)	
1936	Sandia Cave, N.M.		(point) (crossed tools) (point) (fire)	(mammoth) (bison) (sloth) (camel) (horse)
1936–1937	Cerro Sota Hill, Chile	(skull & crossbones)	(point)	(sloth) (horse)
1936–1937	Fell's Cave, Chile		(point) (fire)	(sloth) (horse)
1936–1937	Palli Aike Cave, Chile	(crossbones)	(point) (fire)	(sloth) (horse)
1937–1945	Borax Lake, Calif.		(point) (tool) (fire)	
1938	Bee County, Tex.		(point) (fire)	(mammoth) (bison) (horse)
1938	Lipscomb County, Tex.		(point)	(bison)
1939	Ventana Cave, Ariz.		(point) (point)	(bison) (sloth) (horse)
1939	Mortlach, Sask.		(point) (blade)	(bison)
1940	Eden, Wyo.		(blade)	(bison)
1941	San Jon, N.M.		(point) (crossed tools) (point)	(bison)
1941	San Luis Valley, Colo.		(point) (crossed tools)	(bison)
1941	Fairbanks, Alaska		(blade)	(mammoth)
1941	Circle, Alaska		(crossed tools)	(mammoth)
1941	Cook Inlet, Alaska		(crossed tools) (fire)	(mammoth)
1945	Plainview, Tex.		(crossed tools)	(bison)
1946	Monument Site, Concord, Calif.	(skull & crossbones)	(point)	
1946–1947	Tequixquiac, Mex.		+	(mammoth) (camel) (sloth) (camel) (horse)
1947	Tepexpan, Mex.	(skull & crossbones)	(point)	(mammoth)
1948	Totolzingo, Mex.		(triangle)	(mammoth) (horse)

139

8

EARLY MAN AND THE GREAT EXTINCTION

And prate about an Elephant
Not one of them has seen!

—J. G. SAXE

A Twofold Problem   A mammoth in Colorado . . . a giant sloth near Boulder Dam . . . spear points of early man involved with both. Those two remote and spectacular animals roaming our own United States set our minds far back on the trail of time. The weapons, crude as they were and pitifully small, carry us forward again tens of thousands of years. I am describing the reaction of the layman who first learns of these things, but the opinions of science veer almost as widely when it tries to date the traffic of man and mammoth in the New World. The range is from 100,000 years ago to 2500 B.C.

The dating of the life of early man by the death of mammals now extinct is one of the major tasks that face the American prehistorian. It is doubly difficult because, in the first place, evidence of when these animals died off is not yet available, and may never be, and, secondly, because we must also know how long man hunted them *before* they became extinct. We know that a few skulls have been found in strata containing the fossils of these animals, and we know that all but one of the skulls are long-headed and beetle-browed like those of the Australians and the Melanesians, instead of round-headed like those of most Mongoloids. We know that Sandia and Folsom points have

140

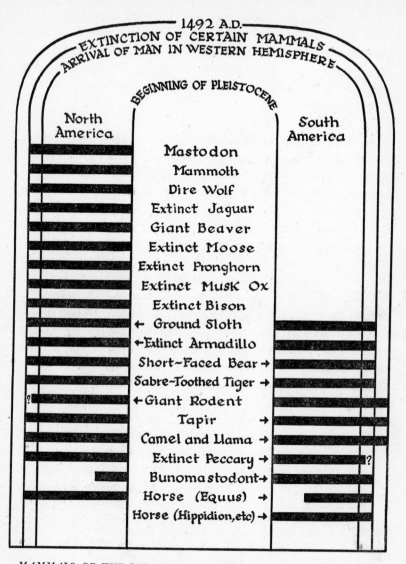

MAMMALS OF THE ICE AGE IN NORTH AND SOUTH AMERICA

A chart of the chief animals that became extinct after the arrival of man. The "extinct armadillo" and "giant rodent," above, are more correctly known as glyptodont and capybara. (After Colbert, 1942, with some rearrangement.)

been found with the fossils of extinct elephants, horses, camels, and bison. If we knew when such mammals became extinct, we should know the latest possible date of most of the archaic skulls and of Sandia and Folsom man. But we should still not know just how much earlier some of these humans lived, or when they or their predecessors discovered America.

Myths and Mammoths The subject has been thoroughly confused by too many guesses and too little evidence. Besides a great variety of geologic theories and some amazingly stubborn conservatism, we have had some extraordinary Indian myths as well as the dreams of innocents and eccentrics.

If the Spanish churchmen were a bit upset at finding in the Indies both a new world and a race unaccounted for in the Bible, later explorers and settlers of the mainland were quite as astonished over the discovery of huge bones in swamps and creeks, prairies and badlands. Laymen and divines sought explanations, and of course they found dozens, most of them as absurd as Cotton Mather's dictum of 1712 that the bones were those of the giants of Holy Writ. By 1782 Thomas Jefferson knew they belonged to a kind of elephant, but on "the traditional testimony of the Indians" he was inclined to believe "that this animal still exists in the northern and western parts of America. . . . He may as well exist there now as he did formerly where we find his bones." [1]

The bridge from sacred fiction to profane fact, from giants to mammoths and mastodons, seems to have been the work, oddly enough, of Negro slaves. Mark Catesby wrote in 1743:

At a place in *Carolina* called *Stono* was dug out of the Earth three or four Teeth of a large animal, which by the concurring Opinion of all the *Negroes,* native *Africans,* that saw them, were the Grinders of an Elephant, and in my Opinion that could be no other; I having seen some of the like that are brought from *Africa.*[2]

On the basis of this statement Loren C. Eiseley—who has written much on the problem of the extinction of American mammals—believes that the Negro slaves told the Indian as well as the white man about the animal that had such gigantic bones, and described its shape and habits.

The eighteenth century white man—eager for knowledge of zoology and many other things—pumped the Indian, and doubtless with leading questions. The Indians, "involved in their own vast animal mythology," as Eiseley puts it, were likely to respond "to these myriads of questions with elaboration and a desire to please." [3] Thus, when our ancestors asked where the elephants had gone, the Indians answered, "Across the lakes." Soon the belief that the mammoth still lived in the remoter portions of northeastern Canada grew so strong in white men that early maps indicated his home in western Labrador. By the time that the ethnologists of the last half-century began collecting Indian myths there were numerous traditions of the elephant in the native folklore. In a summary of the material Duncan Strong lists more than a dozen instances.[4] An Algonquin tribe told of a great animal "with an arm coming out of its shoulder," and of another that left "large round tracks in the snow" and "struck its enemies with its long nose." Penobscot Indians had a myth in which a culture hero saw "moving hills without vegetation," which proved to be "great animals with long teeth, animals so huge that when they lay down they could not get up." There were stories of "a great moose with a fifth leg." Elephant myths turned up among the Alabama Indians in the South. The Chitimacha said: "A long time ago a being with a long nose came out of the ocean and began to kill people. It would root up trees with its nose to get at people who sought refuge in the branches." The Eskimos of Alaska joined their Siberian brothers in tales of a behemoth that burrowed underground and died if he breathed air—a tale derived, no doubt, from the carcasses of mammoths found frozen under the snow. "These stories," writes Eiseley, "show a suspicious growth in numbers just at the time when White interest and enthusiasm were keenest." [5]

Whatever germ of truth may lie in some of the Indian traditions, certain theorists of the last century and a half were quite as absurd as Cotton Mather in their conclusions. In 1806 an Englishman named Thomas Ashe wrote of "incognita, nondescript animals" of the Middle West, and suggested that "as the immense volume of the creature

would unfit him for coursing after his prey through thickets and
woods," nature had "furnished him with the power of taking a
mighty leap." [6] Then there was John Ranking, who published in
1827 *Historical Researches on the Conquest of Peru, Mexico, Bogota,
Natchez, and Talomeco, in the Thirteenth Century, by the Mongols,
Accompanied with Elephants.* Perhaps he was religious enough to
believe, like Jefferson, that "no instance can be produced, of her
[nature] having permitted any one race of her animals to become
extinct." [7] At any rate, Ranking remembered the "divine wind" that
balked Kubla Khan's invasion of Japan, and he allowed it to blow
some of Kubla's vessels to the New World. A son of the Khan
became the first Inca, another Mongol noble founded Montezuma's
line, and the Khan's elephants of war spread all up and down the
two continents—a notion reported in 1778 by Johann R. Forster.[8]

In 1880, worried over how the Mound Builders could have transported so much earth, Frederick Larkin suggested that the Indians
must have domesticated the mammoth: "We can imagine that tremen-
dous teams have been driven to and fro in the vicinity of their great
works." As evidence he offered a "copper relic" with an elephant
engraved on it "in harness." [9]

Archaeological Evidence of Recent Man and the Mastodon   The
American archaeologist has found no evidence of the mammoth as a
living factor in the life of the American Indian since the time of
Christ. He looks askance at two elephant pipes of doubtful provenience
which turned up near Davenport, Iowa, around the eighties. He is not
impressed by a carved head, which might be either elephant or
macaw, on a stone stela in Copan, Honduras. But he must give more
respectful attention to certain evidence concerning the mastodon—
that early form of elephant which alone of all the order penetrated
to South America and was unknown in much of the Old World during
the Great Ice Age. Its bones have been found in peat bogs of the
Great Lakes area which formed after the glaciers began to melt, and a
skeleton has been unearthed near Quito, Ecuador, cheek by jowl with
broken pottery.

The South American mastodon was found twelve miles from Quito in a district where the bones of the horse, the extinct sloth, and an extinct relative of the armadillo have also been discovered. Franz Spillman of the University of Quito made the find, and Max Uhle cooperated in the excavation. Uhle states that the scientific facts recorded are beyond question. The animal lay on his left side, apparently mired in what is now a yellow clay which lies upon a thick layer of blue clay. A small landslide had covered the skeleton and the clay. There were a number of evidences of man. The ribs of the right side had been cut away. There were remains of fire which had been lighted in the belly and around the feet and tail, and which had baked some of the clay touching the animal. Spillman and Uhle found parts of flint artifacts, a shaped bone tool, and some lengths of wood beside an erect block of stone, which suggested levers and a fulcrum used in an attempt to lift portions of the mastodon. They also found—and this is the important point so far as dating is concerned—more than 150 pieces of broken pottery.[10]

Eiseley maintains that the site's "archaeological neglect has been scandalous. If this site had been claimed to be 'Pleistocene' many experts would undoubtedly have journeyed even to this out-of-the-way location." Because of the claim that the find was Neolithic, it has not received the thorough study which a Folsom find would unquestionably have received in North America. If the mastodon actually survived until the time of pottery in South America, says Eiseley, this does not demonstrate that the animal lingered as late in North America.[11] But it plays hob with the antiquity of a South American skull from Punin.

There are two curious factors in this discovery. The first is that coal was found in the remnants of the fire. Did the Indians of Ecuador use that fuel before the Spaniards came? Was there a deposit nearer than that in Peru? The second questionable factor has to do with the pottery. Although there were no fewer than 152 broken pieces, they could not be fitted into even one restored pot. Why? Further, 140 of the sherds were from a primitive type of pottery, imperfectly fired, while 12 pieces were from an advanced and decorated type which, in other locations, is supposed to show Maya influence. Why should two varieties of pottery—so widely separated in technique and, presumably, age—appear at this one time?

If the Quito mastodon and pots were indeed neighbors in time, then they provide the only evidence—ex post facto, at that—for the remarkable statement of the geologist William B. Scott in 1913: "Many Pleistocene mammals were in existence only a few centuries ago, in what is called 'historic time' in the Old World. Several skeletons of the American Mastodon have been found in bogs, covered by only a few inches of peat, with more or less of the hair and recognizable contents of the stomach preserved." [12] Eiseley has questioned the evidence that the mastodon had hair, and he has pointed out that a peat bog is an ideal place for the preservation of vegetable matter such as that animal lived upon.[13] The bogs and their fossils lie to the south of the Great Lakes, which formed as the ice fields began to retreat into Canada. Since the retreat began between 20,000 and 25,000 years ago, it is obvious that bogs could have formed and mastodons been trapped in them far longer ago than a few centuries—whether "few" means five, ten, or even fifteen.

A hundred years ago Charles Lyell commented on the profusion of mastodon bones in North American bogs compared with the paucity of such fossils in the bogs of Europe; and argued for the late survival of these animals in the New World.[14] Answering him Eisley points out first of all that for many centuries such skeletons were hunted out and salvaged by Europeans in search of ivory or the *materia medica* of the unicorn's horn. Further, the mastodon, which was a forest lover and fell a natural victim to bogs, was unknown to Europe, while the mammoth kept mainly to dry, open steppes. We know that bogs both in our Great Lakes area and in northern Europe were postglacial, "and that is all. There exists no evidence, at present, which seems to demand in the New World a lingering extinction of the American elephants in a way much different from the course of events in Europe." [15]

Sloth and Camel in Dry Caves   When we turn from the mastodon preserved in wet peat bogs, we come upon the camel and the sloth in dry caves. There, buried in dust, are skin, hair, and ligaments, as well as bone. Not a great deal of such remains exist, however, and only in a few caves—and this time "few" means less than five. It happens that dry and dust-filled caves are almost as good embalmers as the bogs of the Great Lakes or the ice of Siberia and the Alaska muck beds. "In a perfectly dry limestone cave," says Howard, "covered by three to ten feet of dust, there seems to be no reason why the hair and tissue of the sloth, camel, horse, or bison could not have been preserved for several thousands of years." [16]

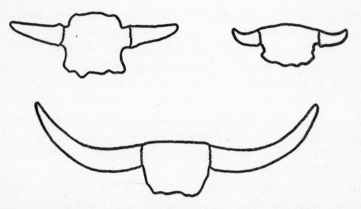

Prehistoric and modern bison. Above at the left is an outline of typical horn cones of *Bison antiquus antiquus,* whose bones have been found with Folsom points. Its horns were longer and straighter than those of the buffalo of today, *Bison bison,* shown at the right. Below is a still larger and more ancient type, *Superbison latifrons,* with an eighty-inch span.

The Folsom Bison Not Extinct?   Neither elephant nor sloth, neither horse nor camel, is such a common companion of the points of Folsom man as is an extinct form of bison. It was larger than the historic animal, and had longer and straighter horns. Though it is known variously as *Bison taylori, Bison antiquus antiquus,* and *Bison occidentalis,* it was probably of a single type. Now one of the significant things about Folsom is that the point never turns up with the modern variety of buffalo which goes by the interesting name of *Bison bison* [17] —unless, of course, lack of skull material has led scientists astray. Therefore, if we seek the latest date of Folsom, it would seem as if we must seek the death day of the extinct bison.

Protagonists of early man have argued that Folsom must date far,

far back, or there would not be time for the evolution of the modern bison of the High Plains. Lately, however, Eiseley has developed a theory which does away with the long period of evolution from *Bison taylori* into *Bison bison,* and yet pins down Folsom to the end of the glaciers. There is some evidence that the kind of bison Folsom man hunted migrated up into Canada when the glaciers melted, and that the "modern" variety, which we call "buffalo," came up from the south and took over the High Plains. As the temperature moderated over the whole northern hemisphere the plains of Canada began to resemble the plains of the United States, where the prey of Folsom man had flourished. The climate and the vegetation of the High Plains, moving north behind the ice, took *Bison taylori* along. The same northward movement of climate and vegetation occurred from Mexico to the High Plains, and it carried to their historic habitat the buffalo that have left their bones in old soils south of the border. The only place where we meet the two varieties of bison together is a peat bog in Minnesota.[18]

The evidence that *Bison taylori* moved to Canada is not complete, but it is suggestive. There are accounts of bison horns from Athabasca "nearly twice the length of the Plains' ones and much straighter." [19] Ernest Thompson Seton provides the same kind of evidence.[20] The Canadian bison and the Folsom variety seem "suspiciously similar," says Eiseley. Unfortunately, in 1925, before the bison of Athabasca had been properly measured and observed, *Bison bison* from the High Plains were brought north to breed with the Canadian variety. Eiseley feels it is a possibility that the Athabascan animals "represented, at least in a mixed form, the last of the Ice Age bison which early man had hunted in the western plains." [21] If this is true, it means that Folsom man was fully developed in the period before the melting of the glaciers drove his favorite game north to Canada. It means, further, that he may have entered the plains 40,000 years ago when a corridor opened through the western ice fields. (See illustration, page 22.)

The Folsom bison may also have gone northeast to the edge of New England. Grasslands extend from the High Plains of the Classic Folsom point northeast to Illinois and Indiana, and ancient steppes once ran through Ohio to New York State and probably to New

Jersey and southern New England.[22] Antevs suggests that late bands of Folsom men pursued their bison across this area. Certainly they left their cruder form of point in this part of the Middle West and the East.[23] But where, in this area, are the fossils of the extinct bison?

The Mystery of Extinction   A hundred years ago the French scientist Cuvier, who gave much time to the study of the fossils of extinct mammals, presented the "cataclysmal" explanation of their end. They were destroyed by sudden great geologic changes. To us, perhaps, these changes seem to have ignored certain other animals in a most disquieting way. Cuvier was at a disadvantage, of course, for he was working in a Bible-ridden world which had to accept the Book of Genesis as fact. Even as late as 1887, Henry H. Howorth wrote in *The Mammoth and the Flood:*

These facts . . . prove in the first place that a great catastrophe or cataclysm occurred at the close of the Mammoth period, by which that animal, with its companions, were overwhelmed over a very large part of the earth's surface. Secondly, this cataclysm involved a very widespread flood of water, which not only killed the animals but also buried them under continuous beds of loam or gravel. Thirdly, that the same catastrophe was accompanied by a very great and sudden change of climate in Siberia, by which the animals which had previously lived in fairly temperate conditions were frozen in their flesh underground and have remained frozen ever since.[24]

In the hundred years since Koch found a mammoth and a spear point in Missouri we have learned little that is definite about the reasons for the extinction of mammoth, mastodon, camel, horse, sloth, and the rest. We merely know that they died out as the glaciers began to melt. The most natural guess for either scientist or amateur is that change of climate was the lethal factor. Yet we know that many of them had already survived drastic changes of climate and lived through interglacials as well as glacials in the Great Ice Age. Further, how do we account for the survival of deer, antelope, fox, rabbit, moose, beaver, bear, and so many other animals? How could climate be so selective? If the dire wolf died, why not the timber wolf? If the short-faced bear, why not the grizzly? If one form of rabbit and three forms of antelope, why not all rabbits and all antelopes? If disease instead of climate was the great eliminator—as some have suggested —we face the same dilemma.

The mysteries of extinction are so many and so baffling that it is small wonder no book in English has been written on the subject. Since 1906, when Henry Fairfield Osborn summed the matter up in his paper of fifty-odd pages, "The Causes of Extinction of Mammalia," Eiseley credits only two theories with contributing anything new to the discussion.

One is the hypothesis of Sewall Wright and his co-workers that when an animal was greatly reduced in numbers it would suffer fatally from inbreeding.[25] This, however, leaves us still searching for what reduced its numbers so radically.

The other theory is Sauer's: Man, the hunter, destroyed the larger, clumsier, and more gregarious animals largely by means of fire drives, and these fires made the grasslands.[26] Or, at least, the fire drives "broke the back" of mammalian resistance.[27] Eiseley objects on a number of grounds. It was not alone the large, clumsy, and gregarious animals that disappeared. Certain mollusks, a variety of toad, a subfamily of rabbits, the dire wolf, the saber-toothed tiger, three forms of antelope, the short-faced bear, and a small horse also disappeared. More damaging still to Sauer's theory is the fact that a number of birds became extinct. Eiseley asks, "Why, if this method was so deadly, did the living bison and the living antelope roam the plains in countless numbers?" He points out that, while there is abundant evidence of extinct bison caught and killed in fire drives, there is no proof of mass kills of mammoth, horse, camel, and antelope.[28] He also mentions the mastodon, the giant beaver, and the sloth, which frequented eastern forests or northern bogs and died in them. "Though man was on the scene at the final perishing, his was not . . . the appetite nor the capacity for such gigantic slaughter." [29] Though Sauer believes that the numbers of hunting man in the New World were comparatively large when he killed *Bison taylori,* most authorities disagree. Alfred S. Romer believes that if man had been numerous enough and deadly enough to play a major part in the killing, we should find more evidences of his association with the extinct mammals.[30]

Romer and Edwin H. Colbert have put forward another explanation for the extinction of the mammals. They suggest that the advent of man in the New World may have upset a nicely balanced state of nature.[31] But man had been living with just such animals in the Old World for hundreds of thousands of years before they became extinct. What, then, destroyed the mammoth in Europe?

The most puzzling of all the fossils of extinct animals are those in the deep Alaska muck beds. Their numbers are appalling. They lie frozen in tangled masses, interspersed with uprooted trees. They seem to have been torn apart and dismembered and then consolidated under catastrophic conditions. Yuma and Plainview spear points and perhaps one Generalized Folsom have been found in these chill beds. Skin, ligament, hair, flesh, can still be seen.[32] If scientists can solve this mystery before the high-pressure water stream of the miner disperses the evidence, perhaps we shall be nearer solving one of the greatest and most tantalizing problems involved in the story of early man—the date of the extinction of the great mammals.

This problem of when the mammoth died should puzzle the Old World as well as the New and cause us to question the dating of Neanderthal and Cro-Magnon quite as much as Folsom man. Oddly enough, it does nothing of the kind. In Europe the mammoth is accepted as diagnostic of the glacial period. The fact that a Magdalenian man of southern France sketched a mammoth on the wall of a cave proves that the man existed in the Great Ice Age. But in America, if a spear point turns up with the bones of a mammoth, too many anthropologists accept it as proof that the animal died after the ice fields had melted. The mammoth proves the antiquity of man in Europe; man proves the modernity of the mammoth in America. The only shred of evidence to support such reasoning is the questionable pottery and coal that lay beside the mastodon bones in Ecuador. We should have more and better proof. Carbon 14 may provide it. This new time-clock should certainly give us a final date for the great extinction.

9

PYGMIES, AUSTRALOIDS, AND NEGROIDS — BEFORE INDIANS?

Let us have all the skeletons out of the closet.

—EARNEST A. HOOTON

The Mythical Indian Race   Science has found a great many artifacts and a few skulls that seem to have belonged to early man. Was he an Indian? Was he a Paleo-Indian—whatever that may imply? Was he a Mongoloid with an admixture of Australoid, Negroid, and White? Was he Mongoloid at all?

Among the most blatant misnomers of popular science is "Indian race." Even in North America it is an absurdity. Throw in Middle America and South America, and the attempt to fit the people of the New World into this or any one racial pigeonhole becomes laughable. Living Indians of pure breed show an immense variety in all physical features except their eyes, their hair, their cheekbones, and their upper front teeth. Some of their skulls and some of the skulls of their dead —particularly those that belonged to early man—show marked differences from those of the Mongoloid race of which the Indians are all commonly supposed to be a part. The differences are so marked that some of our physical anthropologists believe that other races than the Mongoloid contributed to the discovery and settlement of the Americas. They see at least one and possibly three such contributions. If we discount transpacific migration, we must accept the fact that all the peoples of northern Asia did not always belong to the now ubiquitous Mongoloid race.

The Mongoloid has four physical traits that are definitely dominant. Which means that, in any mixture with another race, four traits seem likely to be transmitted to immediate descendants. One trait is the peculiar shovel shape of the upper incisor, or front, teeth. The second is brown eyes. The third is straight black hair. The fourth is prominent cheekbones, or malars. Of course, there are minor irregularities. Not all the millions of incisors of our Indians are shovel-shaped. The hair of the Lacandon Indians of southern Mexico may have a reddish tinge.

The eye of a Chinese with the Mongoloid fold, contrasted
with the eye of a White man. (After Hooton, 1931.)

But the great majority of New World Indians share these traits, including prominent cheekbones, and, by so much, they share also a very considerable amount of Mongoloid blood.

In addition, there are many traits typical of Asiatic Mongoloids which appear very irregularly in the Americas. The "Mongoloid fold" —an overhanging fold of skin on the upper eyelid—is found in some tribes and not in others, and in certain individuals of a tribe and not in others. The bony structure of the face varies greatly. Some tribes have strong chins; some, weak ones. The nose of the typical Plains Indian is hawklike—a violent departure from the Mongoloid's rather flat nasal equipment. The "Semitic" nose of the Maya is Japanese but not at all Chinese. "The Indian type," says Nelson, "is distinguishable in one way or another from its nearest Mongoloid relations, and at the same time is separable according to some authorities into about ten more or less distinct varieties." [1]

Looked at in terms of resemblances to Old World peoples, the American Indian becomes a very crazy quilt of races. Hooton sees "an almost pre-Dravidian look" about the Lacandons which vaguely reminds him of the Veddas of India. He finds that many Indians of the

Northwest coast resemble Alpine Europeans, and that eastern Indians have a "European look," and are "by no means as Mongoloid as the Plains and Southwestern Indians":

> For years I have been troubled by the types depicted in the splendid series of oil portraits of Indians in the Peabody Museum. The most of these represent Indians of the eastern and southeastern United States, and, although the portraits are the work of an excellent painter, his subjects look very European. The features of most are very un-Mongoloid, with prominent noses and oval faces. . . . some Plains Indians are included in the series, and these seem to be accurate representations of types familiar today. I am, therefore, disposed to think that the European-like types are not the result of an artistic convention, but actually did exist.[2]

Racial Definition—the Field of the Physical Anthropologist   Physical anthropology has its difficulties and uncertainties when it tries to reach back deep into time. But the tests by which it distinguishes races seem as sound and dependable as those of any of the disciplines that deal with early man. Some of the results are certainly striking.

There are problems, of course, as to the order in which the various races developed and spread throughout the world. In the opinion of some authorities, the Pygmy came first, although we must face the fact that one of the very earliest forms of man was the gigantic type of which Koenigswald has found evidence in Java and southeastern China; and the Pygmy, although resembling the Negro in most respects, has in general one of the roundest heads of all mankind, while the Negro's is preeminently long and narrow. Many anthropologists pick the Australoid as the second race to leave a homeland in Central Asia and spread far abroad, and they think that he was closely pursued by the Negro. Alfred S. Romer and Griffith Taylor place the Negro ahead of the Australoid;[3] although Taylor is more a geographer than an anthropologist, he has given many years of study to the Australasian area where Pygmy, Negro, and Australoid are so closely involved. Beyond these three races lies the story of the White and the Yellow peoples. Here the physical anthropologists split more widely. The White race is divided into certain groups by one authority, and into other groups by another. Hooton puts the beginnings of the

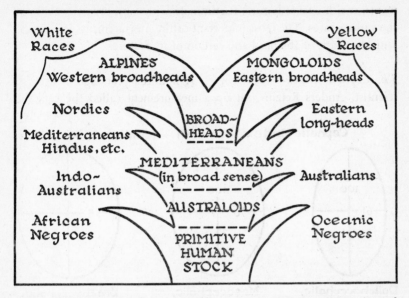

The "twin" nature of the races. The Negritos, or Pygmies, who are lumped with the Negroes in this chart but probably preceded them, are also "twinned": a western branch is found in the Congo and an eastern in the Andaman Islands of the Indian Ocean, in the Philippines, and in New Guinea. Except for the round-headed Pygmies, the races progress, as this chart indicates, from long-headed to round. (After Romer, 1941.)

White race far back by calling the Australoid "an archaic form of modern White man." [4] As to the Mongoloids, Roland B. Dixon calls them old, too; for he finds traces of them in Tasmania and says that the Bushman and Hottentot present a blend of Mongoloid with Pygmy.[5] Taylor, on the other hand, sees the Mongoloid as the last of the races to evolve and spread. He includes in its ranks the puzzlingly round-headed and sallow Alpines who obtrude into central Europe. Just ahead of them in migration from the center where man originated, he places the white Mediterranean,[6] a type found in the neighboring shores of that sea. (Remember that a single homeland for man has not been scientifically established.)

But, in spite of all these conflicts of opinion, the physical anthropologist has fairly firm ground to stand on. He can bring to bear on the skull or the fleshed bone of man certain tests, certain measurements, which enable him to discriminate with some accuracy between the various races. The most important of the measurements have to do with the shape of the head and certain of its features.

The Cephalic Index—and Others A hundred years ago a Swedish scientist, Anders Retzius, set up a measurement called the cephalic

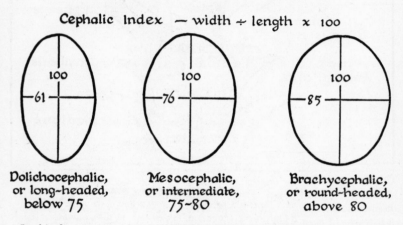

Cephalic Index — width ÷ length x 100

Dolichocephalic, or long-headed, below 75

Mesocephalic, or intermediate, 75~80

Brachycephalic, or round-headed, above 80

In this diagrammatic description of one of the most important measurements of the head, the length is given as 100, instead of 18 centimeters or some other actual measurement, in order to make the matter simpler to comprehend.

index which indicates whether a head is dolichocephalic or brachycephalic—long-headed or round-headed, narrow or broad. The width of the skull, divided by its length, and multiplied by 100, gives the cephalic index—as 15.0 cm. ÷ 17.6 cm. x 100 = 85.23. The long-headed, or dolichocephalic, skull, lies below 75; the round-headed, or brachycephalic, at or above 80. Between lies the intermediate ground of the mesocephalic. (It is rather easy to keep "dolichocephalic" and "brachycephalic" straight if you note that the longer word applies to the long-headed skulls.)

Once the Pygmy is out of the way, we find long-headedness common to early peoples and then gradually giving way to round-headedness. Round-headedness is a progressively modern tendency; there seem to be more round heads than there used to be. Among modern

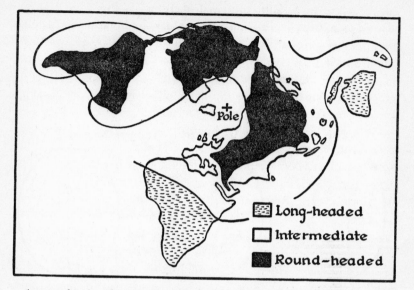

A map showing the centrifugal dispersal, first of long-headed Negroes and Australoids, then intermediate to long-headed Mediterraneans, and finally round-headed Mongoloids and Alpines, from an Asiatic homeland. The maker of this map prefers "narrow-headed" for "long-headed," "broad-headed" for "round-headed." (After Taylor, 1937, with some modifications.)

peoples, the Australian, the Negro, the Nordic, and the Mediterranean are long-headed. The Pygmy, the Alpine of Central Europe, and the Chinese are generally round-headed. Most Indians, being heavily Mongoloid, are likewise round-headed. The cephalic index alone is not too good a means of determining races today, but it has definite value in dealing with early man in the Americas. Here, as in the Old World, he seems to have been, with two exceptions, as long-headed as the modern Australian.

There are other important measurements, which I shall not describe at such length. The facial index tells us whether the face is relatively broad or narrow, the breadth is measured from cheekbone to cheekbone, and the length from the root, or topmost point, of the nose between the eyes to the bottom of the chin. This facial index is not so useful as the cephalic in determining race, because some of the bones involved are affected by age and sex. The nasal index tells us whether the nose—or, in a skull, the nasal aperture—is broad or narrow, adapted to a warm, moist climate or to a dry, cold one. Then there is the matter of prognathism, or protrusion of the jaws. Heavy brow ridges, which usually go with a retreating forehead, and the shape of the vault may be important indications of race. No one of these measurements or observations can definitely denote race, but a number of them taken together are rather reliable.

There is a certain difficulty, however, in applying the detective methods of physical anthropology to the skulls of early man in the New World. It is only a matter of terminology, but sometimes this affects our understanding of what scientists are talking about when they describe early American skulls as Australoid, Melanesian, Papuan, Caucasoid, or Negroid. The difficulty stems back to the southwest Pacific. The Australians—a race as primitive as the Neanderthal and perhaps more primitive—are spoken of as Australoid. They are also described by some writers as Caucasoid on the theory that they are a blend of an archaic white race with Negroid elements. The Oceanic Negroes, who inhabit large parts of New Guinea and near-by islands, are called Melanesian. Some of the men of this area who are a mixture produced by the interbreeding of native Australians and Oceanic Negroes are known by a confusing number of names. They used to be called Papuan—which is really only a word for a language. When the characteristics of their skulls turn up in the Americas, these craniums may be called Papuan by an older writer or Australoid, Melanesian, Caucasoid, or Negroid. I shall use the term Australoid-Melanesian.

What do the tests of the physical anthropologist tell you about skulls which come from the southwest Pacific or resemble specimens

$\rightarrow$

THREE TYPES OF SKULLS

Generalized impressions of the cranial traits of three races which may be presumed to have contributed to the peopling of the Americas. Certain Mongoloid tribes, represented by the Eskimo and peoples of northern Asia, differ from the race in general in having long, narrow skulls with keeled vaults and flat sides. (The Australoid after Leakey, 1935; the Negroid after Leakey, 1935, and Martin, 1928; the Mongoloid after Stibbe, 1938, and Hooton, 1931.)

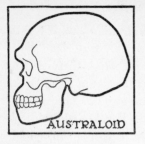  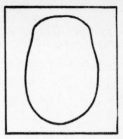

Forehead: low, receding
Brow ridges: heavy
Face and jaws: protruding
Rear: protruding

Forehead: narrow
Vault: keeled
Sides: flat
Sockets: low, oblong

Dolichocephalic
(very long and
narrow head)

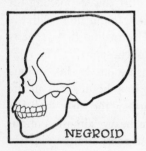  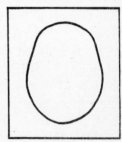

Forehead: low, rounded
Brow ridges: slight or
    absent
Face and jaws: protruding
Rear: bulging

Forehead: narrow
Vault: curved
Sides: flat to slightly
    convex

Dolichocephalic
(narrow head,
    medium to long)

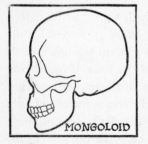 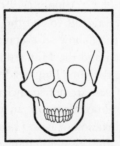 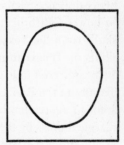

Forehead: somewhat high
Brow ridge: absent
Face: flat
Rear: flat

Forehead: broad
Vault: broad, globular
Sides: convex to bulging

Brachycephalic
(round)

from that area? If you find a skull that has protruding jaws, a low or depressed nose root, and straight sides, you may say with some assurance that it belonged to an Oceanic Negro, an aboriginal Australian, an Australoid-Melanesian, or—if the owner has been dead many thousands of years—an Australoid. If the skull also has a heavy, continuous brow ridge, a retreating forehead, and a low, keeled vault, you can forget the Negroid. The man was an Australian, or an Australoid-Melanesian, or an Australoid.

What Skull Measurements Tell Us About Early Man   These peculiarities of southwest Pacific skulls are important if you are looking for early man in the Americas. As I have said, a skull found along with the bones of extinct mammals or in a geological formation that suggests great age is almost always long-headed, or dolichocephalic. The typical, round-headed Mongoloid Indian is conspicuous by his antique absence. (The only early skulls that are not long-headed fall in the intermediate division, the mesocephalic.) Further, the early skull has most, if not all, of the following features: a heavy, almost continuous brow ridge; protruding jaws; a low nose root; straight sides; a retreating forehead, and a keeled vault.

On the score of long-headedness, there can be no question about all but two of the early skulls mentioned in Chapter 6 or illustrated on page 161. The Confins has a cephalic index of 69.1, which is hyper-dolichocephalic, or extra long; the female skulls of the Pericú in Lower California average 68.50 and the male 66.15, while sixteen skulls from the Texas coast show an average of 65.37. Except for the skulls of Tepexpan man and the Minnesota girl, all the other skulls I have referred to have the same long-headed character. If those from Texas and the Pacific Coast are not so ancient as the rest, at least they seem to represent the descendants of an old strain forced off into marginal areas by the invasion of newer peoples. To be sure, we have now—and have had—Indians with long skulls, particularly in the eastern part of the United States and to some extent on the Great Plains. But their number is not large, and can never have been large, compared with the great bulk of round-headed Indians of the two Americas.

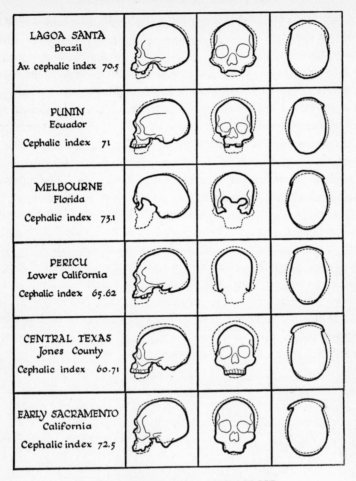

LAGOA SANTA Brazil Av. cephalic index 70.5			
PUNIN Ecuador Cephalic index 71			
MELBOURNE Florida Cephalic index 73.1			
PERICU Lower California Cephalic index 65.62			
CENTRAL TEXAS Jones County Cephalic index 60.71			
EARLY SACRAMENTO California Cephalic index 72.5			

EARLY MAN VS. THE MONGOLOID

In this comparison, the Mongoloid skull—indicated by dotted lines—and the skulls of early man are not drawn to true scale, because the former is an abstraction and the measurements of all the latter are not available. For comparison the nose root and the back of the skull are made to agree in the profiles, and the other views are drawn from this relationship. (The Mongoloid skull, after Stibbe, 1938, and Hooton, 1931; the Early Sacramento, courtesy Robert F. Heizer; the Pericú, after ten Kate, 1884, and Woodbury, 1935; the Punin, after Sullivan and Hellman, 1925; the Lagoa Santa, after Hrdlička, 1912; the Central Texas, after Hooton, 1933.)

Apart from long-headedness, our early skulls share a number of other peculiarities of the Australoid-Melanesian: the quite heavy brow ridges, the keeled vault, the straight sides, the retreating forehead, the low nose root, and the protruding jaw. Some have the round vault and the fuller forehead of White and Mongoloid peoples, but these are also a feature of the Negroid strain that united with the Australoid in Melanesia.

In one respect only do the skulls of early American man follow a Mongoloid pattern: almost all have prominent cheekbones. We must remember, however, that prominent cheekbones are found in other races—though not so commonly—and we must recognize that they cannot weigh too heavily against those un-Mongoloid peculiarities which I have dwelt on.

The peculiarities of our early skulls must make us think twice about the Indian as the only pre-Columbian inhabitant of the Americas south of the Eskimo. They bear witness to another invader from the Old World. Such skulls—even if they were only a thousand years old —would tell us that the typical Mongoloid Indian was not the only arrival from Asia who left descendants. Since many of the skulls are definitely the oldest that have been found in the New World, we must recognize that early man bore some relationship to other peoples than the forebears of the noble red man.

Europe Recognizes the Australoid in America   The earliest recognition of non-Indian traits in the Americas came from scientists of the Old World—Mochi, Biasutti, Hansen, Quatrefages, ten Kate (who found the Pericú skulls in Lower California), Rivet, Gusinde, Lebzelter, Mendes Correâ, Hultkrantz. The first American and British students to accept the idea were Roland B. Dixon in 1923, A. C. Haddon in 1925, and Sir Arthur Keith and Earnest A. Hooton in 1930; the last two were physical anthropologists, and naturally knew more than archaeologists about the meaning of bones. Toward the end, even Hrdlička was diluting the Mongolism of the Indian with some Aurignacian and Magdalenian ancestry, though the Australoid and the Melanesian were too much for him.

In the English-speaking world the case for the Mongoloid Indian as the sole heir of early man was definitely and finally thrown out of court in 1930 by statements from two men eminent in their field— Keith and Hooton.

Keith's statement was simple and short, but his position as a sound and skillful anatomist gave it considerable weight. He confirmed the judgment of Louis R. Sullivan and Milo Hellman that the Punin skull from Ecuador resembled the skulls of native women of Australia. The points of resemblance, he wrote, "were too numerous to permit us to suppose that the skull could be a sport produced by an American Indian parentage." Here follows Keith's decisive dictum: "This discovery at Punin does compel us to look into the possibility of a Pleistocene Glacial invasion of America by an Australoid people." [7]

Hooton and Dixon on Early Invaders   Hooton's pronouncement in 1930 against the pretensions of the Mongoloid Indian resulted from a study of a number of old skulls found at Pecos Pueblo in New Mexico. In terms of early man they were not so very aged; in fact, they were slightly younger than the Basketmakers of the first Christian centuries. But in these skulls Hooton found traces of seven types of men. They included, as one might expect, the Basketmaker, the Plains Indian, and a "large hybrid" type which was thoroughly Indian. In addition he listed a "Pseudo-Australoid," a "Pseudo-Negroid," a "Long-faced European," and a "Pseudo-Alpine" type. From this analysis of skulls little more than a thousand years old, Hooton went on boldly to picture the kind of men that first discovered and invaded the Americas:

Briefly, then, my present opinion as to the peopling of the American continent is as follows: At a rather remote period, probably soon after the last glacial retreat, there straggled into the New World from Asia by way of the Bering Strait groups of dolichocephals in which were blended at least three strains: one very closely allied to the fundamental brunet European and African long-headed stock called "Mediterranean"; another, a more primitive form with heavy browridges, low broad face and wide nose, which is probably to be identified with an archaic type represented today very strongly (although

mixed with other elements) in the native Australians, and less strongly
in the so-called "Pre-Dravidians" such as the Veddahs, and also in the
Ainu; thirdly, an element certainly Negroid (not Negro). These
people, already racially mixed, spread over the New World carrying
with them a primitive fishing and hunting culture. Their coming must
have preceded the occupation of eastern Asia by the present predominantly Mongoloid peoples, since the purer types of these dolichocephals do not show the characteristic Mongoloid features.

At a somewhat later period there began to arrive in the New World
groups of Mongoloids coming by the same route as their predecessors.
Many of these were probably purely Mongoloid in race, but others
were mixed with some other racial element notable because of its
high-bridged and often convex nose. This may have been either
Armenoid or Proto-Nordic (or neither one). These later invaders
were capable of higher cultural development than the early pioneers
and were responsible for the development of agriculture and for the
notable achievements of the New World civilization. In some places
they may have driven out and supplanted the early long-heads, but
often they seem to have interbred with them producing the multiple
and varied types of the present American Indians—types which are
Mongoloid to a varying extent, but never purely Mongoloid. Last of
all came the Eskimo, a culturally primitive Mongoloid group, already
mixed with some non-Mongoloid strain before their arrival in North
America.[8]

In 1947 Hooton stated this in simpler terms: "I am fairly sure that
the earliest arrivals here were non-Mongoloids carrying archaic White
strains ('Australoids,' if you like) probably mixed with Negritic
elements and with whatever else was kicking around in Asia before
they crossed Bering Strait." [9]

Dixon's position, which he took in 1923, is in some ways a more
radical one than Hooton's. He introduces "Proto-Australoid," "Proto-
Negroid," and Mediterranean elements, and also Caspian and Alpine;
but, where Hooton recognizes a general stock in which Australoid,
Negroid, and Mediterranean were blended before their arrival, Dixon
brings in his races separate and pure, and he assigns them definite
areas in the New World.

Dixon's Proto-Australoid originated in tropical southeast Asia. It
spread westward "through India and the Arabian coasts to Africa,

and by way of the Mediterranean passed into western Europe, where it appeared in early Paleolithic times." "Another branch spread southeast into Australia, where its early presence is proved by the Talgai skull," perhaps 150,000 years old. "A third branch drifted slowly northward up the eastern Asiatic littoral, and, crossing into America, spread thinly through the continents, and perhaps mainly along the western shores." "On the Pacific Coast in California and Lower California it appears to constitute the oldest stratum, characterizing as it does the crania from the lower layers of the shell-heaps, from the islands of Santa Catalina and San Clemente off the Coast, and from the extinct Pericue [now Pericú] isolated on the southern tip of the peninsula of Lower California." Dixon places some of his Proto-Australoids among the ancestors of the Iroquois and the southern Algonquin tribes of the East. He puts most of his Proto-Negroids in that same eastern area and with the same tribes. He finds them generally east of the Rockies, but also among the Basketmakers in the Southwest and the peoples of the Coahuila Caves of northern Mexico, in the Lagoa Santa area in Brazil, and in Patagonia.[10]

Two of the White types—the Caspian and the Mediterranean—seem rather scattered and rather early. Dixon thinks that a Caspian strain may have appeared as soon as the Proto-Australoid, perhaps sooner. It crops up among the Eskimo and at spots in British Columbia, and widely in South America. The Mediterranean influence, Dixon says, is found also among the Eskimo and among Shoshonean and Siouan tribes.

Dixon does not think much of the Mongoloids. Believing they were a very old people that drifted into Europe in early paleolithic times, he says they "contributed little of value either to the sum of human achievements or the blood of existing races." He gives them only scant space in North America. Instead he introduces two other round-headed peoples. They are first the Paleo-Alpines, and later the Alpines. These, who seem to take on the role played by the Mongoloids of Hooton and others, spread through to South America and "displayed striking ability. . . . To them seems to be attributable most of the higher achievements of the aboriginal American peoples." [11]

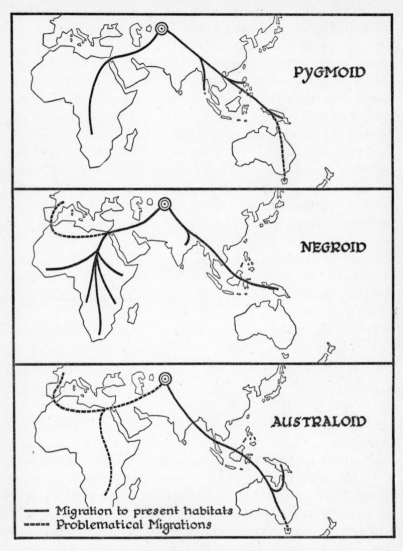

PYGMOID

NEGROID

AUSTRALOID

——— Migration to present habitats
----- Problematical Migrations

THE MIGRATIONS OF EARLY MAN

An indication of how the first three races to develop may have left a supposed homeland in southwestern Asia to reach their present habitats. The dotted lines continue the paths to areas where skulls or peoples have been found that seem related to the parent stock.

The theory of an Australoid strain in both Australia and America, and a Negroid strain in Africa, Melanesia, and America is not so far-fetched as you might at first suppose. It is not a matter of Negroes transporting themselves from the center of Africa to New Guinea and then on up the Asiatic coast to Alaska and points south. It is not a matter of Australians journeying to Asia and then over the same route as the Negroes to the New World. Many authorities believe that mankind originated in southwestern Asia—the Australoid and the Negroid quite as much as the other races. We know that Negroids managed to reach such widely separated places as central Africa and New Guinea and even Easter Island. It is not hard to believe that they might have sent off a branch to the New World, or that one strain of Australoids could have gone to Australia from their original home-land in Asia while another journeyed northeast and crossed to the Americas.

Such theories, as well as some that I shall refer to shortly, are doubtless much too simple; also, they depend too much on other theories, such as the idea that all the races originated in southwestern Asia. R. Ruggles Gates, who writes of "American Neanderthaloids" and "pseudo-Australoids," believes that the craniums of the men of Lagoa Santa and Punin—"the earliest wave of interglacial Americans"—"represent a parallel stage in skull development of a widely different race" from the one that began as the Neanderthal or the one that ended as the Australian.[12]

A Potpourri of Races   The theories of Dixon and Hooton and others conflict in many places; but they present, on the whole, an arresting and convincing case for early man as a predecessor of the Mongoloids and as quite a different sort of creature. There are many side issues to the general theory, and they increase as we begin to deal with living peoples. Hooton finds close resemblances to Egyptian skulls among the Arizona Basketmakers and in the Coahuila Caves of northern Mexico,[13] and Dixon identifies ancient Egyptian skulls with skulls from California and skulls of the Iroquois. W. W. Howells sees similarities between "many forest tribes of South America and certain Indonesian groups in Borneo and the Philippines," and believes the non-Mongoloid features of the Indians point, "not to the Australoids or the Negroes, but towards the White group." [14] Hooton finds Indians of the Northwest coast who "resemble Alpine Europeans." He says that certain Plains Indians seem to be basically White with Mongoloid added, and he points out that although the Eskimo are the most Mongoloid of all the inhabitants of the Americas, they are long-headed, which is a most un-Monogoloid trait.[15] On the basis of skulls from Chancelade, France, and certain late-paleolithic traits, Sollas saw the ancestors of the Eskimo living in Europe in Magdalenian times.[16] M. R. Harrington also picks a Magdalenian forebear for the Eskimo.[17] Authorities differ as to whether the Botocudo tribe of Brazil is descended from the people that left their skulls in the Lagoa Santa Caves, but on the basis of R. N. Wegner's description of a Bolivian tribe, the Qurunga, Griffith Taylor believes these people may be living representatives of an early Australoid migration.[18] Hooton puts forward the picturesque and amusing theory that the Maya, with their large, curved noses and their mania for flattening their heads between boards, picked up both the nose and the mania from the Armenoids of the Iranian plateau. The Mongoloids provided the characteristic skin, hair, and eyelids.[19]

The backwardness of certain living American tribes suggests to Sauer that they came to the New World a very long time ago. Their lack of a number of useful skills argues that they branched off from the men of the Old Stone Age when the Australoid ancestors of the abysmal Blackfellows of Australia looked like an up-and-coming people. These early men had the enterprise to reach the New World, but they stuck to old and limited habits of life. They would not learn from new invading peoples, and so they were forced into refuge areas as remote as Newfoundland, Lower California, Amazonia, and Tierra del Fuego. As an example of cultural backwardness and of an inability to learn which recalls the Australians, Sauer cites a people in the Brazilian interior who get along without boiling any of their food. He believes that this tribe acquired its cultural habits in the days before man began to put heated stones into water in pitch-sealed baskets. The primitive resistance of these "Indians" to borrowing new cooking skills like boiling comes out in other directions. "Long in contact with pottery-making peoples, they make casual or no use of pots, but restrict their cooking to roasting and baking, with gourds, a late acquisition, used for carrying water." [20]

Griffith Taylor once wrote to Earl W. Count that, because certain of the now extinct mammals inhabited both sides of Bering Strait in the days of the glaciers, "it is almost impossible that the Australoids (who preyed on them) did not cross into America in Pre-Würm times." Count supports Taylor with the suggestion that the most primitive of the many stocks that invaded the Americas came "at a time, say, when Talgai man and Wadjak man were en route to their *cul de sac* in Australia." [21] This may have been in the neighborhood of 150,000 years ago.

Radical as these last two suggestions are in point of time, they are conservative compared with theories held by A. A. Mendes Correâ and Paul Rivet. Like many another student, Mendes Correâ saw Australian, Caucasoid, Polynesian, Melanesian, and Asiatic affinities among the American Indians; but he struck into a new field of theory in 1926 by transporting the Australians to South America over a now-vanished land-bridge to the south. Using Wegener's hypothesis of the drift of continents, he found his bridge in a severed and displaced Antarctica. He conceded that this was only a conjecture, but thought it "very probable." [22] That same year Rivet—approving migrations of Australian, Malayan-Polynesian, Asiatic, and Ural elements—suggested that glaciation in the southern hemisphere might have aided the Australians in passing from island to island until they reached the mainland of South America.[23] He dated their journey at only 6,000 years ago,[24] so that glacial assistance beyond the present extent of Antarctica seems just a little unlikely. Rivet, following many a student from Leibnitz to Thomas Jefferson, proposed to trace the origin of the American peoples through comparing their languages with those of the Old World. In 1925 he came up with something more than the usual random identities between words.[25] Indeed, the parallels which he drew between the present speech of the Tshon of Patagonia and the Australians seemed to Dixon to be impossibly close after centuries upon centuries of separation from one another and of contact with other peoples.[26] Only sheer coincidence could account for such identity.

There remain two champions of multiform and multitudinous migrations—José Imbelloni of Argentina and Harold S. Gladwin. They go further than any of their predecessors in peopling the New World with varied races, and further in advancing transpacific migrations as an important factor in the history of the Americas.

Pygmies Before Australoids in the New World?   Both Imbelloni and Gladwin begin with a suggestion that Pygmies deserve consideration. These primordial migrants trod their tiny paces from some unknown fatherland to the forests of the Congo and the jungles of New Guinea, to islands like the Andamans and possibly to Tasmania. The presence of five-foot Yahgan in Tierra del Fuego suggests to both Imbelloni and Gladwin that Pygmies may have preceded the Australoids to the New World. The advent of Pygmies in Tierra del Fuego as well as in Tasmania may be open to question; for in both places the natives, though short, exceeded the average of Pygmy height by a few inches, and their heads, instead of being round like those of the Pygmies, are recorded as of medium cephalic index.

After the Tasmanian strain, Imbelloni carries over by land a Melanesian type to lay their skulls in Lagoa Santa, Punin, Texas, and Lower California. Next came tall people, "comparable partly to the Australian type," who seem to be the Indians of plains and pampas. These were the last of the land-borne migrants until the present era. Hereafter they came by sea. The fourth element was a Proto-Indonesian people that settled exclusively in South America and mainly in Amazonia. With the fifth group Imbelloni presents the first frank Mongoloids, round-headed and inclined to agriculture; they settled in the Southwest, in Middle America, and along the Andean coast. An almost identical people—whom Imbelloni calls the Isthmid—spread through the center of the same area shortly after the birth of Christ and brought to fruition the civilizations which Cortez and Pizarro found in the New World. To top off his list, Imbelloni brings over the Eskimo and men for the American Northwest—but by no longer sea voyage than Bering Strait.[27]

Gladwin's theories appeared first in the second volume of *Excavations at Snaketown,* and are now presented in altered and amplified form through his rather antic book *Men Out of Asia.* They are completely heretical, completely fascinating, and in some respects uncommonly plausible. They are certainly a tonic.

Gladwin begins with what might be called a Pygmoid visitation. He does not dignify it with the word "migration." He is careful to say that there are only "rather vague indications." There is "just enough to make one wonder if there may not have been a few Pygmy groups who strayed over here long, long ago and were pushed off to the edges and the ends when the Australoid tide flowed in." [28]

If a scientific study is ever made in the Guayana highlands of Venezuela, some support may be given to the theory of an early Pygmy migration. Carl Sauer on a visit to Venezuela in 1946 saw photographs of a Pygmy-like people taken by a Venezuelan army officer who had paddled and packed the Guayana River for some years. This tribe, which does not interbreed with other tribes, appears to be Pygmoid in stature and type. Further, it lacks "clothing, weaving, netting, baskets, boats, and fishing skills, and also houses." [29]

Australoids, Negroids, and Men from Europe   Gladwin is definite about the Australoids. They came over Bering Strait somewhere around 25,000 years ago, and drifted down the west coast. They spread out in the southwestern part of the United States below a line from San Francisco to the Texas coast, and flowed on down into Mexico and South America. For evidence he has more than the Australoid-Melanesian skulls of Lower California, Texas, Punin, Paltacalo, and Lagoa Santa. He cites a number of things used and made by the Australians of recent times and also found in the area between southern California and eastern Texas. They include an Aurignacian flint industry, bunt points for darts, bull-roarers, string made by spinning human hair, twisted rabbit's fur, curved throwing sticks with parallel grooves, sand paintings, amputation of finger joints as shown in pictographs, and similarities in spear-throwers and darts with foreshafts (see illustration, page 172).[30] I should like to find them nearer Lagoa Santa.

Gladwin's next migration, the Proto-Negroid of Dixon, leans upon

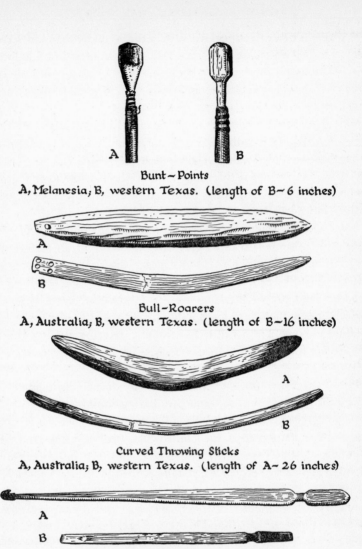

Bunt ~ Points
A, Melanesia; B, western Texas. (length of B ~ 6 inches)

Bull ~ Roarers
A, Australia; B, western Texas. (length of B ~ 16 inches)

Curved Throwing Sticks
A, Australia; B, western Texas. (length of A ~ 26 inches)

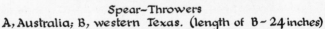

Spear ~ Throwers
A, Australia; B, western Texas. (length of B ~ 24 inches)

FROM THE OLD WORLD AND THE NEW

Implements from Australoid areas of the Eastern Hemisphere resembling implements from western Texas (after Gladwin, 1937).

the Pseudo-Negroid traits of Hooton. It comes in about 17,000 years ago, also over Bering Strait, but down through the corridor between the retreating ice fields of western Canada. Having seen Aurignacian qualities in the Australoids, Gladwin sees Solutrean ones in the Negroid invaders. They bring—or, rather, make—the Folsom point. Unlike the Australoids, who were mostly food gatherers, the Negroids —or Folsom men—are primarily hunters. Although they come trickling in for many, many years, they are few; for, in spite of their hunting prowess and their fine flint knives and spear points, they never invade the Australoid territory that is staked out south from the Mexican border.[31]

The next migration is the Algonquin. It reaches North America somewhere between 1000 and 500 B.C. These people bring in the cord-marked pottery of the Woodland culture of the eastern United States—unpolished and unpainted, its only ornament impressed in the clay. Such pottery has now been traced to western Canada, up into Alaska, across to Siberia, west through Russia to the beakerwares of Europe, and finally down into Africa about 3000 B.C. The Algonquins are such a mixture as the long trip of their pottery might indicate. They are generally long-headed, and they are not today wholly Mongoloid.[32]

No Mongoloids till 300 B.C. The first Mongoloids, as Gladwin sees it, were the Eskimos. They came to the northern edge of North America about 500 B.C. But, because they clung to that edge, we must look elsewhere and later for a Mongoloid invasion of the cultural areas of the New World.

Gladwin believes that these second Mongoloids were thrust out of northern China and on into the New World by the ferment of the Huns. They reached Alaska about 300 B.C. Ultimately, supplemented by the Uto-Aztecans, they supplied the man power on which the Mexican and Maya civilizations were built; and some reached the west coast of South America.[33] Without a good many of them it seems to me difficult to account for such Andean peoples as the Quechua and the Aymara, who were the working population of the Chimu, Nasca, Tiahuanaco, and Inca cultures. By Gladwin's dating, the Mongoloids had only a little more than a thousand years to stamp their hair and eyes and teeth upon five million to fifty million men and women in both Americas.

By the time of the Algonquin—let alone the Eskimo and the Aztec—we are far out of the era of early man. But we are not yet through with the theories of Gladwin as to the peopling of the Americas; for, not content with the stimulating activities of the Huns in northern China, he rediscovers the sailors and the Asiatic fleet of the late, great conqueror Alexander of Macedon, and leads them on expeditions through the East Indies and Oceania even to the Gulf of Darien.[34]

However heretical Gladwin's suggestions may be, they deserve serious attention because they bear heavily upon an old quarrel of the archaeologists, and because this old quarrel bears upon the antiquity of man in the Americas. To be sure, it has to do with the Indians who made the civilizations of Middle America and Peru two thousand years ago, and not with the earlier men who did no more than hunt or gather, and who made nothing more remarkable than Folsom points or milling stones. But by studying certain aspects of those civilizations we may recognize that the Indians had been in the Americas 3,000 to 5,000 years before Columbus. By so much we may reenforce the theory that their forerunners or their forebears came to the New World at least 15,000 years ago and probably 25,000 years ago.

10

DID THE INDIAN INVENT OR
BORROW HIS CULTURE?

American anthropologists usually deny that Old World cultures have influenced to any great extent the pre-Columbian development of the American Indian. We have set up for Aboriginal America a sort of ex post facto Monroe Doctrine and are inclined to regard suggestions of alien influences as acts of aggression. This is probably a scientifically tenable position, although I am afraid it has often been maintained in part by an emotional bias—an "America for Americans" feeling.

—EARNEST A. HOOTON

Diffusion vs. Independent Invention I hope you have not been skipping the choice thoughts that I have placed at the beginning of chapters. Some of them are merely amusing, but certain ones make an important point. Such is the above remark from Hooton. It calls our attention to an unscientific emotionalism which often lies behind one of the dogmas of American archaeology.

This dogma is called the autochthonous origin of Indian cultures. It asserts that practically all the traits, discoveries, and inventions which Columbus, Cortez, and Pizarro found in the New World were home-grown products—importations barred. The question at issue between the friends and the opponents of this dogma is commonly expressed as Independent Invention versus Diffusion. But the phrasing is not quite accurate: it needs a little amplification. Anything invented by man is in a sense an independent invention. In the present case we are talking of an invention made in one center, the New

175

World, independent of a similar invention in another center, the Old. We are concerned, not with independent invention, but with *parallel* independent invention. "Diffusion" is still more inaccurate. Normally it means the gradual transfer of some trait or technique from one people to another, often through the intervention of a third or of a third and a fourth people. In the present discussion it is more a matter of a people's carrying the trait or the technique to a new home. The question is not merely, "Did the Indian invent pottery?" or "Did the American Australoid invent the bull-roarer?" It is rather, "Did he invent it in the New World or the Old?" or "Did he invent it in the Old World and carry it to the New?" or "Did he invent it in the New World while another fellow invented it in the Old?"

This problem of parallel independent invention versus diffusion is important to any discussion of early man, because it can also be phrased: "Did he or did he not bring traits from the Old World that may indicate his racial ancestry?"

Both the theory of diffusion and the theory of parallel, independent invention arise from the same scientific fact. This fact is that different primitive peoples often make similar tools, build similar buildings, enjoy similar institutions, live by similar customs, or believe similar myths. And they do this although the tribes may be widely separated from one another. To pin the matter down to our own present concern, certain objects found in the New World and dated before Columbus are almost exactly like objects in the Old World. For instance, a spear-thrower from western Texas not only employs the same principle as one from Australia, but has practically the same physical shape. Curved throwing-sticks and bull-roarers come from both these localities (see illustration, page 172). Star-shaped mace heads of Melanesian type turn up in Peru. Looms that have the same eleven working parts are found in areas of the New World as well as the Old. Easter Island has polygonal stonework with locked joints which matches a form of masonry in Andean Peru, and a certain people of Easter Island stretched their ear lobes in the same fashion as the Incas. Pan-pipes of the Old World type appear in South America, Panama, and California; some from western Brazil are identical in

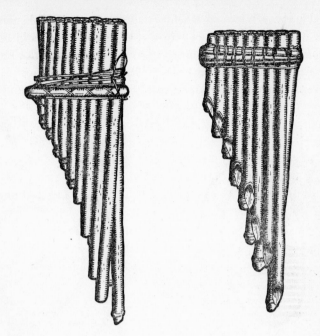

FROM BURMA TO MELANESIA TO AMERICA?

Among the most curious resemblances between traits in the New World and in the Old are those of Pan-pipes. Certain pipes from the Solomon Islands have been found to have the same scale and the same absolute pitch as specimens from pre-Columbian Peru. Double rows of pipes come from the hinterland of Burma, from the Solomon Islands, and from Panama and the Andean highlands; and in all these areas the two rows are tuned in the same relation to each other. The two sets may be lashed together, like these from the Solomon Islands, left, and from Bolivia, right, or they may be merely connected by a cord and blown by two men or, alternately, by one. (Left, after von Hornbostel, 1912; right, after Nordenskiöld, 1924.)

tonal scale and absolute pitch with some from the Solomon Islands (see illustration, page 177). In Hawaii and in Peru, as in Egypt and ancient Japan, brothers married to sisters were of superior status. The digging stick of certain Polynesians has a step like that of the Indians of Peru. The quipu, or knotted-string record, spreads from Polynesia

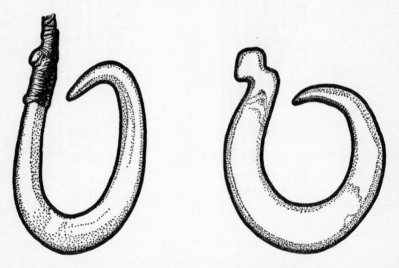

The material used in these fishhooks—pearl shell in Tahiti, abalone shell on San Nicolas Island off southern California—dictated the slight difference in shape. Objects like these are found only in these general areas. (Courtesy of the American Museum of Natural History and the Santa Barbara Museum of Natural History.)

to Peru, and the decimal system is found in both areas, though the more northerly part of the New World employs the vigesimal system based on progression by twenties. The Hindu game of pachisi resembles the Mexican game of patolli. Lists have been published of as many as fifty such similarities between Oceania and the Americas.[1]

Bastian's "Psychic Unity"   Those who argue for independent invention rest their case largely on a distortion of the theory of "psychic unity" put forward by Adolf Bastian in mid-Victorian days. From studies of African and Asiatic cultures, Bastian developed the thesis

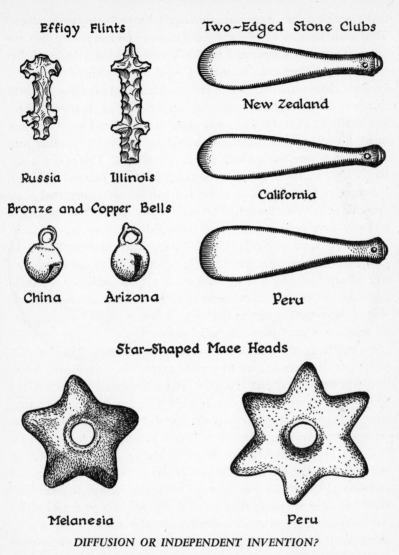

Effigy Flints

Russia   Illinois

Two-Edged Stone Clubs

New Zealand

Bronze and Copper Bells

California

China   Arizona

Peru

Star-Shaped Mace Heads

Melanesia   Peru

DIFFUSION OR INDEPENDENT INVENTION?

Striking resemblances exist between Old World and New World artifacts. The stone clubs are about 14 inches long. (Upper left, after Gladwin, 1937; the Chinese bell after Gladwin, 1937, the Arizona bell after Elmore, 1945; upper right, the New Zealand club, after Wickersham, 1895, the California and Peruvian clubs after Imbelloni, 1930. The mace heads after Gladwin, 1937.)

that "psychic unity" everywhere produced similar "elementary ideas."
Thus early man in France and early man in Java might harden the
point of a wooden spear in a fire, or knock chips off a lump of flint
to make a sharper tool, or make a rope out of twisted vines. But
beyond "elementary ideas," said Bastian, man would develop different
things in different places, depending on different physical conditions;
and finally, as he reached a higher plane of mental and social development, his ideas and his behavior would be influenced by other men
and other cultures with which he came in contact. This was a sound
thesis. Unfortunately, however, Bastian's followers ignored the words
"elementary ideas," as well as the last half of his theory, and made
"psychic unity" the provider of all good things from pots to pyramids.

There have been opponents to independent invention, of course.
There were some in Bastian's day. They pointed out—as Robert H.
Lowie has done recently—that the champion of the theory must prove
that different peoples making similar things were subjected to similar
stimulants in both areas. Otherwise "all the societies of the world
should share the features in question." [2] Lowie might have said that
all cultures of man should be alike today.

By and large, the diffusionists were in the minority. The distorters
of Bastian triumphed. They triumphed even in the Old World, where
distances were not always very great, and where traffic between Africa
and Eurasia seemed not so very difficult. You can imagine, therefore,
what a happy hunting ground the independent inventionists have
made of the Americas. The New World is remote indeed from the
Old. You must go back to the time of the glaciers to find a land-bridge
and up to the Arctic to bring the two worlds within hailing distance of
each other. Otherwise you must be willing to accept thousands of
miles of ocean voyaging. The physical fact of the remoteness of the
Americas has stopped many a mental adventurer among the anthropologists. He rereads with respect—perhaps too much respect—these
words of Spinden's: "The fact that no food plant is common to the
two hemispheres is enough to offset any number of petty puzzles in
arts and myths." [3]

If the physical fact of the Pacific Ocean had not been enough to
stifle talk of diffusion, the extravagant theories of Sir Grafton Elliot

Smith would have done the job. Here was a diffusionist indeed! Echoed by W. J. Perry, Smith found the beginnings of all culture of any importance in Egypt, and from there he sent its traveling salesmen abroad to sell it to Europe, Asia, and the Americas. Pearls and pyramids, gold and dolmens, initiations and totemism, sun worship and the marriage of brother and sister, mummies—even if they were no more than desiccated bodies wrapped in a bag—these traits and many more all "proved" that the Children of the Sun had sold their cultural goods to lesser peoples.

There were other theorists as wild and whirling. Augustus Le Plongeon brought the Maya from Atlantis to found Egypt. Ignatius Donnelly reversed the procession and dragged Greeks to Atlantis and then Mexico. Lewis Spence transported Atlas across the Atlantic as the Mexican god Quetzalcoatl. Leo Wiener, as Spinden has put it, "derives everything of importance in the New World from the highly civilized coasts of Gambia and Sierra Leone . . . brightest Africa." [4] And then there was Churchward with his continent of Mu.

Smith's and Perry's uncritical use of evidence and their distortion of fact—plus these fantasies of Africa and Atlantis and Mu—put the friends of independent invention even more firmly in the saddle than the single and simple fact of the Pacific Ocean. The diffusion of Smith *et al.* was a diffusion to end all diffusion.

Americanists—students of man in the New World—have not yet escaped from the curse of the Children of the Sun, and the terror of Atlantis and Mu. One of the best, Baron Erland Nordenskiöld, a distinguished Swedish scientist, gave a great deal of energy to the cataloguing of the many evidences of analogies; and yet he came to the conclusion that, by and large, Indian culture was a product of independent invention in the New World.[5] He granted that the Indians may have received from Oceania through random voyages "one or two cultivable plants and possibly a few more culture elements"—knowledge of how to make crude clay vessels, for example.[6] Hrdlička, too, conceded a small number of sea-borne visitors before Columbus: "It is . . . probable that the western coast of America, within the last 2,000 years, was on more than one occasion reached by small parties of Polynesians, and that the eastern coast was similarly reached by

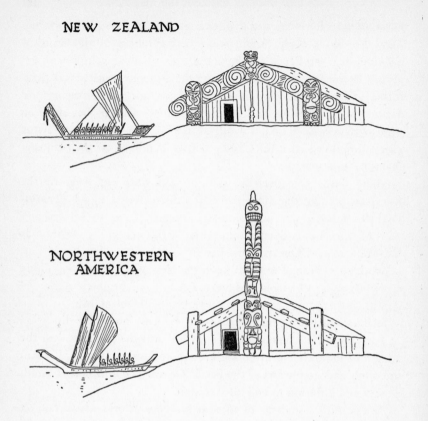

NEW ZEALAND

NORTHWESTERN
AMERICA

CIRCUMPACIFIC NAVIGATION?

There are marked resemblances between the traits of the Maori of New Zealand and of the Indians of the northwest coast of North America. Among these are sailing ships and houses. (After figures on a map by Covarrubias, 1940.)

small groups of whites, and that such parties may have locally influenced the culture of the Americans." [7] But Hrdlička considered such voyaging of very little importance.

Only two anthropologists of any standing favor diffusion. The first of these, Earnest A. Hooton, rejects "the supposition that these various Asiatic invaders brought with them to the New World nothing but a repressed desire to indulge in independent invention, that they came with culturally empty hands, but brains stuffed full of patents to be filed only after arrival. . . . I have no use at all for the anthropological isolationists who are determined to maintain the incredible dogma that there was no diffusion of inventions and ideas from the Old World to the New, but only of naked human animals." [8]

Complexity an Argument for Diffusion   The chief modern American proponent of diffusion is Harold S. Gladwin. What is his case? How does he come to his conclusions? He begins, of course, by noting a large number of random resemblances. Some are in simple objects. Some are in complex ones. As he seeks a scientific basis for his argument, he concentrates on the complex things. Complexity seems to rule out coincidence. If a tool has only one or two parts—like a curved throwing stick or a hafted knife—it is not difficult to conceive of two different men inventing it on opposite sides of the world. A bow and arrow with three essential parts presents a little more of a problem, but not too much, for the three parts are dependent on one another. If the bow has a back reinforced by sinew, if the arrow has feathers and a foreshaft, and the foreshaft has a flint arrowhead—making seven elements in all—then one begins to wonder at the mathematical chances of two men exactly duplicating the whole arrangement. Then, consider the vertical loom with nine separate elements, and eleven if it sports a shuttle and reed fork.

From citing such coincidences, Gladwin turns to the second step of the diffusionist's argument. This has to do not alone with one complex object, but with unrelated things grouped around it—let us say a vertical loom and bark cloth, painted tripod pottery, and metal casting by the lost wax method. Now if all these disconnected objects can be found in another locality and in use by another people, the suggestion of diffusion becomes far stronger than even in the case of a single complex machine. As Gladwin puts it:

If . . . a man should report to the Chinese police that some copper bells, a vertical loom, some tripod trays, and a roll of bark cloth had been stolen from his house, and if, after broadcasting the details, the American police should find all these articles in the possession of a man in America, where such things had hitherto been unknown, would the authorities be satisfied with the explanation that the possessor had independently invented each item? I am inclined to think that, if I should happen to be the attorney for the defense, knowing that my client had recently come over from Asia, a plea of insanity might carry more weight with the jury than my client's explanation.

He argues his point still more vividly:

If a Scotsman uses a split-bamboo trout rod, a waterproof silkline, and a barbed hook, it is not necessarily a case of diffusion if a man in Saskatchewan is found to be fishing with a willow twig, a piece of string, and a bent-pin, since each item is dependent upon the others. But if in addition to their fishing tackle, the Scotsman and the man in Saskatchewan are found to possess a shot-gun, a flask, a brier-pipe and bagpipes, then it would look like a case of diffusion since no one item of the assemblage is dependent upon any other.[9]

Dispersion As Well As Diffusion   The difficulty of this second step in the diffusionist's argument lies in the fact that it is hard indeed to find a complex of traits in *one* American locality that resembles exactly a complex of traits in a *single* Old World one. If the traits are all together in Peru, some may come from one place in the Old World and some from another. Or, if we take a group of traits from a single Old World locale, we find them spread out widely and separately in the Americas. An excellent example of this may be drawn from Oceania and South America. Dixon writes of the diffusionists:

When in South America, they say, you find not only coca-chewing, plank canoes, and tie-dyeing, but also terraced irrigation, Pan-pipes, and the blow gun—all traits widespread in the western Pacific and southeastern Asia—how can you deny that their occurrence is due to diffusion, or believe for a moment that so many similar and parallel inventions could take place? The challenge is a formidable one. Is there anything that can be said in reply?

Dixon points out that these Oceanic traits are not found *together* in the New World. The plank canoe is confined to the Santa Barbara Islands and southern Chile; tie-dyeing, to the arid coasts of northern Peru; coca-chewing, originally to the Andean highlands and the tropical forests along its eastern border; terraced irrigation, to the Andes of Peru and Bolivia; the blow gun, to the upper Amazon and Orinoco forests, the Antilles, and the eastern United States; the Pan-pipe, to the Amazon-Orinoco drainage and southward through Bolivia to northern Chile and the Peruvian coast, and to one or two isolated spots in Ecuador and Colombia. "With one exception the only area where the distribution of any two of these traits is found to overlap lies in the Andean highlands and the tropical forest area to the eastward. Only tie-dyeing and the Pan-pipe are found together on the coast." Further, the two traits we find on the coast are separated in the Old World. Tie-dyeing is found specifically in Indonesia "and known in Melanesia only in degenerate form in one small area, whereas the Pan-pipe is primarily Melanesian and almost unknown in Indonesia." [10] He seems to be ignorant of double Pan-pipes connected by a cord which are found in the hinterland of Burma and also in Panama and South America. [11]

No opponent of diffusionism is so blind as to deny the importation of some culture traits by the migrants from northern Asia. Kroeber concedes the fire drill, the spear-thrower, stone chipping, twisting of string, the bow, the throwing harpoon, simple basketry and nets, hunting complexes, cooking stones in vessels of wood, of bark, or of skin, body painting and perhaps tattooing, the domestication of dogs. [12] But, except for these and a few other examples, most anthropologists deny that the American Indians, early or late, brought any objects of their culture from the Old World. Alfred V. Kidder has phrased very neatly their antagonism to "non-stop journeys by bag-and-baggage culture carriers." [13] This phrase is aimed at a weak chink in the diffusionist's armor—the fact that Old World traits found, say, in the Southwest, Middle America, or farther south leave no trail across Alaska and down through Canada and over the Great Plains.

In addition, the opponents of diffusion like to point out that certain things in the Indian culture of the northern part of the New World are like certain things in the Indian culture of the southern part, while in between lies an area—Mexico, Middle America, and Peru—of entirely different culture traits. Here we find none of the northern and southern things. Nordenskiöld observes that, while some of the identical northern and southern traits may be due to the stimulus of similar cold climates, there are numerous traits that have nothing to do with temperature and humidity. He doubtless feels he is delivering the coup de grâce when he writes:

It is a very characteristic fact that incomparably greater similarity exists between civilizations as far apart as those of the Calchaquis of Argentina, and the Pueblos of North America, than between the culture of any Indian tribe and that of any people in the whole of Oceania.[14]

If such traits were diffused from one American area to the other, they left no trace between. When we add this to the fact that from Alaska to Middle America there are no traces of even the simplest beginnings of the cultures of the central area, the advocate of independent invention has a pretty good case. In answer, the diffusionist has been tempted to argue that when men are moving rather steadily across an area, they do not leave evidence that is easy to find some millenniums later. Only a hundred years have passed since Brigham Young led his people from Independence, Missouri, to Salt Lake City, and yet there is a singular paucity of spinning wheels and first editions of *The Book of Mormon* along their trail.

The Trap of Time   Gladwin has a better answer, which is also an attack on a basic weakness of his opponents. For almost ten years he has been pointing out that friends of the inventive Indian have been getting squeezed tighter and tighter in a trap of their own independent invention. It is the trap of time.

When the Spaniards found the New World, they found it full of inventions and discoveries. There were cities of stone, carved temples, painted pyramids. Metal workers smelted ores, made alloys, and cast elaborate ornaments of gold by a most intricate process. There was a complex despotism in Mexico and as complex and despotic a communism in Peru. The Maya had a calendar more accurate than the one Columbus used. They had devised a hieroglyphic writing and knew how to make cement. The Indians of both continents had developed an extensive agriculture, with potatoes and fertilizers in Peru and corn and beans and tomatoes all over the place.

As soon as the archaeologists decided that all this had been invented in the New World with no help to speak of from the Old, they had to recognize that it would take quite a little time. At first this posed a difficulty, for there was no very early evidence of man in Mexico. In 1917, however, came the discovery of skeletons and pottery under a lava flow at Copilco near Mexico City and of a primitive pyramid half buried under the same flow at near-by Cuicuilco; and the archaeologists promptly dated the eruption of the lava at 4000 B.C.

Then, unfortunately, new evidence narrowed the trap of time once more. George C. Vaillant and his wife dated other sites with the same kind of pottery as Copilco considerably later than the birth of Christ. The dates in the Maya calendar began to shrink, too. Herbert Spinden's correlation of this calendar with the Christian was torn from its moorings by Eric Thompson and Martínez Hernández, and ritual cities were moved up 257 years; a date in Uaxactun advanced from A.D. 68 to 325. On the basis of pottery in the Maya area, Vaillant tentatively suggested that the correlation ought to move up another 257 years. The Basket-makers advanced from an estimated 2000 B.C. to a tree-ring date about A.D. 217. And all this time, nobody could find any really primitive beginnings of pottery in Middle America, and nothing that seemed earlier than the birth of Christ. The trap of time was growing tighter and tighter. A very elaborate civilization would have to develop in 1,500 years, without any roots. For ten years Gladwin has been pointing out this difficulty and urging that man came into the Americas not only as a primitive paleolithic 15,000 or 25,000 years ago, but as a fairly civilized and perfected neolithic close to the beginning of the Christian era.

Escape from the Trap   The similarity between the traits of the north and the south which Nordenskiöld points out, and the fact that a different lot of traits were dropped in between the others are grist to Gladwin's diffusion mill. In 1937, when he wrote *Excavations at Snaketown,* he was only beginning to see an answer. By 1947, when *Men Out of Asia* appeared, he had a fairly complete and certainly an ingenious explanation.

His first proposition is that the Mongoloids came late—very late—and that they brought not much more than the brawn and brains which someone else would later direct. His fifteenth chapter begins with the following parody of a baseball score:

Score at the End of the Fourth Inning

NORTH AMERICA 4	SOUTH AMERICA 1
Australoid, Folsom, Algonquin, Eskimo	Australoid
No Discoveries No Inventions	*No Mongoloids*

By 300 B.C.—two hundred years after the Eskimo—Gladwin is will-ing to add 1 run to the North American score and make that run Mongoloid. But he does not believe that the Mongoloids reached South America in any numbers, or contributed anything but labor to the culture which Columbus found. They did not make black-on-white pottery in the Pueblo country or red-on-buff pottery and irriga-tion canals in southern Arizona, create incised pottery, pyramids, carved jade, or a calendar system and hieroglyphs in Middle America, pound bark cloth in Central America, or produce stone fortresses and superb weaving and portrait jugs in Peru. Left to their own devices, the Mongoloids would have accomplished no more in the New World than they had in the Old before the Huns made things unpleasant for them in northern China. Gladwin believes that the people who created the culture of Middle America and Peru came overseas, spreading north and south from the isthmus of Panama. The suggested invasion by water explains the odd fact that many of the traits of northern North America are like some of those of southern South America, and not at all like most of the traits of the area between. Some of these northern and southern traits, says Gladwin, are the property of the Australoids who came far back; others in North America find analogies in China and northern Asia. His overseas peoples thrust

themselves and their culture into the central part of the New World, changing or obliterating the Australoid traits that they found there, and isolating those that lay to the north and south. He believes that these people brought with them certain objects and customs from the islands in the Pacific, from southeastern Asia, and from China and points west. Among them is the habit of squeezing a baby's head between boards to give it an elegant elongation; this head deformation is not practiced in northern Asia, from which the Indians are presumed to have come.

It is hardly necessary to point out that Gladwin's hypothesis disposes of the question: "Why are there no traces of Middle American and Peruvian traits on the trail down from Alaska?" But we might ask: "Why are there not more of them in the Pacific islands?"

Gladwin has not worked out his maritime invasions too thoroughly; but he sees the Melanesians—who are believed to have reached Easter Island—continuing on to Central America and becoming the Caribs and spreading into South America and the West Indies. He sees the Polynesians taking much the same route and turning into the Arawaks.

What started these South Sea islanders off on their career of civilizing the central part of the Americas? Where did they get some of the traits and some of the physical features that Melanesians and Polynesians do not now possess, as well as their inventive brains? Here Gladwin has a startling and fabulous theory to put forward. Here is where Alexander the Great and his sailors and ships come in.

Dead Alexander Invades America Before Alexander died in 323 B.C. he brought 5,000 Levantine and Greek shipwrights and sailors to the Persian Gulf and built a navy of 800 vessels. We hear a good deal about what his army did after his death, of the quarrels of generals and the dissipation of their forces—but not a word about the 5,000 nautical men or their fleet. As Gladwin points out, it is hard to imagine that sailors with sound vessels under them would take shore leave and walk home to Greece. If they sailed away from the Persian Gulf, which way would they have gone? They would hardly have sailed southwestward along the Arabian coast; for Alexander died at a

BEARDED WHITE GODS?

Middle American portraits of men who, unlike the generality of Mongoloids, wear beards. Upper left, the back of a Totonac slate mirror probably from the state of Vera Cruz. Upper right, a carving from Tepataxco, Vera Cruz. Center, a figure on a pottery vase from Chama, Guatemala. Lower left, a pottery head found at Tres Zapotes in Vera Cruz. Lower right, a carving on a stela at La Venta, Vera Cruz, which appears to have an artificial beard such as was worn by the Egyptians. (The first three after Vaillant, 1931; the fourth after Stirling, 1940; the last after Covarrubias, 1946.)

season when the winds would have been against them, and the coast is lacking in fresh water and harbors at any time. A southeastward voyage would have been another matter. The wind would have been behind them, and they had already found the coast attractive in that direction.

With this much to go upon, Gladwin sends the fleet of the dead Alexander down the coast of India, past the Spice Islands, and out through Melanesia, Micronesia, and Polynesia. On the way the fleet picks up men and women of various races, and stimulates the whole South Seas into a navigating era. The end result is another discovery of America. It is a discovery by a varied and talented people. Along with the Melanesian-Carib and Polynesian-Arawak, the fleet of Gladwin and Alexander finally brings to our western shores those bearded white men with civilizing propensities who are found in the legends of the Toltec and Maya and the peoples of Colombia and Peru. They it is who teach the Mongoloids how to build stone edifices, work metals, weave textiles, and make fine pots. Gladwin documents all this assiduously and even goes to his opponents for evidence.

He bolsters his argument with the "Q Complex"—that list of traits in the cultures of Middle America and the southeastern portion of the United States which Vaillant and Lothrop compiled as being very old indeed and unaccounted for in present theory. *Men Out of Asia* suggests that the Levantine voyagers brought these things or shaped them after they landed.

He uses with the greatest relish the mass of material on Oceanic traits in the Americas that Nordenskiöld drew together in "Origin of the Indian Civilizations in South America." Of the forty-nine elements of culture which the Swede found common to both regions, Gladwin points out that more occur in Colombia and Panama than in any other New World era—thirty-eight in all—and that Colombia and Panama surround the spot where ships would have landed if they had followed the Equatorial Counter Current to the Gulf of Darien. From this region as a center the Melanesian and Polynesian traits gradually thin out to the north, the south, and the east.

Against Gladwin's argument must be set, however, the evidence that Gonzalo Aguirre Beltrán has recently developed showing that,

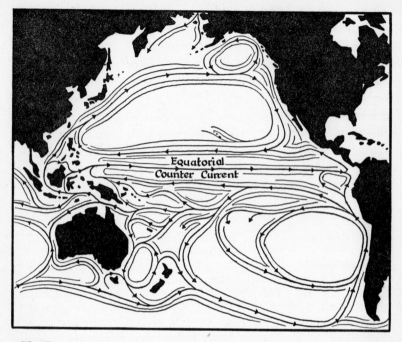

The Equatorial Counter Current, which flows just north of the equator, varies in width from 150 to 500 miles. The winds in this area are light and blow from south of east over its southern area and north of east over its northern area.

among the slaves sent to Mexico from Manila during the sixteenth and seventeenth centuries, there were many from New Guinea and other Pacific islands.[15] Was there a similar trade with Colombia, where Oceanic traits are slightly more plentiful than in Mexico and Central America, and with Amazonia, where they are almost as plentiful? It is vitally important, however, to remember that Melanesian slaves cannot possibly be credited with the importation of objects that have been found in pre-Columbian burials—certain Pan-pipes and mace heads, for example.

There are plenty of other objections, of course, to Gladwin's theory, even though it does explain much that has been a mystery; but there are also defenses that he has not made. If the islands of the Pacific are not too well provided with pottery, pyramids, cement, metallurgy, and textiles, he might have pointed out that they were imperfectly supplied with the proper raw materials. If the white voyagers left their triremes behind in favor of double canoes, and if they did not build Greek temples in the New World, he might have suggested that some generations of sojourn in the South Seas led them to forget a few things. Indeed, it is surprising that they remembered so much of weaving, metal working, and pottery (though without the potter's wheel). It is equally surprising and just a little disquieting that the white gods, almost as soon as they landed, invented a complex and unique calendar and a hieroglyphic system like nothing they were familiar with. (Perhaps they could not agree on which of the many Old World varieties to use and had to devise something new.)

Before pouncing too heavily on Gladwin and his Alexandrians, it may be well to reread some sentences in his Introduction:

We are going to offer an explanation that will be a radical departure from those in current circulation, and I shall be the first to admit that this tale will need a great deal of patching and strengthening before it will carry much weight. This may seem a strange way to launch a new theory, but I am more concerned in opening up new channels of inquiry than in trying to provide pat answers to all the questions that are plaguing us. . . . I do not know of anyone who has yet been rash enough to try to connect the origins of American civilizations with definite causes, at definite dates, in the progress of Old World history, and it is for this reason that I have said this tale will need support and will undoubtedly need to be changed. This, however, is the way that every theory should be treated, and no harm will be done if when a new idea is launched it is regarded with due reserve, but also without prejudice.[16]

My next chapter will return to rather formidable arguments for inventiveness in the American Indian; but first I should perhaps point out that Gladwin is not an Elliot Smith riding the hobby of diffusion to the end. He admits independent invention in many important fields. Pottery was invented, he believes, at least twice in the Old World. He concedes a number of origins for agriculture in the New. But he believes that the really inventive men of the New World—the men who developed corn, and devised the Maya calendar—were the men who brought brains as well as cultural equipment in the ships of

Alexander, and put those brains to work devising more cultural equipment. Gladwin simply does not consider that early man and his successors before the birth of Christ were smart enough to produce much more than exceptionally good spear points and rather inferior milling stones. He does not believe that the Australoids or the Folsom men or the Algonquins or the Mongoloids who came over just before our era—let alone the Uto-Aztecans or the Athabascans a little later— were capable of inventing much in the way of neolithic civilization. He points out that the Indian—bereft, presumably, of the brains and blood of the men of Alexander's fleet—has not done much invent- ing in the past four centuries. An opponent might remark that many an inventive, creative people has lapsed from grace—the Egyptians and the Greeks, for instance. The Polynesians and the Melanesians have not done much more inventing than the Indians since the days when the Alexandrians turned them into pre-Columbian pioneers of America culture.

Independent Inventions Neither Parallel nor Diffused   It will be some years before the debate of diffusion versus independent invention comes anywhere near settlement. Much of Gladwin's evidence for diffusion is striking and not to be laughed aside—particularly the group of Australian traits in our Southwest, and the Polynesian and Melanesian traits in the area around the Gulf of Darien. His injection of Old World voyagers between the northern and southern areas of the New World explains certain puzzling matters; but the theory presents puzzles of its own. Many culture traits of Middle America and Peru are not found in Oceania: the use of cement in masonry and the vigesimal system of numeration in Middle America; the amazingly intricate Maya calendar and hieroglyphics with the first invention of zero; baked brick in two Mexican sites; bronze in Peru; the hammock; the whistling jar; the manioc press. Some of these New World traits must have been invented here, but we have to believe that the others were forgotten in Oceania and remembered in the Americas. One argument for trans-Pacific diffusion is clear and cojent, however. It is hard to believe that the men who voyaged as far as the Marquesas and Easter Island stopped there, and so missed

our long coast line. Certainly the sweet potato made the ocean crossing in the reverse direction.[17]

Other things went with the sweet potato, according to the great
chemist Gilbert N. Lewis. Without believing that man originated in
South America, he thinks that man first reached the neolithic level in
the area east of the Peruvian Andes while his fellow man in the rest
of the world was wandering in paleolithic darkness. In the Andean
highlands, man developed architecture, numeration, metallurgy, weaving, sculpture, and so forth. He spread these things to Middle America
6,000 or 8,000 years ago, and then carried them across the Pacific to
the Old World.[18] As a whole, Lewis's theory may be unacceptable;
but his arguments for diffusion and against independent invention
are cogent.

In 1947 six Scandinavians demonstrated the possibility of an east-
west crossing by sailing and drifting 4,300 miles in 101 days on a
primitive raft of balsa logs from Peru to an atoll not many days from
Tahiti.[19]

The position of the American partisans of independent invention is
a curious one. It is both weak and strong. Man *is* inventive—even
primitive man. But his inventions often have a unique quality: they
are not always duplicated, or they are not duplicated at the same
level of cultural development. Consider the cave paintings and the
sculpture of the Aurignacians, Solutreans, and Magdalenians in the
Late Paleolithic. It is an art of remarkable perfection that utterly disappeared, and was not equaled again for thousands upon thousands
of years. At Bonampak in southern Mexico a Maya painter used consummate perspective and foreshortening seven hundred years before
they appeared in the Italian Renaissance. Then there are the unique
Folsom point, the perfection of the Solutrean and Yuma points, the
Maya calendar and hieroglyphs, the mosaic walls of Mitla in Mexico,
Egyptian architecture and sculpture as well as writing, the beautifully
expressive masks of the Negro and the Eskimo. These were independent inventions, but they were unique ones. They were not independent, *parallel* inventions. And they were not diffused.

As for early man in the New World, we may believe if we wish
that the shape of the Sandia point was diffused from the Solutreans of

Europe. We may deny the independent invention in our Southwest of spear-throwers, bull-roarers, bunt points, and curved throwing sticks that look more as if they had been brought from Australia. The Yuma point may have come from Siberia, or Siberia may have got it from North America. The Folsom point, however, looks definitely like an independent invention, for it is found nowhere else in the world. This argues that the people who ultimately succeeded in making it must have been in the New World for many, many generations before one of them lashed a Folsom point to a spear and thrust it into a bison. Where are the flints they shaped before the Folsom? Can they have evolved the craft of flint knapping here in the New World? When we know this, we shall probably know whether they came before or after the last glaciers.

Meantime it is interesting to observe that the log-jam of the independent inventionists is breaking up. When the International Congress of Americanists met in New York in 1949, the hitherto conservative and autochthonous American Museum of Natural History presented for the instruction and delectation of the Congress a rather elaborate exhibition of parallelisms between the cultural traits of the Old World and the New.

11

THE INDIAN IN AGRICULTURE

Corn, which is the staff of life.

—EDWARD WINSLOW, *Good
Newes from New England,*
(1624)

Inventions—Some New, Some Old   Let us forget, for the moment,
white conquerors like Alexander and white gods like Quetzalcoatl.
Let us suppose that the Indian actually invented his own culture.

This does not mean that we throw diffusion out of the window;
for the Indian may have invented things in the Old World and
brought them to the New—which is one kind of diffusion. On the
other hand, he may have invented in the Americas the same things
that other peoples were inventing—before or after him—in Eurasia.
That, of course, is independent invention.

There is a third possibility: that the Indian invented things in the
New World which none of the peoples of the Old World ever invented. If he could do this, then it is obvious that he could invent
some things which other people had also invented. The Indian's ability to invent uniquely is a far stronger argument for independent
invention than the theory of "psychic unity." It is also an argument
for early man, if the things invented can be dated far back in time.

Nordenskiöld and others list a number of inventions that are unique
to the New World.[1] Among them are the hammock; the tube of
diagonally woven fibers which enabled the lowland Indians of South
America to squeeze the poison from the manioc and produce whole-

some tapioca; the bola of Argentina and the Arctic; the ventilating and cooling system of the kivas (the subterranean religious chambers of the pueblos); the Peruvian whistling jar; the cigar, cigarette, tobacco pipe, cigar holder, the quipu (a set of knotted strings for counting); the enema syringe; the hollow rubber ball; elastic rings; the toboggan; the Maya calendar and hieroglyphs; and possibly the snowshoe. If the list is not very impressive, consider how few unique inventions the Old World could muster in the same kind of stone age.

The significance of the list is reinforced by our knowledge of certain parallel inventions which the Indian is presumed to have made without aid from the Old World. One is metallurgy. In South America, he discovered rather late how to smelt metals and make bronze. This lateness, according to Nordenskiöld, proves independent invention. If migrants brought over the knowledge of metallurgy, they left no trace of it along their journey, either in North America or in the South Seas; and there is no Indian folklore telling of how their forefathers or their gods brought bronze to the New World. Nordenskiöld makes the further point that, having invented the casting of metal, the Indians must also have invented the forms in which they cast it— the socketed ax, for example, the bell, and the pincers. On the basis of these inventions in metallurgy, and other inventions, Nordenskiöld writes, "It is surely a matter of logical reasoning to suppose that independent inventions may have been made by them in the realms of architecture, weaving, ceramics, etc." [2] This would be a very much better argument, of course, if bronze had never been invented in the Old World. Then no boatload of Alexandrians could ever refute it.

Nordenskiöld might have added agriculture to his list of unique Indian inventions—or rather the products of agriculture. The Indian discovered and cultivated plants unknown to the Old World. He developed special varieties suited to special conditions of soil and climate. In a sense he even invented two plants, for botanists have been unable to find any wild ancestor of Indian corn or the white potato.

American Plants and Their Cultivation   The list of important plants that made up the Indian's agriculture is impressive. It is also unique,

THE INDIAN'S NEW WORLD PRODUCTS

CULTIVATED
   FOOD CROPS
maize (Indian corn)
white potato
sweet potato
tomato
pumpkin
squash
peanut
lima bean
kidney bean
tepary bean
chili pepper
cacao (for
   chocolate)
agave (for pulque)
sunflower seed
custard apple
pineapple
chayote (vegetable)
quinoa (cereal)

strawberry
arracacha (root)
avocado
manioc (for tapioca)
Jerusalem artichoke

WILD FOOD-
   STUFFS
persimmon
papaw
papaya
wild rice
guava
arrowroot
cashew nut
jacote (plum)
Paraguay tea (maté)
soursop
vanilla bean
tonka bean
capulin (a cherry)

FIBERS
New World cottons *
henequen

DYES
cochineal (red) *
arnotto (red and yellow)
anil (indigo blue)

GUMS
rubber
copal
balsam of Peru
chicle

DRUGS
tobacco *
coca * (for cocaine)
cinchona (for quinine)
cascara sagrada
ipecac
_____
* Cultivated

A more exhaustive list could include many natural products which the Indian used locally, such as honey in Middle America and flour made from acorn and mesquite in California.

for it contains no Old World species. In the northeastern United States there were a few wild fruits and berries—grapes and black-berries, for example—that are common to the north temperate zones of both hemispheres. In Middle America were two plants which are found in Asia and the South Sea Islands—the bottle gourd and the coconut palm—and cotton of a different species from that of Eurasia and Africa. Otherwise, "of cultivable plants," says Nordenskiöld, "the ancient American higher civilizations possessed none in common with the Old World." [3]

There are two very curious facts about primitive husbandry in the

New World. The Americas provided the Indian with few animals that could be domesticated, and no draft animals at all. Because he had no ox and no horse, he could not use a plow, and did not invent one. Fortunately, on the other hand, the Americas had no plants that required plow cultivation and field sowing. Wild rice grew in lakes. The rest of the plants responded to hoe culture. Or, rather, since the Indian used the hoe only in limited areas—and probably quite late, at that—the seeds could be placed in the ground with a planting stick, and after a little hand cultivation the shade of the abundant leaves would take care of the weeds. Beans, corn, manioc, and potatoes—the four major crops—were ideally suited to the only means the Indian possessed for planting and cultivating.

This difference between agriculture in the Mediterranean area and the New World is quite as great as the difference between the pastoral activities of the Fertile Crescent and the scanty domestication of animals in the Americas. Here there is no solace for the diffusionist. As Lowie has said, "There is more resemblance between the Ionic capital and a Papuan headrest than between the sowing of cereals and the planting of a banana shoot." (If he had been thinking specifically of our present problem, he would have substituted corn kernel or potato eye for banana shoot.) "Bee-keeping is not the same as training elephants or herding horses; and sowing seeds is not equivalent to planting a side-shoot or a tuber, let alone ridding a tuber [manioc] of its prussic acid." [4]

When and Where Did Our Agriculture Begin?   There are two questions to be asked about agriculture in the New World: Where did it originate and with what plants? Did it have a multiple origin—which would entail a sort of independent invention? These questions have a bearing on how much time man spent in the inventing and perfecting of agriculture, and therefore on how long he had been thoroughly settled in the Americas when the Spaniards came.

Not so many years ago, Indian corn, or maize, was carelessly considered the first plant cultivated in the Americas—probably because it was the most spectacular—and was supposed to have originated in the highlands of Mexico or Guatemala. Now we know that beans preceded corn, and so, in all probability, did most of the commoner food plants. Beans and melons, with their free-running vines and prominent flowers and seed pods, would seem most likely to have first attracted man—or, perhaps, woman—and led him to assist the processes of nature.

When corn was king, semiarid farm lands were supposed to be the place of its origin. Spinden saw "irrigation as an invention which accounts for the very origin of agriculture itself." [5] Semiarid land, however, is notoriously hard to clear; though its plants are few, they have deep, tenacious roots. The flood plain of the Sonora Desert in Mexico —ideal by Spinden's standard—yields no evidence of long or extensive occupation, according to Carl Sauer. Where irrigation was used in our Southwest, dates are not early. The evidence of the plants themselves, he writes, "overwhelmingly points not to desert or steppe but to several humid climates for their origin.[6]

There has never been much enthusiasm for the humid tropic lowlands as the seedbed of agriculture. Of late years the students of botany have turned to the temperate forest area and particularly to the mountain valley as the seat of agriculture. This has been championed by N. I. Vavilov and a group of Russian scientists, sent to the Americas in the 1920's, who made a most elaborate study of our native cultivated plants. Much of their evidence is too technical for presentation here, but their conclusions have seemed convincing to many students.[7] A mountain valley provides a wider range of temperature and rainfall and a greater variety of native plants. Its forest trees, before they are cleared by girdling and burning, store up a rich humus under their shade. Costa Rica and El Salvador—full of isolated mountain valleys—contain, according to Henry J. Bruman, as many species of plants as the United States, in spite of the fact that the United States is a hundred times the size of the two countries together.[8] The Russians believe that agriculture took early shape in certain mountain valley areas, including southern Mexico, Central America, Colombia, highland Peru, western Bolivia, and southern Chile. Though they do not commit themselves as to whether agriculture originated in one place and spread later to others, "their evidence," Sauer thinks, "may be interpreted in favor of multiple independent beginnings." [9] But

Bruman, writing of their work, points out that the "enormous spread of maize and beans, of cotton and tobacco, for example, show that there is 'something of the undivided whole' in the great cultures of the New World, as Vavilov well expresses it." [10] So, as to single or multiple origin, you may take your choice.

It is amusing to note that the diffusionists and the partisans of independent invention change places on the subject of corn. Spinden diffuses all corn from Middle America. Gladwin plumps for various areas of independent invention, including the Mississippi Valley. [11]

The Indian's Accomplishment in Agriculture   There can be no argument over the remarkable nature of certain things that the Indian farmer accomplished. Through long cultivation he produced the seedless pineapple. When he found that one form of manioc was poisonous, he took thought and devised a press for squeezing out the deadly cyanide while retaining the starch. Bruman calls this "one of the outstanding accomplishments of the American Indian." [12] He says further:

The original process of plant selection seems to have been carried on more intensively in the Americas than elsewhere. The major crop plants were farther removed from their wild ancestors than those of any other part of the earth at the time of the discovery. Mention need only be made of corn, which is so distinct as to require classification in a unique genus, and of the potato, which resulted probably from the crossing of many and various Solanaceae.

[The Solanaceae include nightshade, jimson weed, tobacco, and others.]

On November 5, 1492, two Spaniards whom Columbus had sent into the interior of Cuba told him of "a sort of grain they call maiz which was well tasted, bak'd, dry'd, and made into flour." Thus came the first news of "a cereal treasure of immensely greater value than the spices which Columbus traveled so far to seek." [13]

The fact that corn is today the second most important food crop of the world is due to its unique adaptability. In 1492 at least seven hundred different varieties of this grain were growing in widely varied areas of half the western hemisphere. Today corn is grown on

TVRCICVM
FRVMENTVM.
Türckisch korn.

THE FIRST ILLUSTRATION OF THE CORN PLANT

From Fuchs's *De Historia Stirpium*, published in 1542, only fifty years after Columbus's men first saw maize. Seven years earlier Oviedo printed a drawing of an ear of corn. (Courtesy of Harvard University Library.)

all the continents, and its habitats range from 58° north latitude in Canada and Russia to 40° south of the equator in Argentina.

Fields of maize are growing below sea level in the Caspian plain and at altitudes of more than 12,000 feet in the Peruvian Andes. Corn is cultivated in regions of less than ten inches of annual rainfall in the semi-arid plains of Russia, and in regions with more than 200 inches of rain in the tropics of Hindustan. It thrives almost equally well in the short summers of Canada and the perpetual summer of tropical Colombia.[14]

For the Gaspé Peninsula in the province of Quebec and for the Pyrenees Mountains there is a variety that matures in two months. For Colombia there is one that requires ten or eleven months. The height ranges from two feet to twenty; the leaves vary from eight to forty-eight; the number of stalks by a single seed, from one to twelve; the ears from three inches to three feet. Authorities used to list from five to eight basically different types of corn; the five are sweet, flour, dent, flint, and pop. "The Russians," write P. C. Mangelsdorf and R. G. Reeves, "have already collected more than 8,000 varieties." [15]

All the chief types of corn known today were developed by the Indians to suit the wide variety of lands and climates in which they lived. The feat seems all the more remarkable because botanists tell us that all these varieties had to be developed by keen observation and hard work from a single parent species—*Zea mays* L.—and modern man has never found corn in a wild form. This amazingly varied plant, which cannot properly seed itself and will die without man's intervention, was evolved from a plant that is now apparently extinct.

In spite of the old saw about the staff of life, a starchy grain is not the ideal food; but corn, says Sauer, is the most useful of all American starches because in addition to its ease of storage "it contains also fat and protein and is a more nearly complete food than the others." [16]

How Old Is Corn?   Obviously it must have taken many long years for the Indian to develop corn from its unknown ancestor into its many and widespread varieties. One botanical authority, G. N. Collins, thinks 20,000 years would not be enough—if a gross mutation, or sudden genetic change, were ruled out.[17] Other botanists do not accept

CHAP. X.

Of Turkie Corne, or Indian wheat.

The kindes.

Turkiſh wheat is of one, and of many ſorts. A man ſhall not find in this coun-trey (in faſhion and growing) moꝛe than one kind, but in colour the ſæde oꝛ grayne doth much differ : foꝛ one beareth a bꝛowne grayne oꝛ coꝛne, the other a red, the third a yellow, and the fourth a white coꝛne oꝛ grayne: The which colour doth likewiſe remayne both in the eares and floures.

The deſcription.

This Coꝛne is a maruellous ſtrange plant, nothing reſembling any other kind of grayne : foꝛ it bꝛingeth foꝛth his ſæde cleane contrarie from the place whereas the Floures grow, which is againſt the nature and kinds of all other plants, which bꝛing foꝛth their fruit there, whereas they haue boꝛne their Floure. This Coꝛne beareth a high helme oꝛ ſtemme, and very long, round, thicke, firme, and below to-wards the roote of a bꝛowniſh colour, with ſundꝛie knots and ioynts, from the which dependeth long, and large leaues, like the leaues of Spire oꝛ Poleræde : at the higheſt of the ſtalkes, grow idle and barren eares, which bꝛing foꝛth nothing but the floures oꝛ bloſſomes, which are ſometimes bꝛowne, ſometimes red, ſome-times yellow, and ſometimes white, agræable with the colour of the fruit, which commeth foꝛth afterward. The fruitfull eares do grow, vpon the ſides of the ſtems amongſt the leaues, the which eares bæ great and thicke, and couered with many leaues, ſo that one cannot ſee the ſayd eares, vppon the vppermoſt part of the ſayd eares there grow many long hayꝛie thꝛædes, which iſſue foꝛth at the ends oꝛ poynts of the leaues, couering the eare, and doe ſhew themſelues about the time that the fruit oꝛ eare waxeth ripe. The grayne oꝛ ſæde which groweth in the eares, is about the quantitie oꝛ bigneſſe of a Peaſe, of colour in the out-ſide, ſometimes bꝛowne, ſometimes redde, and ſometimes white, and in the in-ſide it is in colour white, and in taſte ſweet, growing oꝛderly about the eares, in nine oꝛ ten ranges oꝛ rowes.

The place.

This grayne groweth in Turkie, whereas it is vſed in the time of dearth.

The time.

It is ſowne in Apꝛill, and ripe in Auguſt.

The names.

They doe now call this grayne, Frumentum Turcicum, and Frumentum Aſiati-cum : in French, *Blé de Turquie,* oꝛ *Blé Sarazin:* in high Dutch, Turkie Koꝛn : in baſe Almaigne, Toꝛckſehcoꝛen : in Engliſh, Turkiſh Coꝛne, oꝛ Indian-wheat.

The nature, and vertues.

There is as yet no certayne experience of the naturall vertues of this coꝛne.

The bꝛead that is made thereof is dꝛye and hard, hauing very ſmall fatneſſe oꝛ moyſture, wherefoꝛe men may eaſily iudge, that it nouriſheth but little, and is euill of digeſtion, nothing comparable to the bꝛead made of Wheat, as ſome haue falſly affirmed.

"TURKIE CORNE"

By 1578 maize had spread so widely in the Old World that in Dodoens's *A Newe Herball* the habitat of this "marvelous strange plant" was attributed to Turkey. (Courtesy of Harvard University Library.)

CHAP. XXIV.

Milium Indicum maximum Maiz dictum, sive Frumentum Indicum,
vel Turcicum aliquorum. Indian or Turkie Wheate.

AS a kinde of Millet although farre greater and differing notably from the former I must joyne this graine although some have made divers sorts thereof, yet I cannot perceive any more then two speciall differences, the one beareth eares at the joynts of the stalkes, the other at the toppe following the flowers: the other differences consist not in any other things then the colours, of the blooming first and of the graines afterwards.

1. *Maiz Frumentum Indicum vel Turcicum vulgare.*   The usuall Indian or Turkie Wheate.

This Indian Wheate shooteth from the roote which is thicke and bushie, sundry strong and tall stalkes six or eight foote high, as thicke as a mans wrest if it grow in any ranke ground, full of great joynts with a white pith in the middle of them, the leaves are long, twise as large and great as of Millet; at the toppes come forth many feather-like sprigs, bending downewards like unto the toppe of Millet, which are either white or yellow or blew, as the graines in the eares will prove, which fall away, nothing appearing after them; but while they are in flower at the joynts of the stalkes with the leaves, from within two or three of the lower joynts up towards the toppes, come forth the eares one at a joynt which have many leaves foulded over them smallest at the toppe, with a small long bush of threads or haires hanging downe at the ends, which when they are ripe are to bee cut off: which foulds of leaves being taken away, the head appeareth much like unto a long Cone or Pineaple, set with six or eight or ten rowes of Cornes, orderly and closely set together, each being almost as bigge as a Pease not fully round, but flat on the sides that joyne one unto another, of the same colour on the outside as the bloomings were, hard but brittle and easie to bee broken or ground, with a white meale within them somewhat dry and not clammy in the chewing. Lobel expresseth the figure of another sort as he thinketh because as hee saith it grew greater and higher, and the roote grew greater, and with more separate tufts, the roote not differing in any thing else: but I thinke it no specificall

1. *Milium Indicum maximum Maiz dictum sive Frumentum Indicum vel Turcicum.* The usuall Indian or Turkie Wheate.

difference, not understanding by any that it is taken for another sort, and therefore I have omitted it and speake no more thereof.

2. *Frumentum Indicum alterum sive minus.*   The other lesser Indian Wheate.

This other Indian Wheate is like the former both in stalkes and leaves, but not halfe so high or great, the eares likewise are not halfe so bigge, of as differing colours as it, but they doe not grow at the joynts of the stalkes as the other, but at the toppes following the flowers, which maketh a specificall difference betweene them: the graine it selfe is being made into bread not of that nourishing qualitie that the greater sort, is but weaker by much, nor is so strong to breede so much blood as it.

A SEVENTEENTH CENTURY PICTURE OF CORN

Part of a page from Parkinson's *Theatrum Botanicum*, published in 1640.
(Courtesy of Harvard University Library.)

such a figure. The development of corn may have taken a good many centuries or, more likely, a few millenniums. Behind corn must lie more centuries or more millenniums during which the first agriculturists of the New World discovered how to grow other plants. For whether corn originated in Middle America, Colombia, or Paraguay —independent inventionists argue for each locality—or in all three with the Mississippi Valley thrown in, there can be no question that it came later than most of the other cultivated plants; and this adds more years to the story of the civilizing of man in the Americas. Bruman writes:

> Whether this high specialization of cultivated plant life can be used as an indication of greater age on the part of American agriculture in comparison to that of the Old World is a difficult point. In the writer's opinion it may indicate merely a greater agricultural awareness on the part of the Indian, a cultural trait no doubt strongly furthered by the relative unimportance of domesticated animals.[18]

Sylvanus G. Morley believed that the Maya cultivated corn at a time close to 1000 B.C.[19] which is, of course, no more than a guess. The earliest *firm* date that we have is A.D. 217, fixed by the tree rings in wood found together with corn in a Basketmaker cave of Utah.[20] But a far earlier time, "not later than 2500 B.C.," is given by Ernst Antevs for a layer of refuse in Bat Cave, New Mexico, in

Corn of 4,500 years ago, as reconstructed from a cob found in Bat Cave, New Mexico. Natural size. (After Mangelsdorf and Smith, 1949.)

which Herbert W. Dick found the cobs and kernels of a primitive form of maize that is both a pod corn and a pop corn. These 4500-year-old cobs range from 2⅜ inches to 3¾ inches in length. Though probably not specimens of the long-sought wild corn, they are not far removed in characteristics.[21]

In coastal Peru—where corn could not have started—Julio C. Tello found kernels in the ruins of Paracas, along with manioc roots, sweet potatoes, and beans. Paracas may have flourished around A.D. 400.

Among the vegetable relics of an earlier culture, Coastal Chavin, which Duncan Strong dates before the birth of Christ,[22] no corn has been found. In the Virú Valley of the Peruvian coast, Strong and Junius Bird have found evidences of a people who had neither corn nor pots but raised cotton, squash, and other plants, and Bird thinks these people may have lived 5,000 years ago.[22]

It seems unlikely that any form of agriculture could have been developed from native plants in coastal Peru, for it is as arid a spot as can be found anywhere in our hemisphere. Only an elaborate system of irrigation canals enabled this area to grow extensively corn, beans, and other plants. In the highly developed civilization of the coast—so close to the guano islands—the Indians started the use of fertilizers. This was later a feature of Peruvian agriculture. The development of irrigation and fertilizer, plus city architecture and the finest pottery in the Americas, spells many years of slowly growing civilization in coastal Peru, and behind these beginnings must have lain centuries upon centuries of earlier agricultural discoveries and improvements in the hinterlands. The only alternative is to accept the diffusion of a full-blown culture across the Pacific.

There are those who believe that corn did in fact come from Asia to the Americas. Sauer points out that Asia has more kinds of the wild grasses, Gramineae, akin to corn, Zea mays L., than the New World.[23] Another argument is that though the Chinese kept a careful record of the importation of various plants such as tobacco and the opium poppy, there is no mention of corn, implying that they had long been familiar with some variety of it.[24] The botanist Edgar Anderson believes it could have originated in Burma, and could have come across the Pacific "along with cotton, pottery, weaving, etc." [25]

Anderson's evidence, as he himself maintains, is not conclusive; but it is certainly suggestive. Popcorn is found today among primitive or backward peoples in the remoter parts of Formosa, Sumatra, Java, Borneo, and Burma. From the Naga Hills, where Burma meets Assam, Anderson has had brought to the United States cobs and kernels of popcorn which are identical with the corn found in the earliest graves in Peru. Was this Burmese popcorn carried eastward over the Pacific 2,000 to 4,000 years ago and then crossed with some American plant, such as Tripsacum, to produce the great variety of larger and more useful types that the Spaniards found? Or was popcorn, imported from the New World, the only maize that the primitive Naga of Burma would cultivate?

The argument for a Burmese origin for popcorn is strengthened by some habits of the Naga tribesmen which carry us back to the dispute over diffusion versus independent invention. These people, living in the Stone Age today, follow the agricultural pattern of the pre-Columbian Indian. They burn trees and underbrush to clear their fields. They use a digging stick to plant their corn in the charred rubbish. In amongst the corn they grow cereals and cotton.[26]

Yet, if it should prove true that popcorn came to the Americas as the first form of maize, we should still have to credit the Indian with the tedious centuries—even millenniums—that went into the production of the many varieties which covered thousands of square miles of the New World when Columbus heard of "a sort of grain they call maiz." And, before the coming of corn from Asia, we should still have to recognize the tens of centuries that went into the discovery and development of the agriculture of beans, squash, melons, potatoes, and manioc.

The story of corn and of agriculture does not tell us when early man reached our hemisphere; but it suggests that he must have settled in South America thousands of years before the birth of Christ. He needed many millenniums to evolve from a hunting and gathering savage into a farmer and to reach the cultural level at which he would develop and perfect the many varieties of corn.

12

PUZZLES, PROBLEMS, AND
HALF-ANSWERS

*One swallow does not make a summer,
but two lead one to suspect an abiding
change in the weather.*

—R. A. DALY

The Pendulum Swings   This chapter might have been headed "Summary." I could not have called it "Conclusions," for, as an amateur of archaeology, I have tried—sometimes unsuccessfully, I'm sure—to avoid appraisals. The final pages will review the more important evidence of early man in the New World, including, at some length, his relation to Old World peoples and to certain geologic phenomena.

The study of early man in America has suffered from alternate spasms of unscientific enthusiasm and far too "scientific" caution. It has ranged from the parading of rumor and guesswork to the blind cranioclasm of Hrdlička. In the nineteenth century the talk was of man in the Americas before the Great Ice Age and far back into the Tertiary era that ended 1,000,000 years ago. At the beginning of the twentieth century anthropologists gave him no more than 4,000 years in the New World. Now they generally concede him 10,000 or 15,000 years, and many grant him 25,000.

Clark Wissler, dean of American anthropologists, wrote in 1944, "The first great migration of Old World peoples to the New can be set down as not only beginning but culminating within the limits of late Pleistocene Time." [1] Frank H. H. Roberts, Jr., long a protagonist of

Folsom man, wrote the next year, "The belief that the Folsom complex developed towards the end of the Pleistocene, or Late Glacial, period and carried over into the beginning of the Recent is now more or less generally accepted." [2]

On the whole, the archaeologists—developing a new and sound technique in stratigraphic excavation and pottery study—have held back more than the physical anthropologists from the acceptance of a variegated array of early men at quite early dates. Geologists and paleontologists, in whose hands must lie the final dating of the Indian's predecessors, have inclined to a more radical attitude. A few scientists are talking of the possibility that man crossed Bering Strait before the last glaciation—Würm in Europe, Wisconsin in America—and possibly even while the Riss-Illinois was laying a land-bridge across from Siberia to Alaska.

When you look at the evidence behind these opinions—skulls, tools, fossils, earth strata—you see why there has been disagreement. We have facts about early man, plenty of them. Some are conflicting facts. Most of them raise serious problems. A few leave us with grievous puzzles. Let us reexamine the facts and the puzzles.

The Puzzle of the Skulls   We have quite a few skulls that may have belonged to early man. On the whole, they do not look as Mongoloid as good Indian skulls should. Except for two—Minnesota man and Tepexpan man—they are long-headed instead of round-headed, and those exceptions lie between the two extremes. The skulls have heavy brow ridges. Most of them have keeled vaults like the Australoid-Melanesians of today. Many have retreating foreheads. It is true that skulls like these can be found in the variegated ranks of what is supposed to be the homogeneous "Indian race"; but they are far from plentiful. For instance, Hrdlička's catalogue of Indian craniums shows only a small percentage that are long-headed. If early man was indeed more Australoid-Melanesian in type than pure Mongoloid, it would be only natural to find some reflection in the descendants of the Mongoloid immigrants with whom early man may be presumed to have bred.

There is no agreement as to the racial affinities of the earliest migrants. Most anthropologists still believe they were Mongoloids and therefore what they call Indians. Some go to the other extreme and declare they were Australoid, Negroid, and/or Caucasoid. Some, like Hooton, say the stock was drawn from a mingling of the three races in Asia. He thinks they "may have received some Mongoloid admixture before reaching the New World, but this is doubtful." [3]

Many of the skulls of early man resemble in certain respects those of that late arrival, the Eskimo, just as the Eskimo resembles some specimens of Magdalenian man. The skulls of the Eskimo are longheaded, and have keeled vaults and prominent cheekbones. But most early craniums have three features that are lacking in the Eskimo—jutting jaws, slanting foreheads and heavy brow ridges—all stigmata of the Australoid-Melanesian.

It is rather puzzling to note that these early skulls are found with the bones of extinct animals in South America, but seldom with such fossils in North America, while they are not found with Folsom or Sandia or any form of ancient point. (There seems to be no especially ancient type of point in South America.) It is possible, as Howard suggested, that the North American hunters practiced exposure of the dead instead of burial, while early man to the south left more burials for us than the few that have been found.

The Puzzle of the Querns   The next puzzle lies in the milling stones. Man in America not only starts off with an exceptionally fine type of spear point to thrust into elephant or camel, and uses pressure flaking far more extensively than man in the Old World; in addition, he develops the type of milling stone, or quern, that does not appear in Europe until man is coming out of the Old Stone Age and entering the neolithic period of agriculture. Milling stones might be used as an argument against the early appearance of man in America if it could be proved that they were made to grind agricultural products; but no kernels of corn or other cultivated seeds have been found with these querns.

Except for milling stones that seem to have been used to grind paint in Chile,[4] the preagricultural querns occur mainly in the area of

California, the Southwest, and upper Mexico. Through California, from Borax Lake and the Mohave Desert, to the Cochise area of southeastern Arizona and the Edwards Plateau of central Texas, and on into northwestern Mexico, these grinding tools turn up with artifacts and in geological strata that may be from 6,000 to 25,000 years old. If those dates are correct, then we have milling stones in the New World many years before there was any agriculture. The explanation must be that some of the earliest of the Americans were food gatherers and grinders of nuts and seeds as well as hunters. In addition to their querns, they have left us hearths on beds of collected stones, rude knives, rough percussion tools such as scrapers and choppers, but very few spear points. There is no early culture of this sort in Asia or Africa. It is not Folsom. Is it Australoid? Does it go back to a type of people who, in some hybrid and degenerate form, settled Australia? At least we know that the culture of the Australians is a curious mixture of very primitive traits with some elements of the polished stone work of the New Stone Age such as milling stones. They are nearer being food gatherers than hunters.

The Puzzle of the Points   With the first hunters in the New World— the men who made the Sandia, the Folsom, the Plainview, and probably the early Yuma points—we come to another puzzle. The Sandia is shaped like a much superior point made by the Solutreans of Europe and an equally crude one made in Africa, but the best Folsom is better than the best Solutrean. The fluted channels of the Folsom are remarkable enough; in addition, the edges are sharpened by the removal of almost microscopic flakes, and the base is often carefully ground. We know that such points were being made at least 15,000 and perhaps 25,000 years ago. The Yuma point is doubtless newer, yet it must antedate the only chipped weapons that can equal it, the daggers of neolithic Egyptians 7,500 years ago or of the still later Danes.

A point with Yuma-like chipping has been found in a neolithic site in Siberia.[5] What does this mean? Obviously Sandia man or his forebears came from Asia across Bering Strait, but too early to leave the Siberian Yuma behind him. Someone has been bold enough to suggest that the descendants of the man who developed the Folsom point may have returned to Siberia; after all, as George Gaylord Simpson has pointed out, a bridge works both ways.[6] If Yuma man was too late for the land-bridge of the last glaciation, he still had the ice-bridge of winter. But "ice" suggests a doubt. Would a hunter of

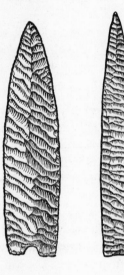

At the left, a point with oblique chipping in the Yuma style, found near Lake Baikal, Siberia, in a neo-lithic culture, compared with a Yuma point from Colorado. Is the resemblance accidental, or could Yuma man have migrated to the Old World after developing his characteristic style of flint knapping in the New? The size of the Siberian point is not recorded. (The Yuma point after Howard, 1935; the Siberian, after Okladnikov, 1938, and Collins, 1943.)

the temperate High Plains be likely to trek north through the chill of winter to deposit a spear point in Siberia? Yet we know that traces of Yuma, Plainview, and Folsom have been found in Alaska. Were they left by summer transients fishing Cook Inlet or hunting Alaskan jaguar around Fairbanks? It is safer, on the whole, to ask where this type of early American came from than to ask where he went.

The points of early man present a double puzzle. How did it happen that the art of working flint was brought to higher perfection in the New World during the Old Stone Age than it was in the Old World? And where did these consummate flint knappers come from? The first question may never be answered. The second presents interesting possibilities. They revolve around the brief appearance of the Solutreans in Europe. Only a great deal of very thorough excavation in Siberia will give us more than provocative or provoking theories about the origins of the men who made Sandia and Folsom points.

Was Our Early Man a Solutrean?   Let me stress again that the Folsom and Yuma chipping reached a perfection unknown in Europe until neolithic man brought in agriculture. Indeed, if the paleolithic Solutrean points had never been found, *all* American archaeologists—instead of just one or two—would unhesitatingly have called Folsom and Yuma neolithic, even though they were found with extinct animals. In the history of Europe's Old Stone Age—and in Africa's, too, for that matter—we have no more than one hint of such work. It was only the men of the Solutrean culture—thrust between the late Aurignacian and the early Magdalenian—who took much true advantage of pressure flaking, and who made spear points with Sandia-like shoulders. (While the flint chipping of the Solutreans is fine, it is not so minute or so perfect as the work of the men who made Folsom and Yuma points.) With the disappearance of the Solutreans, the art of fine flint knapping and point making faded away, not to appear again with any vigor until neolithic times.

The Solutreans are not a part of the flow and development of prehistoric European culture. They seem to come as invaders, and then fade out after 500 years, or, at the most, 10,000. Where they came from is uncertain. Because crude points called Proto-Solutrean are much more plentiful along the Danube than they are in France—where the finest Solutrean work is found—it has long been argued that the people who made them came from western Asia. Lately, flint work of the Solutrean type has been discovered in Morocco and also in Egypt;[7] and, since it is intermixed with the products of a much older culture, the Mousterian, it may be argued that the Solutreans came from Africa. The theory of an eastern origin remains strong, however; for among the African flints are shouldered points, and shouldered points were not developed until the end of the Solutrean period in Europe. We do not know the date of the Mousterian in Africa; it may have been late.

If the Solutreans did, in fact, originate in Asia, can we believe that an Asiatic people with an unusual flair for flint knapping fathered both the Solutreans and the men who made the Sandia and the far finer Folsom and Yuma points? Did this parent stock send a group of migrants across Bering Strait and down into the High Plains to give us Folsom, Sandia, and Yuma points? Did it throw off toward the west a group that practiced the Solutrean arts in Europe? Even after archaeologists have dug Siberia thoroughly we may never know how much earlier or later the American offshoot appeared on the High Plains than the Solutreans in Europe. There is even more disagreement about dating the Solutrean than about dating Sandia and Folsom; figures range from 9,500 to 67,000 years ago.

It is a curious fact that the Solutreans were as negligent as the Folsom and Yuma men in providing us with skulls. C. S. Coon writes, "There are no skulls which all authorities accept as definitely belonging to that short and far from widespread cultural phase." [8] Hunters in Europe, like hunters in America, seem to have taken little interest in formal obsequies and proper burials. Nature consumed their remains.

Or Was the American Aurignacian or Magdalenian? Even before the discovery of Folsom made early man in America look like a fugitive from that village in France called Solutré, anthropologists were struck by other resemblances. In 1924 the Englishman Sollas compared the Eskimo culture with the Magdalenian.[9] In 1932 Hrdlička was writing of an Aurignacian and Magdalenian ancestry for the American Indian.[10] In 1933 N. C. Nelson was playing with such comparisons, and writing of our "wooden spear and spear-thrower, perhaps of Magdalenian affinity; our three out of four forms of Solutrean chipped blades; our ordinary Aurignacian-like endscraper; our simple Mousterian type flake; and, finally, our Acheulean and Chellean varieties of the *coup-de-poing*." [11] In the same year Harrington was going further. Recalling that in 1921 he had reported flint work in Cuba that was Aurignacian in style, Harrington pointed out that the Solutrean never reached the West Indies. "Man in a Magdalenian stage of development . . . reached America, probably via Asia, but perhaps from Europe via Iceland and Greenland. These bands kept to the north, following up the retreating glaciers, and became the an-

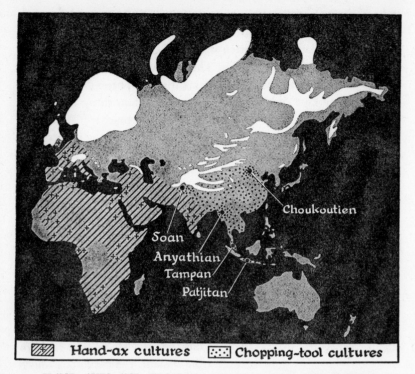

Soan
Anyathian
Tampan
Patjitan

Choukoutien

▨ Hand-ax cultures   ⋯ Chopping-tool cultures

HAND AXES AND CHOPPING TOOLS OF THE OLD WORLD

Showing the areas where the hand ax dominated and those where the chopping tool took precedence. The white portions are the ice fields of the last glaciation. (After Movius, 1944.)

cestors of the Eskimo." [12] Thomas Jefferson had somewhat the same idea when he wrote that the Eskimos "must be derived from the Groenlanders, and these probably from some of the northern parts of the old continent." [13]

Must we add the Aurignacians and Magdalenians of the end of the New Stone Age to the Solutreans and the Australoids as early invaders of America? The answer is dubious, for as yet northern Asia has yielded only a little evidence of the Aurignacian and the Magdalenian.

Chopping Tools Instead of Hand Axes in Asia   Throughout most of Asia the men of the Old Stone Age developed a very different core industry from that of Europe. Instead of the hand ax (*coup-de-poing*), they made an implement now called a chopping tool. This was a large and somewhat flat pebble with a sharpened edge made by striking off flakes alternately from either side. They had also large, crude scrapers, flaked on a single side, which are now called choppers. Only in India and the Near East did the hand ax seem to flourish as in western

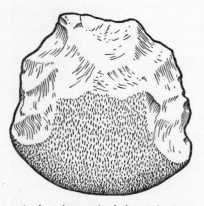

Europe and much of Africa. In the border area of the Upper Punjab, Helmut de Terra found both hand axes and chopping tools in the early Soan culture, which seems to lie in the Second Interglacial. In upper Burma the hand ax disappears, leaving the field to the chopping tool and the chopper. The same seems true of Java and northern China.[14] Here there are flake artifacts, but they were

A chopping tool of the early Soan culture in northwestern India. (After Paterson, 1942.)

not chipped by European methods. On the whole, the tools of the Asiatic complex look much more like the choppers and scrapers found at very early sites such as Lake Mohave, southeastern Arizona (Cochise), Sonora, Lower California, and the Valley of Mexico.

Yet—another puzzle—hand axes have been found in central and southern Texas, and in Renaud's Black's Fork culture of Wyoming, without traces of Folsom or Yuma. Can these hand axes, like the Aurignacian and Magdalenian traits of which Nelson and Harrington write, represent an earlier migration than Sandia and Folsom? This is most problematical.

Spinden's Neolithic Blockade   All this is patently absurd to the dean of American archaeologists, Herbert J. Spinden. If tools in the New World resemble the Aurignacian or the Solutrean, it is an accident—perhaps an accident of psychic unity. He is against all talk of paleolithic man in the Americas on the late edge of the Great Ice Age.

In the face of facts presented by Russian and American glacialists, he maintains that "eastern Siberia was rather heavily glaciated." [15] He believes that certain Asiatic peoples with a sudden urge for travel first appeared at the Siberian-Alaskan portal about 2500 B.C.[16] They could not have been men of the Old Stone Age because, he asserts, we have found nothing in Siberia that approaches the paleolithic; indeed, we have found no paleolithic tools north of 54° in England, of 53° in Siberia, or of 43° on the Sea of Japan, while "the portal to America for man and beast lies at 67° north latitude." We have, then, "a no-proof barrier zone a thousand miles deep extending clear across the Old World." [17] This "rules out invasion of America until relatively modern times because it shows that a wide zone of the Old World, blocking the road to America, was itself unused by man until long after the last continental ice sheet . . . had disappeared." [18] Obviously, Spinden's argument is not based on evidence in the Americas, but rather on lack of evidence in little studied Siberia. He ignores the presence of paleolithic tools in northern Manchuria together with the fossils of extinct mammals.[19] He concedes that even in the regions of "the most ancient civilization" in the Old World there is no trace of such high technical skill in flint chipping as the Folsom "before the fourth millennium before Christ." But—appearing to ignore the geological evidence connected with Sandia, Lindenmeier, Clovis, Abilene, and Lake Mohave—he interprets this as meaning that man cannot have reached the Southwest before the golden age of Ur. He speaks of "the lost cause of paleolithic man in America." He accepts Solutrean flint work as paleolithic, but not Folsom or Yuma. "Now, even if we admit that Folsom man hunted the mammoth, we must place that sporting event not earlier than 2000 B.C." [20]

Was the First Migration Interglacial?   As I think I have shown in Chapter 8, we can never hope to date early man at all exactly by means of elephants or bison or any other extinct mammal. Even if science were able to settle the time of the great extinction, we should be only a little better off. We could say that man was in the New World at that time; but this would give us only an upper limit, not a lower one. Man may have been here for tens of thousands of years before those mammals died off. A few scientists think he was.

The great glaciations presented early man with an opportunity and a difficulty; they threw a land-bridge across Bering Strait, but, for long periods of time, they also laid a barrier of ice and snow across his path to the south. Look at the map at the top of page 22 and you will see that about 65,000 years ago the barrier covered the whole depth of Canada. This would have meant a trip of some 2,000 miles across ice. For a time, as I have explained earlier, a corridor opened up for his passage. By 25,000 years ago, however, it had closed again. To be sure, there was a tongue of ice-free land that ran northward across part of Canada and shortened the journey over snow and ice to a thousand miles; but the invader would have had to be extremely lucky to hit the upper end of the open country. Far more important, none of the animals that he hunted, and that therefore led him on his southward journey, would have taken that thousand-mile trek across a frozen, foodless waste. If early man came in the time of the corridor, his trip would not have been too difficult and he would have found game along the way. At any period he could have come by boat or possibly afoot along the Pacific coast. But, no matter how he came, he would have faced almost insuperable difficulties during the first quarter and the third quarter of the last glaciation.

This fact affects different students differently. Antevs, feeling that man must have come after the ice began to melt, gives our migrant not much over 15,000 years in the New World. If man arrived earlier, he feels, it must have been when the corridor opened through the ice some 40,000 years ago, and he sees no evidence for so early a migration.[21] Kirk Bryan disagrees. Accepting the theory that the last glaciation waxed and waned three times, he places the first invasion by man in the second of these wanings, or interstadials, just before the final burgeoning of the ice 30,000 years ago.[22] Sauer goes further. He suggests that the shores of western Siberia may have been inhabited during the second interglacial, and that during the third glaciation, preceding the Wisconsin, "a first colonization of the New World is not improbable."[23] Erwin H. Barbour and C. Bertrand Schultz say that "evidence is constantly accumulating to show that man actually had reached

North America before the last glacial advance.[24] George F. Carter believes that artifacts in the glacial gravels of Trenton and Lake Lahontan, spear points with musk oxen in New Mexico, the Vero skull partnered in Florida with flora and fauna more appropriate to Pennsylvania, stone implements deeply buried under aged soil profiles, all argue that man was in North America during the last glaciation. He does not believe that primitive hunters—let alone the Cochise food gatherers—would have survived Arctic travel at the height of the glaciations. He thinks that Folsom man came through the ice-free corridor of 40,000 years ago, and that another body of immigrants came during the last of the three great interglacials, which means about 100,000 years ago.[25]

Interglacial migration finds support from Albrecht Penck, the German glacialist who with Eduard Brückner established the four great glaciations of central Europe. Penck gives two reasons for believing that man came to the Americas in the last interglacial. Both theories lie outside his field of special knowledge.

First, Penck doubts that man had time enough after the glaciers melted to adapt himself to the seven or eight climates in which he lived and labored in 1492. In the 25,000 years since the Wisconsin glaciation, people of an arctic habitat could not possibly have adjusted their physical nature so perfectly "first to forests, then to steppes and deserts in temperate zones, then to steaming tropical forests and to the plateaus of the tropics, the steppes and deserts of the southern hemisphere, and finally to the damp, cool south."

Penck's second reason for supporting interglacial migration has to do with the marked changes of climate that took place during the Great Ice Age. As the glaciers grew and moved farther and farther south, the temperature belts of Canada and the United States moved south with them. As these belts moved, vegetation altered. Tundra crept to the south, pursuing grasslands and forest. Deserts and jungle moved before them. When the glaciers began to melt, this movement went into reverse. Penck feels that primitive man migrates easily only within a single climatic zone. Tundra folk avoid forests; forest folk avoid tundra. Man moves with the climate, not against it; a New Yorker goes to Florida in the winter, not the summer. Early man would not have traveled southward through Canada and the United States while the climate was moving northward with the melting of the ice. On the contrary, man would have moved southward only as the glaciers grew and the temperature belts moved southward. When the glaciers melted he would have tended to move northward again. Thus man must have entered the New World toward the end of an inter-glacial, and gone southward with the weather. After that, shifts in the climate would have distributed man all over the Americas. "Under the influence of a number of alternating glacial and interglacial periods, we can understand the gradual settlement, but not solely on the assumption of one glacial migration." With the end of the last glaciers men spread north and south once more, and even drifted back to Asia.[26] Penck's argument becomes all the stronger if we grant that early man followed the animals he killed for food and animals fol-lowed the movements of the vegetation on which they fed.

Further, the presence of early man close to the time and even the edge of the retreating glaciers—if the evidence is read aright—argues that he must have arrived in North America during one of those retreats of the Wisconsin glaciation which preceded its final growth and decline.

Geological Evidence and the Pluvials All this is speculation, of course—reasoned speculation, but no more than that. Are we on firmer ground when we deal with geological evidence? Perhaps, yet there is plenty of room for controversy.

The New World has very few sites in which artifacts or human bones have been found in glacial gravels. A noted one, near Trenton, New Jersey, has been under dispute for seventy years. The Lake Lahontan site and its blade have been too much neglected. There are, however, a number of places where skulls or artifacts have been found linked to other strata than gravels that suggest a relationship with glacial activity.

In these sites we find human skulls or artifacts together with signs of much rainfall or of large lakes and rivers which now have no more existence than the mammoth. The evidence of man lies undisturbed beneath sterile layers of material deposited by water. A typical case is

Sandia Cave. Here Folsom points were found beneath a floor of a stalagmitic limestone created by so heavy a seepage of calcium-charged water that the stratum holding the Folsom material had been partially consolidated. Below lies another sterile layer—of yellow ocher earth, indicating a very moist period and the presence of trees which would provide certain chemical agents and which are no more common now in this arid area than are heavy, continuous rains. Another example of man's association with a much moister time than the present comes from the cave in Brazil where the Confins skull was found. The skull lay under six feet of alluvial soil carried in by water. Later a layer of stalagmitic limestone sealed the sepulcher. It may be presumed that artifacts found on the shore or in the clay of Lake Cochise, Lake Mohave, and Pinto Basin—now dry and gone—must have been made during a time of great waters.

What do such evidences of unusual moisture mean? They mean that the men of these sites lived before or during a period of heavy rainfall not known there for at least the last 15,000 years. Beyond that bare fact, debate begins. Walter, Cathoud, and Mattos, who described the Brazilian find, took a most conservative attitude and wrote that Confins man lived "a few thousands of years ago." [27] Bryan, who studied Sandia Cave, placed the later wet period after the end of Pleistocene, or Great Ice Age, and the first wet period—along with the Sandia points—in the Late glacial. [28]

Glacial experts call a period of unusual and widespread rains a pluvial. They believe that the growth of the glaciers was accompanied by pluvials, and some maintain that pluvials also marked the melting of the ice. Antevs lists a great pluvial—the Bonneville—which formed Lake Bonneville and Lake Lahontan during the first maximum of the last, or Wisconsin, glaciation, 65,000 years ago. He places another period of great moisture, the Provo Pluvial, at the last glacial maximum, about 25,000 years ago, and believes it was all but spent 13,000 to 15,000 years ago. [29] Thus he dates Lake Mohave and its early artifacts about 15,000 years ago. His point is that annual precipitation is about the same throughout the globe, but that the pluvials shift at various times. "It is essentially the location of the rainfall that changes." [30]

All authorities do not agree that annual rainfall is constant, and some deny Antev's late date for the last pluvial. Sauer writes, "I know of no climatologic basis for postulating a postglacial pluvial period," either in New Mexico or the Lake Mohave and Pinto Basin area of southern California.[31] Some European authorities believe that pluvials are entirely glacial. M. C. Burkitt, for example, cites the fact that the same type of tools is found in Africa during pluvials as in Europe during glacials.[32] According to Simpson's theory of the formation of the glaciers, rainfall increased enormously during two periods of the Great Ice Age; the last pluvial was at its height during the building up of the Würm-Wisconsin ice sheets. (See page 49.) The pluvials make a rather good case for early man in the New World during the last glaciation.

In Sum   We know definitely that American men once killed, skinned, and ate animals that are now extinct, for we find men's weapons and a few of their bones mingled with the fossils of extinct mammals. We cannot question the association, because it is often combined with the remains of campfires; spear points and fossils might be moved about in the course of time, but not fragile heaps of charcoal. We know that the bones and tools of man have been found sealed from our times by the chemistry of the ages. But when we try to date man by the animals that are dead and gone, or by the earths that lie above him, we begin to guess. The guesses of conservative glacialists give him at least 15,000 years in the New World. Other speculations— supported by plausible evidence as well as plausible theory—place man on this continent before the chill of the last ice settled upon the land.

REFERENCES IN THE TEXT

Chapter 1

1. Alfred L. Kroeber, "Native American Population," *American Anthropologist*, 36:24 (1934). Herbert J. Spinden, "The Population of Ancient America," *Smithsonian Institution Annual Report for 1929* (1930), 470.
2. Nels C. Nelson, "The Antiquity of Man in America in the Light of Archaeology," in *The American Aborigines*, ed. Diamond Jenness (1933), 97.
3. Alfred L. Kroeber, *Anthropology* (1923), 98.
4. Franz Boas, "Relationships Between Northwest America and Northeast Asia," in *The American Aborigines*, 367–368.
5. John P. Harrington, personal communication, 1947, and "Southern Peripheral Athapaskawan Origins, Divisions, and Migrations," *Smithsonian Miscellaneous Collections*, 100:504 (1940).
6. Edgar B. Howard, "An Outline of the Problem of Man's Antiquity in North America," *American Anthropologist*, 38:398 (1936).
7. W. W. Howells, "The Origins of the American Indian Race Types," *The Maya and Their Neighbors* (1940), 5.
8. Albrecht Penck, "Wann kamen die Indianer nach Nordamerika?" *Proceedings, 23rd International Congress of Americanists* (1930), 23–30.
9. Kroeber, *Anthropology*, 336–339.
10. Clark Wissler, "Ethnological Diversity in America and Its Significance," in *The American Aborigines*, 188.

Chapter 2

1. Nels C. Nelson, "The Antiquity of Man in America in the Light of Archaeology," in *The American Aborigines* (1933), 89.

2. Padre Joseph de Acosta, *The Natural and Moral History of the Indies* (transl. Edward Grimston, 1604), ed. Clements R. Markham (1880), 1:45, 57.

3. Edward Brerewood, *Enquiries Touching the Diversity of Languages, and Religions, Through the Chief Parts of the World* (1622—1st ed., 1614), 96, 97.

4. Fray Gregorio Garcia, *Origen de los Indios de el Nuevo Mundo* (1719—1st ed., 1607), 315.

5. Voltaire, *La Philosophe de l'Histoire* (1765), 46.

6. Alexander von Humboldt, *Political Essay on the Kingdom of New Spain* (1822), 153, 155.

7. Reginald A. Daly, *The Changing World of the Ice Age* (1934), 47, 182. Ernst Antevs, *The Last Glaciation* (American Geographical Society Research Series, No. 17, 1928), 81. Richard F. Flint, *Glacial Geology and the Pleistocene Epoch* (1947), 432–433.

8. Aleš Hrdlička, "The Coming of Man from Asia in the Light of Recent Discoveries," *Proceedings, American Philosophical Society*, 71:399 (1932).

9. Richard F. Flint and H. G. Dorsey, "Glaciation in Siberia," *Bulletin, Geological Society of America*, 56:98 (1945).

10. James W. Gidley, "Paleontological Evidence Bearing on the Problem of the Origin of the American Aborigines," *American Anthropologist*, 14:22 (1912).

11. Hrdlička, *op. cit.*, 398.

12. Frank Hibben, "Evidence of Early Man in Alaska," *American Antiquity*, 8:254–259 (1943). Hrdlička, *op. cit.*, 399.

13. Philip S. Smith, "Certain Relations Between Northwestern America and Northeastern Asia," in *Early Man*, ed. G. G. MacCurdy (1937), 87.

14. Hibben, *op. cit.*, 255–257.

15. Frederick Johnson, "An Archaeological Survey Along the Alaska Highway, 1944," *American Antiquity*, 11:183–186 (1946).

16. Douglas Leechman, "Prehistoric Migration Routes Through the Yukon," *Canadian Historical Review*, 27:383–390 (1946).

17. Ernst Antevs, "Climate and Early Man in North America," in *Early Man*, 125–126.

18. M. R. Harrington, *Gypsum Cave, Nevada* (Southwest Museum Papers, No. 8, 1933), 190.

19. Ellsworth Huntington, *The Red Man's Continent: A Chronicle of Aboriginal America* (1919), 31–35.
20. Stansbury Hagar, "The Bearing of Astronomy on the Subject," *American Anthropologist*, 14:43–48 (1912).

Chapter 3

1. W. C. McKern, "An Hypothesis for the Asiatic Origin of the Woodland Culture," *American Antiquity*, 3:138–143 (1937). Georg Neumann, "The Migration and the Origin of the Woodland Culture," *Proceedings, Indiana Academy of Science*, 54:41–43 (1945).
2. Désiré Charnay, *Ancient Cities of the New World* (1887), 174–175. Gordon F. Ekholm, "Wheeled Toys in Mexico," *American Antiquity*, 11:222–228(1946). Robert H. Lister, "Additional Evidence of Wheeled Toys in Mexico," *American Antiquity*, 12:184–185 (1947).
3. Erland Nordenskiöld, *The Copper and Bronze Ages in South America* (Comparative Ethnographical Studies, No. 4, 1921), 156, 157.
4. Earnest A. Hooton, *Apes, Men, and Morons* (1937), 51.
5. T. A. Rickard, "The Nomenclature of Archaeology," *American Journal of Archaeology*, 48:1 (1944).
6. V. Gordon Childe, "Changing Methods and Aims in Prehistory," *Proceedings, Prehistoric Society, 1935*, 7.
7. Rickard, *op. cit.*, 12.
8. George R. Stewart, *Man: An Autobiography* (1946), 29.
9. John Crawfurd, "On the Supposed Stone, Bronze, and Iron Ages of Society," *Anthropological Review*, 2:313 (1864).
10. Waldemar Bogoras, "The Chukchee," *Jessup North Pacific Expedition*, 7:209 (1904).
11. See, respectively, William Coxe, *Account of the Russian Discoveries* (1780), 78; Edward H. Man, *On the Aboriginal Inhabitants of the Andaman Islands* (1883), 161; Leonard Ray, "The Cave Dwellers of Perak," *Journal, Anthropological Institute*, 26:46. (1887); and *Expeditions into the Valley of the Amazon*, transl. Edward Markham (1859), 80–83.
12. Rickard, *op. cit.*, 15–16.

13. John Lubbock, *Prehistoric Times* (1865), 2.
14. Otto von Kotzebue, *A Voyage of Discovery into the South Seas*, (1821), 2:65.
15. Rickard, *op. cit.*, 11.
16. Nels C. Nelson, "The Antiquity of Man in America in the Light of Archaeology," in *The American Aborigines* (1933), 117.
17. V. Gordon Childe, *Man Builds Himself* (1939), 96–97.
18. *Ibid.*, 102, 101.
19. L. S. B. Leakey, *The Stone Age Cultures of Kenya Colony* (1931), 103–104, pl. 11.
20. E. B. Sayles, *An Archaeological Survey of Texas* (Medallion Papers, Gila Pueblo, No. 17, 1935), Table 9. Wm. Duncan Strong, "Finding the Tomb of a Warrior-God," *National Geographic Magazine*, 91:459 (1947).
21. Childe, "Changing Methods and Aims in Prehistory," *Proceedings, Prehistoric Society, 1935*, 8.
22. Seton Lloyd and Fuad Safar, "Tel Hassuna: Excavations by the Iraq Government Directorate General of Antiquities, in 1943 and 1944," *Journal of Near Eastern Studies*, 4:255–289 (1945).

Chapter 4

1. John Playfair, *Illustrations of the Huttonian Theory of the Earth* (1802), 388–389.
2. A. Bernhardi, "Wie kamen die aus dem Norden stammenden Felsbruchstücke und Geschiebe, welche man in Norddeutschland und den benachbarten Ländern findet, an ihre gegenwärtigen Fundorte?" *Jahrbuch für Mineralogie, Geognosie, und Petrefaktenkunde*, 3:257–267 (1832).
3. Albrecht Penck and Eduard Brückner, *Die Alpen im Eiszeitalter* (1901–1909).
4. Ernst Antevs, *Late Glacial Correlations and Ice Recession in Manitoba* (Canada Geological Survey, Memoir 168, 1931), 2, 33.
5. Richard F. Flint, "Chronology of the Pleistocene Epoch," *Quarterly Journal, Florida Academy of Sciences*, 8:3–4 (1945).
6. Ernst Antevs, *The Last Glaciation* (American Geographical Society, Research Series, No. 17, 1928), 74–82. R. A. Daly, *The*

Changing World of the Ice Age (1934), 46. Richard F. Flint, *Glacial Geology and the Pleistocene Epoch* (1947), 334–335.

7. Eduard Brückner, "Postglaziale Klimaänderungen und Klimaschwankungen im Bereich der Alpen," *Die Veränderungen des Klimas seit dem Maximum der letzten Eiszeit* (Stockholm, 1910), 108.

8. Milutin Milankovitch, "O Rasporedu suneeve Radijacije na Povrsini Zembljie" (On the Distribution of Solar Radiation on the Surface of the Earth), *Glas Srpske K. Akad.*, 91:101–179 (1913), and "Neue Ergebnisse der astronomischen Theorie der Klimaschwankungen," *Bulletin, Royal Serbian Academy of Science,* 1938, p. 4.

9. Frederick E. Zeuner, *The Pleistocene Period* (1945), 167.

10. Kirtley F. Mather, *Sons of the Earth* (1930), 106.

11. Zeuner, *op. cit.,* 161.

12. George C. Simpson, "World Climate During the Quaternary Period," *Quarterly Journal, Royal Meteorological Society,*60:425-478 (1934), and "Ice Ages," *Nature,* 141:591–598 (1938)—reprinted in *Annual Report, Smithsonian Institution, 1938,* 289–302.

13. Zeuner, *op. cit.,* 163.

14. *Ibid,* 164–165.

15. A. Vayson de Pradenne, *Prehistory* (1940), 84–85.

Chapter 5

1. V. Gordon Childe, *Progress and Archaeology.* 1944, 5.

2. John Frere, "Account of Flint Weapons Discovered at Hoxne in Suffolk," *Archaeologia,* 13:204–205 (1807).

3. William Buckland, *Reliquiae Diluvianae* (1823), 82–98.

4. Harold Peake, and H. J. Fleure, *Apes and Men (The Corridors of Time,* Vol. 1, 1927), 84.

5. Gabriel de Mortillet, "Essai d'une classification des cavernes et des stations sous abri, fondée sur les produits de l'industrie humaine," *Comptes Rendus, Académie des Sciences,* 68:553–555 (1869).

6. Edith Plant, *Man's Unwritten Past* (1942), 29.

7. W. B. Wright, *Tools and the Man* (1939), 38.

8. Franz Weidenreich, *Apes, Giants, and Man* (1946), 61. "Giant Ape-Man Fossils," *Science News Letter,* Dec. 11, 1948. Robert Broom, "Another New Type of Ape-Man," *Nature,* 163:57 (1949).

9. Henry F. Osborn, *Men of the Old Stone Age* (1915), 351. Nels C. Nelson, "Succession of Prehistoric Ages in Egypt and in Europe" (chart), in Henry F. Osborn, *The Age of Man* (1944), 44. Kirtley F. Mather, *Sons of the Earth* (1930), 160.

10. Frederick E. Zeuner, *Dating the Past* (1946), 290.

11. Robert Braidwood, personal communication, 1946. Mather, *op. cit.,* 160–161. Peake and Fleure, *Hunters and Artists* (*The Corridors of Time,* Vol. 2, 1927), 91.

12. Zeuner, "The Pleistocene Chronology of Central Europe," *Geological Magazine,* 1935, opp. 357.

13. Mather, *op. cit.,* 161. Zeuner, *Dating the Past,* 200.

14. V. Gordon Childe, *Progress and Archaeology* (1944), 5.

15. *Ibid.,* 6.

Chapter 6

1. "An Extract of Several Letters from Cotton Mather," etc., *Philosophical Transactions* (1714), 62.

2. Peter Kalm, *Travels into North America* (2nd ed. 1772), 1:277–280. Nels C. Nelson, "The Antiquity of Man in America in the Light of Archaeology," in *The American Aborigines* (1933), 90.

3. M. F. Ashley Montagu, and C. Bernard Peterson, "The Earliest Account of the Association of Human Artifacts with Fossil Mammals in North America," *Proceedings, American Philosophical Society,* 87:419 (1944).

4. P. W. Lund, *Blik paa Brasiliens Dyreverden, etc.* (1842), 195–196.

5. M. W. Dickeson, "Fossils from Natchez, Mississippi," *Proceedings, Academy of Natural Sciences of Philadelphia,* 3:106–107 (1846). Charles Lyell, *A Second Visit to the United States* (1st Amer. ed., 1849), 151–152, and *The Geological Evidences of the Antiquity of Man* (2nd Amer. ed., 1863), 202–203.

6. Aleš Hrdlička, "Skeletal Remains Suggesting or Attributed to Early Man in North America," *Bulletin, Bureau of American Ethnology,* no. 33 (1907), 23.

7. Charles C. Abbott, "The Stone Age in New Jersey," *American Naturalist*, 1872, 6:144–160, 199–229 (1872), and "Evidences of the Antiquity of Man in Eastern North America," *Proceedings, American Association for the Advancement of Science,* 37:293–315 (1889), Ernest Volk, *The Archaeology of the Delaware Valley (Papers, Peabody Museum,* no. 5, 1911).

8. Frank H. H. Roberts, Jr., "Developments in the Problem of the North American Paleo-Indian," *Smithsonian Miscellaneous Collections,* 100:52 (1940).

9. Aleš Hrdlička and others, *Early Man in South America (Bulletin, Bureau of American Ethnology,* no. 52, 1912), numerous references in index.

10. Hrdlička, "The Problem of Man's Antiquity in America," *Proceedings, 8th American Scientific Congress,* 2:53 (1942).

11. Earnest A. Hooton, *Apes, Men, and Morons* (1937), 111.

12. *Ibid.*, 112.

13. Roberts, *op. cit.*, 98.

14. Aleš Hrdlička, "Early Man in America: What Have the Bones to Say?" in *Early Man,* ed. G. G. MacCurdy (1937), 93–94.

15. Hrdlička, "The Origin and Antiquity of the American Indian," *Smithsonian Institution Annual Report for 1923,* 491.

16. Hrdlička, "The Problem of Man's Antiquity in America," *Proceedings, 8th American Scientific Congress,* 2:53 (1942).

17. Hrdlička, "Early Man in America," 101.

18. Hrdlička, "The Coming of Man from Asia in the Light of Recent Discoveries," *Proceedings, American Philosophical Society,* 71:401 (1932).

19. Arthur Keith, *The Antiquity of Man* (1920), 286.

20. H. V. Walter, A. Cathoud, and Anibal Mattos, "The Confins Man: A Contribution to the Study of Early Man in South America," in *Early Man,* 345, 348.

21. Louis R. Sullivan, and Milo Hellman, "The Punin Calvarium," *Anthropological Papers, American Museum of Natural History,* 23:308–338 (1925). Paul Rivet, "La Race de la Lagoa Santa chez les populations précolombiennes de l'équateur," *Bulletins et Mémoires, Société d'Anthropologie de Paris,* 5th ser. 9:209–271 (1908).

22. Junius Bird, "Antiquity and Migrations of the Early Inhabitants of Patagonia," *Geographical Review,* 28:250–275 (1938).

23. Albert E. Jenks, *Pleistocene Man in Minnesota* (1936).

24. Ernst Antevs, "The Age of 'Minnesota Man,'" *Year Book, Carnegie Institution*, 36:335–338 (1937), and "Was 'Minnesota Girl' Buried in a Gully?" *Journal of Geology*, 46:293–295 (1938). Kirk Bryan and Paul MacClintock, "What Is Implied by 'Disturbance' at the Site of Minnesota Man?" *Journal of Geology*, 46:279–292. G. F. Kay and M. M. Leighton, "Geological Notes on the Occurrence of 'Minnesota Man,'" *Journal of Geology*, 46:268–278.

25. Earnest A. Hooton, *Apes, Men, and Morons* (1937), 104.

26. Albert E. Jenks and Lloyd A. Wilford, "Sauk Valley Skeleton," *Bulletin, Texas Archaeological and Paleontological Society*, 10:162–163 (1938).

27. Hrdlička, "Early Man in America: What Have the Bones to Say?" 97–98.

28. T. D. Stewart, "A Reexamination of the Fossil Human Skeletal Remains from Melbourne, Florida," *Smithsonian Miscellaneous Collections*, no. 10, 1946, 106:1–28 (1946).

29. George and Edna Woodbury, *Prehistoric Skeletal Remains from the Texas Coast* (Medallion Papers, Gila Pueblo, no. 18, 1935) 43. C. F. ten Kate, "Matériaux pour Servir à l'anthropologie de la presqu'île Californienne," *Bulletin, Société de l'Anthropologie de Paris*, 7:551–769 (1884). Paul Rivet, "Recherches anthropologiques sur la Basse-Californie," *Journal, Societé des Américanistes de Paris*, vol. 6 (1909), nos. 1, 2.

30. R. Earle Storie, and Frank Harradine, An Age Estimate of the Burials Unearthed near Concord, California, Based on Pedologic Observations (unpublished MS.).

31. Robert F. Heizer, personal communication, 1946.

32. Robert F. Heizer and Franklin Fenenga, "Archaeological Horizons in Central California," *American Antiquity*, 41:393 (1939).

33. S. F. Cook and Robert F. Heizer, "The Quantitative Investigation of Aboriginal Sites: Analyses of Human Bone," *American Journal of Physical Anthropology*, new ser., 5:218 (1947).

34. Robert F. Heizer, personal communication. Bailey Willis, "Out of the Long Past," *Stanford Cardinal*, 32:8–11 (1922).

35. Díaz del Castillo, Bernal, *The True History of the Conquest of New Spain* (1908), 1:286.

36. Hellmut de Terra, Javier Romero, and T. D. Stewart, *Tepexpan Man* (Viking Fund Publications in Anthropology, no. 11, 1949), 33–62.
37. Glenn A. Black, " 'Tepexpan Man': A Critique of Method," *American Antiquity*, 14:344–346 (1949).
38. Franz Weidenreich, "Preliminary Report on the Anatomical Character of the Human Skeleton from Tepexpan," in de Terra, *Tepexpan Man*, 123.
39. Javier Romero, "The Physical Aspects of Tepexpan Man," in de Terra, *Tepexpan Man*, 105, T. D. Stewart, "Initial Impressions Regarding the Tepexpan Skeleton," in de Terra, *Tepexpan Man*, 125.

Chapter 7

1. Quoted in John Evans, *The Ancient Stone Implements, Weapons, and Ornaments, of Great Britain* (1872), 57.
2. Michele Mercati, *Metallotheca Opus Posthumum* (1717), 243.
3. C. C. Abbott, "An Historical Sketch of the Discoveries of Paleolithic Implements in the Valley of the Delaware River," *Proceedings, Boston Society of Natural History*, 21:126–127 (1881).
4. I. C. Russell, *The Geological History of Lake Lahontan* (Monograph, U.S. Geological Survey, no. 11. 1885). W J McGee, "An Obsidian Implement from Pleistocene Deposit in Nevada," *American Anthropolgist*, 2:301–312 (1889).
5. S. W. Williston, *"Homo sapiens* in Pleistocene of Kansas," *Bulletin, Kansas University Geological Survey*, 2:301 (1897). E. H. Sellards, "Early Man in America," *Bulletin, Geological Society of America*, 51:387 (1940).
6. J. D. Figgins, "The Antiquity of Man in America," *Natural History*, 27:229-231 (1927). Harold J. Cook, "Definite Evidence of Human Artifacts in the American Pleistocene," *Science*, new ser., 62:459–460 (1925).
7. Figgins, *op. cit.*, 234–239. Harold J. Cook, "New Geological and Paleontological Evidence Bearing on the Antiquity of Mankind in America," *Natural History*, 27:244–247 (1927). O. F. Evans, "The Antiquity of Man As Shown at Frederick, Oklahoma: A Criticism," *Journal, Washington Academy of Sciences*,

234 EARLY MAN IN THE NEW WORLD

20:475–479 (1930). Harold J. Cook, "The Antiquity of Man As Indicated at Frederick, Oklahoma: A Reply." *Journal, Washington Academy of Sciences*, 21:161–167 (1931).

8. Figgins, *op. cit.*, 232–234.

9. Barnum Brown, "Recent Finds Relating to Prehistoric Man in America," *Bulletin, New York Academy of Medicine*, 2nd ser., 4:824–828 (1928). H. Marie Wormington, *Ancient Man in North America* (2nd rev. ed., 1944), 6–7.

10. Edgar B. Howard, "Evidence of Early Man in North America," *Museum Journal*, 24:119–120 (1935). F. de L., "Notes and News," *American Antiquity*, 13:268 (1948).

11. Richard S. MacNeish, "The Pre-Pottery Faulkner Site of Southern Illinois," *American Antiquity*, 13:236–237 (1948).

12. John L. Cotter, "The Occurrence of Flints and Extinct Animals in Pluvial Deposits near Clovis, New Mexico: Part 4 of Report on the Excavations at the Gravel Pit in 1936," *Proceedings, Academy of Natural Sciences of Philadelphia*, 89:2–16 (1937).

13. M. R. Harrington, *An Ancient Site at Borax Lake, California* (Southwest Museum Papers, no. 16, 1948), 61, 63.

14. Edgar B. Howard, "Caves Along the Slopes of the Guadalupe Mountains," *Bulletin, Texas Archaeological and Paleontological Society*, 4:17–18 (1932).

15. Frank H. H. Roberts, Jr., "A Folsom Complex, etc.," *Smithsonian Miscellaneous Collections*, vol. 94, no. 4, p. 6 (1935).

16. Edgar B. Howard, "Early Man in America," *Proceedings, American Philosophical Society*, 76:327–333 (1936). Edgar B. Howard and Ernst Antevs, "The Occurrence of Flints and Extinct Animals in Pluvial Deposits near Clovis, New Mexico," *Proceedings, Academy of Natural Sciences*, 87:299–312 (1935). Kirk Bryan, "A Review of the Geology of the Clovis Finds Reported by Howard and Cotter," *American Antiquity*, 4:113–130 (1938).

17. Roberts, *loc. cit.*

18. Kirk Bryan, "Geology of the Folsom Deposits in New Mexico and Colorado," in *Early Man* (1937), 143–152. Kirk Bryan and Louis L. Ray, "Geological Antiquity of the Lindenmeier Site in Colorado," *Smithsonian Miscellaneous Collections*, vol. 99, no. 2 (1940).

19. Kirk Bryan, "The Geological Antiquity of Man in America," *Science*, new ser., 93:511 (1941). Ernst Antevs, "The Occurrence of Flints and Extinct Animals in Pluvial Deposits near Clovis, New Mexico: Part 2, Age of the Clovis Lake Clays," *Proceedings, Academy of Natural Sciences*, 87:311 (1935), and "Dating Records of Early Man in the Southwest," *American Naturalist*, 70:336 (1936).
20. Edgar B. Howard, "Evidence of Early Man in North America," *Museum Journal*, 24:90 (1935).
21. Edgar B. Howard, "Folsom and Yuma Problems," *Proceedings, American Philosophical Society*, 86:258 (1943).
22. John Paul Moss, *The Antiquity of the Finley Yuma Site: Example of the Geologic Method of Dating* (MS. of paper read at the 29th International Congress of Americanists, New York, Sept. 5, 1949). Edgar B. Howard, "Folsom and Yuma Points from Saskatchewan," *American Antiquity*, 4:277–279 (1939). Frank H. H. Roberts, Jr., "On the Trail of Ancient Hunters in the Western United States and Canada," *Smithsonian Institution, Exploration and Field Work in 1938*, 103–110. Frank Hibben, "Evidence of Early Man in Alaska," *American Antiquity*, 8:257 (1943).
23. E. H. Sellards, "Fossil Bison and Associated Artifacts from Texas," *Bulletin, Geological Society of America*, 56:1196–1197 (1945). E. H. Sellards, Glen L. Evans and Grayson E. Meade, "Fossil Bison and Associated Artifacts from Texas." *Bulletin, Geological Society of America*, 58:927–938 (1947).
24. Froelich G. Rainey, "Archaeology in Central Alaska," *Anthropological Papers, American Museum of Natural History*, 36:390–401 (1939). Frank Hibben, *op. cit.*, 255–258.
25. Alex Krieger, "Artifacts from the Plainview Bison Bed," *Bulletin, Geological Society of America*, 58:940–941, 951 (1947).
26. *Ibid.*, 947, 949.
27. Nels C. Nelson, "Early Migration of Man to America," *Natural History*, 35:356 (1935).
28. M. R. Harrington, *Gypsum Cave, Nevada* (Southwest Museum Papers, no. 8, 1933).
29. Ernst Antevs, "Climate and Early Man in North America," in *Early Man*, 128, and personal communication to H. M. Wormington, 1949. E. W. C. and W. H. Campbell and others,

The Archaeology of Pleistocene Lake Mohave (Southwest Museum Papers, no. 11, 1937), 9–44. E. W. C. and W. H. Campbell, *The Pinto Basin Site* (Southwest Museum Papers, no. 9, 1935), 1–51.

30. Malcolm J. Rogers, *Early Lithic Industries of the Lower Basin of the Colorado River and Adjacent Desert Areas* (San Diego Museum Papers, no. 3, 1939), 70, pl. 21, 74.

31. Robert F. Heizer and E. Lemert, *Observations on an Archaeological Site in Topanga Canyon, Los Angeles County* (University of California Publications in American Archaeology and Ethnology, vol. 44, 237–258 (1947), Heizer, "Notes and News: Pacific Coast Area," *American Antiquity,* 13:270 (1948).

32. Wesley L. Bliss, "An Archaeological and Geological Reconnaissance of Alberta, Mackenzie Valley, and Upper Yukon," *American Philosophical Society Yearbook, 1938,* 136–139.

33. M. M. Leighton, *Geological Aspects of the Finding of Primitive Man near Abilene, Texas* (Medallion Papers, Gila Pueblo, no. 24, 1936), 40–41.

34. *Ibid.,* 34.

35. Harold S. Gladwin, *Excavations at Snaketown* (Medallion Papers, Gila Pueblo, no. 26, 1937), plate 1, pp. 30–31.

36. Cyrus N. Ray, "Report on Some Recent Archaeological Researches in the Abilene Section," *Bulletin, Texas Archaeological and Paleontological Society,* 2:45–58 (1930). Kirk Bryan and Cyrus N. Ray, "Long Channelled Point Found in Alluvium Beside Bones of *Elephas columbi,*" *Bulletin, Tex. Arch. and Pal. Soc.,* 10:267 (1938). Ray, "New Evidences of Ancient Man in Texas Found During Prof. Kirk Bryan's Visit," *Bulletin, Tex. Arch. and Pal. Soc.,* 10:273. Bryan, "Deep Sites near Abilene, Texas," *Bulletin, Tex. Arch. and Pal. Soc.,* 10:274.

37. C. C. Albritton and Kirk Bryan, "The Quaternary Stratigraphy in the Davis Mountains, etc.," *Bulletin, Geological Society of America,* 50:1468 (1939).

38. M. M. Leighton, "The Significance of Profiles of Weathering in Stratigraphic Archaeology," in *Early Man,* 163–172.

39. Kirk Bryan, "Correlation of the Deposits of Sandia Cave, New Mexico, with the Glacial Chronology," *Smithsonian Miscellaneous Collections,* 99:45–64 (1941).

40. Frank Hibben, "Association of Man with Pleistocene Mammals

in the Sandia Mountains, New Mexico," *American Antiquity*, 2:260–263 (1937), and "Evidences of Early Occupation in Sandia Cave, etc.," *Smithsonian Miscellaneous Collections*, 99:- 1–44 (1941).

41. Frank Hibben, "The First Thirty-eight Sandia Points," *American Antiquity*, 11:257–258 (1946).
42. C. Bertrand Schultz and W. D. Frankfurter, "Notes and News," *American Antiquity*, 13:279–280 (1948). "How Old is the Oldest American?" *Science Illustrated*, 3:42–45 (1948). C. Bertrand Schultz, Gilbert C. Lueninghoener, and W. D. Frankfurter, "Preliminary Geomorphological Studies of the Lime Creek Area" and "Preliminary Report on the Lime Creek Sites, etc.," *Bulletin, University of Nebraska State Museum*, 3:31-42, 43–62, (1948). H. M. Wormington, personal communication, 1949.
43. Harold S. Gladwin, *Excavations at Snaketown* (Medallion Papers, Gila Pueblo, no. 26, 1937), 34.
44. E. B. Sayles and Ernst Antevs, *The Cochise Culture* (Medallion Papers, Gila Pueblo, no. 29, 1941).
45. William Duncan Strong, "An Introduction to Nebraska Archaeology," *Smithsonian Miscellaneous Collections*, vol. 93, no. 10 (1935). E. W. C. and W. H. Campbell, *The Pinto Basin Site* (Southwest Museum Papers, no. 9, 1935), 33–34.
46. Carl Sauer, personal communication, 1946.
47. M. R. Harrington, "The Age of Borax Lake" and "Farewell to Borax Lake," *Masterkey*, 8:208–209 (1939) and 19:181–184 (1945), and *An Ancient Site at Borax Lake, California* (Southwest Museum Papers, no. 16, 1948).
48. M. R. Harrington, personal communication, 1948.
49. E. H. Sellards, "Stone Images from Henderson County, Texas," *American Antiquity*, 7:20–38 (1941).
50. Mariano Barcena, "Descripción de un hueso labrado, de llama fosil," *Anales del Museo Nacional de México*, 2:439–444 (1882).
51. Hellmut de Terra, Javier Romero, and T. D. Stewart, *Tepexpan Man* (Publications in Anthropology, Viking Fund, no. 11, 1949), 84–86.
52. Etienne B. Renaud, *The Black's Fork Culture of Southwest Wyoming* and *Further Research Work in the Black's Fork Basin*,

Southwest Wyoming (University of Denver, Dept. of Anthropology, Archaeological Survey Series, Reports 10 and 12, 1938, 1940).

53. Thomas Wilson, "The Paleolithic Period in the District of Columbia," *Proceedings, U.S. National Museum, for 1889*, 12:371–376, and "A Study of Prehistoric Anthropology" and "Results of an Inquiry As to the Existence of Man in North America During the Paleolithic Period of the Stone Age," *Report, U.S. National Museum, for 1887–1888*, 629–636, 677–702. Nels C. Nelson, "The Antiquity of Man in America in the Light of Archaeology," in *The American Aborigines* (1933), 93–94.

54. Frank H. H. Roberts, Jr., "Developments in the Problem of the North American Paleo-Indian," *Smithsonian Miscellaneous Collections*, 100:96–97 (1940).

55. Kirk Bryan, "Prehistoric Quarries and Implements of Pre-Amerindian Aspect in New Mexico," *Science*, new ser., 87:345 (1938).

56. E. B. Sayles, *An Archaeological Survey of Texas* (Medallion Papers, Gila Pueblo, no. 17. 1935), table 4, plate 19. J. E. Pearce, "Tales That Dead Men Tell," *University of Texas Bulletin*, no. 3537 (1935), 25, plate 3.

57. Junius Bird, "Antiquity and Migrations of the Early Inhabitants of Patagonia," *Geographical Review*, 28:273 (1938), fig. 27. Walter Dupouy, "Sobre una punta litica de tipo singular en Venezuela," *Acta Venezolana*, 1:80–87 (1945).

58. Helmut de Terra, "New Evidence for the Antiquity of Early Man in Mexico," *Revista mexicana de estudios antropológicos*, 8:69–88 (1946).

59. F. B. Richardson, "Nicaragua," *Year Book, Carnegie Institution, 1941* (no. 40), 300–302. F. B. Richardson and Karl Ruppert, "Nicaragua," *Year Book, Carnegie Institution, 1942* (no. 41), 269–270.

60. G. F. Becker, "Antiquities from Under Tuolumne Table Mountain in California," *Bulletin, Geological Society of America*, 2:193–194 (1891).

61. W. H. Holmes, *Handbook of Aboriginal American Antiquities* (*Bulletin, Bureau of American Ethnology*, No. 60, 1919, part 1), 62.

62. H. M. Wormington, personal communication, 1949.

Chapter 8

1. Thomas Jefferson *Notes on the State of Virginia* (1801), 77.
2. Mark Catesby, *The Natural History of Carolina, Florida, and the Bahamas Islands* (1743), vol. 2, appendix vii.
3. Loren C. Eiseley, "Myth and Mammoth in Archaeology." *American Antiquity,* 11:86 (1945).
4. Wm. Duncan Strong, "North American Indian Traditions Suggesting a Knowledge of the Mammoth," *American Anthropologist* new ser. 36:81–88 (1934).
5. Eiseley, *op. cit.,* 87.
6. Thomas Ashe, *Memoirs of Mammoth and Various Other Extraordinary and Stupendous Bones of Incognita, or Non-Descript Animals Found in the Vicinity of the Ohio, Wabash, Illinois, Mississippi, Missouri, Osage, and Red Rivers, &c., &c.* (1806), 41.
7. Jefferson, *loc. cit.*
8. John Ranking, *Historical Researches on the Conquest of Peru, Mexico, Bogota, Natchez, and Talomeco, in the Thirteenth Century, by the Mongols, Accompanied with Elephants* (1823), 1–479. Johann R. Forster, *Observations Made During a Voyage Around the World,* etc. (1778), 316.
9. Frederick Larkin, *Ancient Man in America* (1880), 3, 141.
10. Max Uhle, "Späte Mastodonten in Ecuador," *Proceedings, 23rd International Congress of Americanists* (1930), 247–258.
11. Loren C. Eiseley, "The Mastodon and Early Man in America," *Science,* 102:108–109 (1945).
12. William B. Scott, *A History of Land Mammals in the Western Hemisphere* (2nd ed., 1937), 260.
13. Loren C. Eiseley, "Men, Mastodons, and Myths." *Scientific Monthly,* 62:517–524 (1946).
14. Charles Lyell, *Travels in North America,* 1:54 (1845).
15. Eiseley, "The Mastodon, etc.," 109–110.
16. Edgar B. Howard, "The Emergence of a General Folsom Pattern," *25th Anniversary Studies, Philadelphia Anthropological Society* (1937), 1:114.
17. Hans E. Fischel, "Folsom and Yuma Culture Finds," *American Antiquity,* 4:241 (1939).

18. Eiseley, "Did the Folsom Bison Survive in Canada?" *Scientific Monthly*, 56:468–472 (1943).

19. S. N. Rhoads, "Notes on Living and Extinct Species of North American Bovidae," *Proceedings, Academy of Natural Sciences of Philadelphia,* 49:497 (1897). C. Gordon Hewitt, *The Conservation of the Wild-Life of Canada* (1921), 124.

20. Ernest Thompson Seton, *Lives of Game Animals* (1827), vol. 3, pt. 2, p. 707.

21. Eiseley, *op. cit.,* 471.

22. K. P. Schmidt, "Herpetological Evidence for a Post-Glacial Eastward Extension of the Steppe in North America," *Ecology,* 19:398–399 (1938).

23. Ernst Antevs, personal communication, 1946.

24. H. H. Howorth, *The Mammoth and the Flood* (1887), xviii.

25. Eiseley, "The Fire-Drive and the Extinction of the Terminal Pleistocene Fauna," *American Anthropologist,* new ser. 48:54–55 (1946).

26. Carl Sauer, "A Geographic Sketch of Early Man in America," *Geographical Review,* 34:543–554 (1944).

27. Sauer, personal communication, 1946.

28. Eiseley, *op. cit.,* 56–58.

29. Eiseley, "Archaeological Observations on the Problem of Post-Glacial Extinction," *American Antiquity,* 8:214 (1943).

30. Alfred S. Romer, "Pleistocene Vertebrates and Their Bearing on the Problem of Human Antiquity in North America," in *The American Aborigines,* ed. D. Jenness (1933), 76–77.

31. *Ibid.,* 77. Edwin H. Colbert, "The Association of Man with Extinct Mammals in the Western Hemisphere," *Proceedings, 8th American Scientific Congress* (1942), 2:27.

32. Frank Hibben, "Evidence of Early Man in Alaska," *American Antiquity,* 8:255–257 (1943). Froelich G. Rainey, "Archaeological Investigations in Central Alaska," *American Antiquity,* 5:299–308 (1940).

Chapter 9

1. Nels C. Nelson, "The Antiquity of Man in America in the Light of Archaeology," in *The American Aborigines* (1933), 97.

2. Earnest A. Hooton, "Racial Types in America and Their Relations to Old World Types," in *The American Aborigines* (1933), 152–153.
3. Alfred S. Romer, *Man and the Vertebrates* (3rd ed., rev., 1941), 269. Griffith Taylor, *Environment, Race, and Migration*, 98 (1937).
4. Hooton, *The Indians of Pecos Pueblo* (Papers, Phillips Academy Southwestern Expedition, No. 4, 1930), 355–356.
5. Roland B. Dixon, *The Racial History of Man* (1923), 375–376.
6. Taylor, *op. cit.*, 259.
7. Arthur Keith, *New Discoveries Relating to the Antiquity of Man* (1931), 312.
8. Hooton, *op. cit.*, 361–362.
9. Hooton, Introduction to Harold Gladwin, *Men Out of Asia* (1947), xi.
10. Dixon, *op. cit.*, 476, 401–403, 475.
11. *Ibid.*, 402, 507–507, 513.
12. R. Ruggles Gates, *Human Ancestry from a Genetical Point of View* (1948), 284, 290, 312.
13. Hooton, "Racial Types in America, etc.," 158.
14. W. W. Howells, "The Origins of the American Indian Race Types," in *The Maya and Their Neighbors* (1940), 8.
15. Hooton, *op. cit.*, 152, and *Up from the Ape* (1931), 569.
16. W. J. Sollas, *Ancient Hunters and Their Modern Representatives* (1911), 583–594.
17. M. R. Harrington, *Gypsum Cave, Nevada* (Southwest Museum Papers, no. 8. 1933), 190.
18. Taylor, *op. cit.*, 247.
19. Hooton, "Skeletons from the Cenote of Sacrifice at Chichén Itzá," in *The Maya and Their Neighbors* (1940), 277, 280.
20. Carl Sauer, "Early Relations of Man to Plants," *Geographical Review*, 87:10 (1947).
21. Earl W. Count, "Primitive Amerinds and the Australo-Melanesians," *Revista del Instituto de Antropologia de la Universidad Nacional de Tucumán*, 1:123, 133 (1939).
22. A. A. Mendes Correâ, *Homo* (1926), 229, and "Nouvelle hypothese sur le peuplement primitif de l'Amérique du Sud," *22nd International Congress of Americanists*, 1:116 (1926).
23. Paul Rivet, "Recherche d'une voie de migration des Australiens

vers l'Amérique," *Séances publiques, Société Biogéographique* (1926), 3:11-16.

24. Rivet, *Titres et travaux scientifiques de P. Rivet* (1927), 34.
25. Rivet, "Les Australiens en Amérique," *Bulletin de la Société de Linguistique,* 26:1–43 (1925).
26. Roland B. Dixon, *The Building of Cultures* (1928), 239.
27. José Imbelloni, "The Peopling of America," *Acta Americana,* 1:320–324 (1943).
28. Harold S. Gladwin, *Men Out of Asia* (1947), 62.
29. Carl Sauer, personal communication. 1946.
30. Gladwin, *op. cit.,* 56–59.
31. *Ibid.,* 95–103.
32. *Ibid.,* 137–146.
33. *Ibid.,* 147–156, 165–183.
34. *Ibid.,* 221–243.

Chapter 10

1. Erland Nordenskiöld, "Origin of the Indian Civilizations in South America," in *The American Aborigines* (1933), 262–263. Harold S. Gladwin, *Excavations at Snaketown: Part 2, Comparisons and Theories* (Medallion Papers, Gila Pueblo, no. 26, 1937), 137–148. Kenneth P. Emory, "Oceanic Influence on American Indian Culture: Nordenskiöld's View," *Journal, Polynesian Society,* 51:126–135 (1942).
2. Robert H. Lowie, *The History of Ethnological Theory* (1937), 77–78.
3. Herbert J. Spinden, "Origin of Civilizations in Central America and Mexico," in *The American Aborigines* (1933), 225.
4. Spinden, "The Prosaic vs. the Romantic School in Anthropology," in *Culture, the Diffusion Controversy* (1927), 53.
5. Nordenskiöld, *An Ethno-Geographical Analysis of the Material Culture of Two Indian Tribes in the Gran Chaco* and *Modifications in Indian Customs Through Inventions and Loans* (Comparative Ethnographical Studies, nos. 1 and 8, 1919, 1930) and "The American Indian as an Inventor," in *Source Book in Anthropology,* ed. Kroeber and Waterman (rev. ed., 1931), 488–505, and "Origin of the Indian Civilizations in South America," in *The American Aborigines* (1933), 249–311.

6. Nordenskiöld, "Origin, etc.," 287.
7. Aleš Hrdlička, "The Derivation and Probable Place of Origin of the North American Indian," *Proceedings, 18th International Congress of Americanists* (1913), 62.
8. Earnest A. Hooton, Introduction to Harold S. Gladwin, *Men Out of Asia* (1947), xi.
9. Gladwin, *Excavations at Snaketown*, 2:131, 152, 136.
10. Roland B. Dixon, *The Building of Cultures* (1928), 206–207.
11. Curt Sachs, *The History of Musical Instruments* (1940), 178.
12. Alfred Kroeber, *Anthropology* (1923), 386.
13. Alfred V. Kidder, Foreword to Gladwin, *op. cit.,* 2:vii.
14. Nordenskiöld, "Origin, etc.," 256, 249.
15. Gonzalo Aguirre Beltrán, *La Población negra de México* (1947).
16. Gladwin, *Men Out of Asia* (1947), xiv–xv.
17. Peter H. Buck, *Vikings of the Sunrise* (1938), 314.
18. Gilbert N. Lewis, "The Beginning of Civilization in America," *American Anthropologist,* new ser., 49:1–24 (1947).
19. Thor Heyerdahl, "The Voyage of the Raft *Kon-Tiki,*" *Natural History,* 57:264–271, 286–287 (June, 1948).

Chapter 11

1. Erland Nordenskiöld, *Modifications in Indian Customs Through Inventions and Loans* (Comparative Ethnographical Studies, no. 8, 1930), 23–24.
2. Nordenskiöld, "Origin of the Indian Civilizations in South America," in *The American Aborigines* (1933), 278.
3. *Ibid,* 285.
4. Robert H. Lowie, *The History of Ethnological Theory* (1937), 165.
5. Herbert J. Spinden, "The Origin and Distribution of Agriculture in America," in *Source Book in Anthropology* (1931), 228.
6. Carl Sauer, "American Agricultural Origins," in *Essays in Anthropology,* ed. R. H. Lowie (1936), 281.
7. N. I. Vavilov, "Studies on the Origin of Cultivated Plants," *Bulletin of Applied Botany,* vol. 16, no. 2, pp. 218–219 (1926). S. M. Bukasov and others, "The Cultivated Plants of Mexico, Guatemala, and Colombia," 47th Supplement to the *Bulletin of*

Applied Botany, 1930. Other papers listed in Henry J. Bruman, "The Russian Investigations on Plant Genetics in Latin America and Their Bearing on Culture History," *Handbook of Latin American Studies* (1937), 287.

8. Bruman, *op. cit.*, 451.
9. Sauer, *op. cit.*, 288.
10. Bruman, *op. cit.*, 456.
11. Harold S. Gladwin, *Excavations at Snaketown* (Medallion Papers, Gila Pueblo, no. 26, 1937), 2:79.
12. Bruman, *op. cit.*, 456–457.
13. P. C. Mangelsdorf and R. G. Reeves, *The Origin of Indian Corn and Its Relatives* (Bulletin No. 574, Texas Agricultural Experiment Station, 1939), 7.
14. *Ibid.*, 7.
15. *Ibid.*, 8, 7.
16. Sauer, *op. cit.*, 292.
17. G. N. Collins, "The Phylogeny of Maize," *Bulletin, Torrey Botanical Club*, 57:203 (1930).
18. Bruman, *op. cit.*, 457.
19. Sylvanus G. Morley, *The Ancient Maya* (1946), 386.
20. W. S. Stallings, Jr., "A Basketmaker Cave Date from Cave Du Pont, Utah." *Tree-Ring Bulletin*. 1941, 8:3.
21. Paul C. Mangelsdorf and C. Earle Smith, Jr., "A Discovery of Primitive Maize in New Mexico," *Journal of Heredity*, 40:39–43 (1949), and "New Archaeological Evidence on Evolution in Maize," *Harvard University Botanical Museum Leaflets*, Vol. 13, No. 8, 213–247 (Mar., 1949).
22. Wm. Duncan Strong, "Finding the Tomb of a Warrior-God," *National Geographic Magazine*, 91:464, 459 (1947). Junius B. Bird, "Preceramic Cultures in Chicama and Virú," in *A Reappraisal of Peruvian Archaeology* (Memoirs, Society for American Archaeology, vol. 13, no. 4, pt. 2, 1948), 28.
23. Carl Sauer, personal communication, 1946.
24. Oakes Ames, *Economic Annuals and Human Cultures* (Botanical Museum of Harvard University, 1939), 92–93.
25. Edgar Anderson, "What Is Zea Mays?" *Chronica Botanica*, 9:89–90 (1945).

26. C. R. Stonor and Edgar Anderson, "Maize Among the Hill Peoples of Assam," *Annals of the Missouri Botanical Garden*, 36:355–404 (1949).

Chapter 12

1. Clark Wissler, "The Origin of the American Indian," *Natural History*, 53:313 (1944).
2. Frank H. H. Roberts, Jr., "The New-World Paleo-Indian," *Smithsonian Institution Annual Report for 1944*, 406.
3. Earnest A. Hooton, *Up from the Ape*. 1931, 568.
4. Junius Bird, personal communications, 1945–1947.
5. A. P. Okladnikov, "Archaeological Data on the Ancient History of the Lake Baikal Region," *Review of Ancient History*, vol. 1, pt. 2, fig. 5 (Moscow, 1938). Henry B. Collins, Jr., "Eskimo Archaeology and Its Bearing on the Problem of Man's Antiquity in America," *Proceedings, American Philosophical Society*, 86:-229–230 (1943), fig. 5.
6. George Gaylord Simpson, "Mammals and Land Bridges," *Journal, Washington Academy of Sciences*, 40:153. (1940).
7. Bruce Howe and Hallam L. Movius, Jr., *A Stone Age Cave Site in Tangier* (Papers, Peabody Museum, vol. 28, no. 1, 1947). Gertrude Caton-Thompson, "The Levalloisian Industries in Egypt," *Proceedings, Prehistoric Society, 1946*, new ser., 12:57–120.
8. Carleton S. Coon, *The Races of Europe* (1939), 46.
9. W. J. Sollas, *Ancient Hunters and Their Modern Representatives* (2nd ed., 1915), 485–487, 510–513, 520.
10. Aleš Hrdlička, "The Coming of Man from Asia in the Light of Recent Discoveries," *Proceedings, American Philosophical Society*, 71:401 (1932).
11. Nels C. Nelson, "The Antiquity of Man in America in the Light of Archaeology," in *The American Aborigines*, ed. Diamond Jenness (1933), 116.
12. M. R. Harrington, *Cuba Before Columbus*, pt. 1 (Indian Notes and Monographs, Museum of the American Indian, 1921), 1:-205–206, and *Gypsum Cave, Nevada* (Southwest Museum Papers no. 8, 1933), 189–190.
13. Thomas Jefferson, *Notes on the State of Virginia*. 1801, 148.

14. Hallam L. Movius, Jr., *Early Man and Pleistocene Stratigraphy in Southern and Eastern Asia* (Papers, Peabody Museum, vol. 19, no. 3, 1944), 25–27.

15. Herbert J. Spinden, *World Chronology and the Peopling of America* (mimeographed Presidential Address read before the American Anthropological Society, Washington, Dec. 27, 1936), 5.

16. Herbert J. Spinden, personal communication, 1946.

17. Spinden, "First Peopling of America As a Chronological Problem," in *Early Man* (1937), 106, and *World Chronology, etc.,* 5.

18. Spinden, *World Chronology, etc.,* 4.

19. A. S. Loukashkin, "Some Observations on the Remains of a Pleistocene Fauna and of the Paleolithic Age in Northern Manchuria," in *Early Man* (1937), 327–340.

20. Spinden, "Time Scale for the New World." *Proceedings, 8th American Scientific Congress,* 2:39 (1942), and *World Chronology, etc.,* 2, 19.

21. Ernst Antevs, personal communication, 1946.

22. Kirk Bryan, "Geologic Antiquity of Man in America." *Science,* new ser., 93:505–514 (1941).

23. Carl Sauer, "Early Relations of Man to Plants," *Geographical Review,* 37:10 (1947).

24. Erwin H. Barbour and C. Bertrand Schultz, "Paleontologic and Geologic Consideration of Early Man in Nebraska," *Bulletin, Nebraska State Museum,* 1:431 (1936).

25. George F. Carter, The Idea of the Recency of Man in America (unpublished MS.).

26. Albrecht Penck, "Wann kamen die Indianer nach Nordamerika?" *Proceedings, 23rd International Congress of Americanists* (1930), 23–30.

27. H. V. Walter, A. Cathoud, and Anibal Mattos, "The Confins Man: A Contribution to the Study of Early Man in South America," in *Early Man* (1937), 345.

28. Kirk Bryan, "Correlation of the Deposits of Sandia Cave, New Mexico, with the Glacial Chronology," Appendix to Hibben, "Evidences of Early Occupation in Sandia Cave" (*Smithsonian Miscellaneous Collections,* no. 23, 1941, vol. 99), 69.

29. Ernst Antevs, "Correlation of Wisconsin Glacial Maxima," *American Journal of Science*, 243A: 29 (1945) and "Dating Records of Early Man in the Southwest," *American Naturalist*, 70:336 (1936). Chart in Gladwin, *Excavations at Snaketown*, 2:73.

30. Antevs, "Climate and Early Man in North America," in *Early Man*, 128, and "Dating Records, etc.," 333.

31. Carl Sauer, "Geographic Sketch of Early Man in America," *Geographical Review*, 34:538 (1944).

32. M. C. Burkitt, *The Old Stone Age*, 86–87 (1933).

REFERENCES AS TO ILLUSTRATIONS

(In the main, the earliest instances of publication)

PAGE 11. Edward Brerewood, *Enquiries Touching the Diversity of Languages, and Religions, Through the Chief Parts of the World* (1622—1st ed., 1614).

PAGE 15. W. A. Johnston, "Quaternary Geology of North America in Relation to the Migration of Man," in *The American Aborigines,* ed. D. Jenness (1933).

PAGE 19. Carl Sauer, "Geographic Sketch of Early Man in America," *Geographical Review,* Vol. 34 (1944).

PAGES 22 and 23. Harold S. Gladwin, *Excavations at Snaketown: II, Comparisons and Theories* (1937), and Ernst Antevs, personal communication.

PAGE 37. Arthur Holmes, *Principles of Physical Geology* (1945). Earnest A. Hooton, *Up from the Ape* (1931).

PAGE 41. Richard F. Flint, *Glacial Geology and the Pleistocene Epoch* (1947). Ernst Antevs, *The Last Glaciation* (American Geographical Society Research Series, no. 17, 1928). Richard F. Flint and H. G. Dorsey, "Glaciation of Siberia," *Bulletin, Geological Society of America,* Vol. 56 (1945). R. A. Daly, *The Changing World of the Ice Age* (1934).

PAGE 47. Arthur Keith, *New Discoveries Relating to the Antiquity of Man* (1931). Henry Fairfield Osborn, *Men of the Old Stone Age* (1915). Albrecht Penck and Eduard Brückner, *Die Alpen im Eiszeitalter* (1901-1909). Frederick E. Zeuner, *The Pleistocene Period: Its Climate, Chronology and Faunal Successions* (1945). H. N. Fisk, *Geological Investigation of the Alluvial Valley of the Lower Mississippi River* (1944). Henry Fairfield Osborn, *Man Rises to Parnassus* (1927).

PAGE 49. George C. Simpson, "Ice Ages," *Nature, Vol.* 141 (1938). Carl Sauer, "Geographic Sketch of Early Man in America," *Geographical Review,* Vol. 34 (1944).

PAGE 52. W. J. Sollas, *Ancient Hunters and Their Modern Representatives* (1911).

PAGE 55. Harold Peake and Herbert John Fleure, *Apes and Men* (1927). J. Reid Moir, *The Antiquity of Man in East Anglia* (1927). E. Ray Lankester, "Rostro-Carinate Flint Implements," *Proceedings, Royal Society,* Vol. 41 (1912).

PAGE 60. Henry Fairfield Osborn, *Men of the Old Stone Age* (1915). L. S. B. Leakey, *Adam's Ancestors* (3rd ed., 1935). Miles C. Burkitt, *The Old Stone Age: A Study of Palaeolithic Times* (1933).

PAGE 62. Charles Dawson and A. Smith Woodward, "On a Bone Implement from Piltdown (Sussex)," *Quarterly Journal, Geological Society of London,* Vol. 71 (1917). O. G. S. Crawford, *Man and His Past* (1921).

PAGE 65. Henry Fairfield Osborn, *Men of the Old Stone Age* (1915). Hans Weinert, "Zusammenfassung des Pithecanthropus Problems," *Zeitschriften für Anatomie und Entwicklungsgeschichte,* Vol. 87 (1928).

PAGE 66. Gustav H. R. von Koenigswald, "Search for Early Man," *Natural History,* Vol. 56 (1947).

PAGE 68. Franz Weidenreich, *Apes, Giants, and Men* (1946). J. H. McGregor, "Restoring Neanderthal Man," *Natural History,* Vol. 26 (1926). R. Verneau, "Les Grottes de Grimaldi," *Anthropologie,* Vol. 2 (1906). Raymond W. Murray, *Man's Unknown Ancestors* (1943).

PAGE 69. Gabriel de Mortillet, *Musée Préhistorique* (1881).

PAGE 70. W. H. Holmes, *Handbook of Aboriginal American Antiquities* (1919).

PAGE 71. *Ibid.*

PAGE 72. *Ibid.*

PAGE 74. Henry Fairfield Osborn, *Men of the Old Stone Age* (1915).

PAGE 76. John Evans, *The Ancient Stone Implements, Weapons, and Ornaments of Great Britain* (1872).

PAGE 77. Miles C. Burkitt, *The Old Stone Age: A Study of Palaeolithic Times* (1933). George Grant MacCurdy, *Human Origins* (1924).

PAGE 77. Harold Peake and Herbert John Fleure, *Hunters and Artists* (1927).

PAGE 78. George Grant MacCurdy, *Human Origins,* Vol. I (1924). L. S. B. Leakey, *Adam's Ancestors* (3rd ed., 1935).

PAGE 80. Miles C. Burkitt, *The Old Stone Age: A Study of Palaeolithic Times* (1933). George Grant MacCurdy, *Human Origins,* Vol I (1924). Edith Plant, *Man's Unwritten Past* (1942).

PAGE 81. George Grant MacCurdy, *Human Origins,* Vol. I (1924).

PAGE 82. Thomas Wilson, "Prehistoric Art," *Report, U.S. National Museum for 1896* (1898).

PAGE 82. E. Lartet and H. Christy, *Reliquiae Aquitanicae* (1875).

PAGE 82. Michele Mercati, *Metallotheca, Opus Posthumum* (1717).

PAGE 83. Mark R. Harrington, *Gypsum Cave, Nevada* (Southwest Museum Papers, no. 8, 1933).

PAGE 84. Emile Cartailhac and Henri Breuil, "La Caverne d'Altamira à Santillane près Santander (Espagne)," *Peintures et gravures murales des cavernes paléolithiques* (1906). L. Capitan, H. Breuil, and D. Peyroni, "La Caverne de Font-de-Gaume aux Eyzies (Dordogne)," *Peintures et gravures murales des cavernes paléolithiques* (1910).

PAGE 85. Hugo Obermaier and Paul Wernert, *Las Pinturas rupestres del barranco de Valltorta* (1919).

PAGE 86. *Ibid.*

PAGE 87. L. Capitan, H. Breuil, and D. Peyroni, "La Caverne de Font-de-Gaume aux Eyzies (Dordogne)," *Peintures et gravures murales des cavernes paléolithiques* (1910).

PAGES 88 and 89. Harold Peake and Herbert John Fleure, *Hunters and Artists* (1927). Arthur Keith, *New Discoveries Relating to the Antiquity of Man* (1931). Henry Fairfield Osborn, *Men of the Old Stone Age* (1915). Robert Braidwood, personal communication, 1946. Frederick E. Zeuner, *Dating the Past* (1946).

PAGE 109. Charles C. Abbott, "The Stone Age in New Jersey," *American Naturalist,* Vol. 16 (1872).

PAGE 110.   Israel C. Russell, *The Geological History of Lake Lahontan* (U.S. Geological Survey, Monograph no. 11, 1885).

PAGE 111.   J. Graham D. Clarke, "New World Origins," *Antiquity*, Vol. 14 (1940).

PAGE 113.   H. M. Wormington, *Ancient Man in North America* (Denver Museum of Natural History, Popular Series no. 4, 2nd rev. ed., 1944).   Edgar B. Howard, "Evidence of Early Man in North America," *Museum Journal*, Vol. 24 (1935). Alex Krieger, "Artifacts from the Plainview Bison Bed," *Bulletin, Geological Society of America*, Vol. 58 (1947).

PAGE 117.   W. J. Sollas, *Ancient Hunters and Their Modern Representatives* (1911).

PAGE 118.   Edgar B. Howard, "Evidence of Early Man in North America," *Museum Journal*, Vol. 24 (1935).   W. J. Sollas, *Ancient Hunters and Their Modern Representatives* (1911).   Edith Plant, *Man's Unwritten Past* (1942).   Jacques J. M. de Morgan, *Prehistoric Man* (1925).

PAGE 120.   Frank C. Hibben, "Evidence of Early Man in Alaska," *American Antiquity*, Vol. 8 (1943).   Frank H. H. Roberts, Jr., "Developments in the Problem of the North American Paleo-Indian," *Smithsonian Miscellaneous Collections*, Vol. 100 (1940).

PAGE 121.   *Ibid.*

PAGE 122.   H. M. Wormington, *Ancient Man in North America* (2nd rev. ed., 1944).   E. W. C. and H. H. Campbell, and others, *The Archaeology of Pleistocene Lake Mohave* (Southwest Museum Papers, no. 11, 1937)

PAGE 123.   H. M. Wormington, *Ancient Man in North America* (2nd rev. ed., 1944).

PAGE 125.   Frank C. Hibben, "Evidences of Early Occupation in Sandia Cave, New Mexico," *Smithsonian Miscellaneous Collections*, Vol. 99 (1941).   Bruce Howe and Hallam L. Movius, Jr., *A Stone Age Site in Tangier*, Vol. 28 (Papers of the Peabody Museum, 1947).   Edith Plant, *Man's Unwritten Past* (1942).

PAGE 127.   Paul S. Martin, George I. Quimby, and Donald Collier, *Indians Before Columbus* (1947).

PAGE 130.   Mariano Barceno, "Descripción de un hueso labrado, de llama fosil," *Anales, Museo Nacional de México*, Vol. 2 (1882).

PAGE 130.   Helmut de Terra, *Tepexpan Man* (Viking Fund Publications in Anthropology, no. 11, 1949).

PAGE 135.   G. F. Becker, "Antiquities from Under Tuolumne Table Mountain in California," *Bulletin, Geological Society of America*, Vol. 2 (1891).

PAGE 141.   Edwin H. Colbert, "The Association of Man with Extinct Mammals in the Western Hemisphere," *Proceedings of the Eighth American Scientific Congress*, Vol. 2 (1942).

PAGE 153.   Earnest A. Hooton, *Up from the Ape* (1931).

PAGE 155.   Alfred S. Romer, *Man and the Vertebrates* (3rd ed., rev., 1941).

PAGE 157.   Griffith Taylor, "The Nordic and the Alpine Races and Their Kin," *American Journal of Sociology*, Vol. 37 (1931).

PAGE 159. L. S. B. Leakey, *Adam's Ancestors* (1935). Rudolf Martin, *Lehrbuch der Anthropologie, etc.* (1928). E. P. Stibbe, *An Introduction to Physical Anthropology* (1938). Earnest A. Hooton, *Up from the Ape* (1931).
PAGE 161. E. P. Stibbe, *An Introduction to Physical Anthropology* (1938). Earnest A. Hooton, *Up from the Ape* (1947). Herman F. C. ten Kate, *Matériaux pour servir à l'anthropologie de la presqu'île Californienne,"* Vol. 7, *Bulletin, Société d'Anthropologie de Paris* (1884). George and Edna Woodbury, *Prehistoric Skeletal Remains from the Texas Coast* (Medallion Papers, Gila Pueblo, no. 28, 1935). Louis R. Sullivan and Milo Hellman, "The Punin Calvarium," *Anthropological Papers, Amer. Museum of Natural History,* Vol. 23 (1925). Aleš Hrdlička, "Early Man in America," *American Journal of Science,* Ser. 4, Vol. 34, (1912). Earnest A. Hooton, "Notes on Five Texas Crania," *Bulletin, Texas Archaeological and Paleontological Soc.,* Vol. 5 (1933).
PAGE 172. Harold S. Gladwin, *Excavations at Snaketown: II, Comparisons and and Theories* (Medallion Papers, Gila Pueblo, no. 26, 1937).
PAGE 177. Erich M. von Hornbostel, *Die Musik auf den nordwestlichen Salomon-Inseln aus dem Phonogramm-Archiv des Psychologischen Instituts der Universität Berlin* (1912). Erland Nordenskiöld, *The Ethnography of South America As Seen from Mojos in Bolivia* (Comparative Ethnological Studies, no. 3, 1924).
PAGE 179. Harold S. Gladwin, *Excavations at Snaketown: II, Comparisons and Theories* (Medallion Papers, Gila Pueblo, no. 26, 1937). Frances Elmore, "The Casa Grande National Monument," *Arizona's National Monuments* (1945). James Wickersham, "An Aboriginal War Club," *American Antiquarian,* Vol. 3 (1895). J. Imbelloni, "On the Diffusion in America of *Patu Onewa, Okewa, Patu Paraoa, Miti,* and Other Relatives of the *Mere* Family," *Journal, Polynesian Society,* Vol. 39 (1930).
PAGE 190. George C. Vaillant, "A Bearded Mystery," *Natural History,* Vol. 31 (1931). Matthew W. Stirling, "Great Stone Faces of the Mexican Jungle," *National Geographic Magazine,* Vol. 78 (1940). Miguel Covarrubias, *Mexico South* (1946).
PAGE 207. Paul C. Mangelsdorf and C. Earle Smith, Jr., "New Archaeological Evidence on Evolution in Maize," *Harvard University Botanical Museum Leaflets,* Vol. 13, no. 8 (Mar. 4, 1949).
PAGE 214. A. P. Okladnikov, "Archaeological Data on the Ancient History of the Baikal Region," *Review of Ancient History,* Vol. 86 (Moscow, 1938). Henry B. Collins, Jr., "Eskimo Archaeology and Its Bearing on the Problem of Man's Antiquity in America," *Proceedings, American Philosophical Society,* Vol. 86 (1943). Edgar B. Howard, "Evidence of Early Man in North America," *Museum Journal,* Vol. 24 (1935).
PAGE 217. Hallam L. Movius, Jr., *Early Man and Pleistocene Stratigraphy in Southern and Eastern Asia,* Vol. 19, no. 3 Papers, Peabody Museum (1944).
PAGE 218. Thomas T. Paterson, "On a World-Correlation of the Pleistocene," *Transactions, Royal Society of Edinburgh,* Vol. 60 (1942).

INDEX

Various theories concerning the early appearance of man in the New World, the time, the routes by which he came, etc., are listed under "Migrations." Italics indicate illustrations or charts. When a page contains both text and illustration dealing with a single topic, the number appears twice.

Abbeville, France, 53, 54
Abbevillian, 54. *See also* Chellean
Abbott, C. C., 95, 109
Abilene, Texas, 123; points, 123, *123*, 138
Acheulean, *52*, 54, 58, *59, 60, 62, 62, 63*, 64, 69, 71; in New World, 131, 132, 216
de Acosta, José, 10
Adhémar, J., 45–46
Agassiz, Louis, 39
Agriculture, invention of, 32, 33; prepottery, 32
Agriculture in New World, 198–211; when first developed, 204, 207–209; where first developed, 200–201
Alangasi, *138*. *See also* Quito
Alexander the Great, 174, 189–194
Algonquin, 173, 174
Alpera, Spain, 86
Alpine skull traits in New World, 163, 165
Altamira cave, Spain, 84, *84*
Ameghino, Fiorino, 94–97
Anderson, Edgar, 208–209
Anderson, Harold, 116
Anderson, Perry, 116
Angus, Nebr., 138
Antevs, Ernst, 23, 26, 40, 41, 102, 114, 115, 121, 123, 128, 149, 207, 220, 223
Archaic skulls. *See* Brow ridges; Keeled vaults; Long-headed skulls; Low foreheads; Teeth.
Arellano, A. R., 105
Arrowheads. *See* Points

Art, New World, 129–130, *130;* Old World, 74, 75, 79, 83, *84, 85, 86.* 87
Ashe, Thomas, 143–144
Aterian, 79, *80,* 81
Atlantis, 13, 14
Aurignac, France, 75
Aurignacian, 59, 74, 75, 76, 77, *78,* 85; skull types in New World, 97, and in Old World, 75, 76, 77; artifact types in New World, 132, 216–217
Australoid culture traits in New World, 26, *172,* 176
Australoid-Melanesian skull traits, 160, 162; in New World, 162–173 *passim*
Australoid skull traits, *159;* in Neanderthal, 73; in New World, 106; in Punin skull, 163; Hooton's "Pseudo," 163
Aztec blades, 76, 81

Badarians, 33
Bagford, 51
Barbour, Erwin H., 220–221
Barcena, Mariano, 130
Basket Makers, 163, 165, 167
Basket making, 32
Bastian, Adolf, 132, 178, 180
Bat Cave, N.M., 207; corn from, 207
Bâtons de commandement, 74
Bee County, Texas, *139*
Bernhardi, A., 39
Biasutti, 162
Big Bend, Texas, cave dwellers, 32
Bird, Junius, 101, 134, 208
Black, Glenn H., 106
Black's Fork Valley, Wyo., 131–132, *131, 218*
Blades, 75, 76, *78,* 81, *82*

Boas, Franz, 5
Bone preceding stone, 29–30
Borax Lake, Calif., 129, *139*
Botocudo tribe, Brazil, 168
Boucher de Crèvecœur de Perthes, Jacques, 53, 56
Bourgeois, Abbé Louis, 54, 56
Bows, 82–83
Braidwood, Robert J., *54, 59, 79, 88–89*
Brard, 39
Breasted, James H., Sr., 33
Brerewood, Edward, 11, *11*, 12
Breuil, Abbé Henri, 84, 87
Brinton, Daniel G., 27
Bronze Age, 28–29
Bronze in New World, 27
Broom, Robert, 66
Brow ridges, heavy, Calaveras, 93; Confins, 101; Lagoa Santa, 100; Melbourne, 103; Tepexpan, 106
Brown, Barnum, 110–111
Browns Valley, Minn., 102, *120, 138*
Brückner, Eduard, 39, 45, 47
Bruman, Henry J., 201–202, 207
Bryan, Kirk, 26, 102, 105, 114, 115, 125, 132, 220, 223
Buckland, William, 52
Burins, 75–76, 77, 81, *82*
Burkitt, M. C., 60, 77, 80, 224
Burnet Cave, N.M., 114, *138*
Bushman wall painting, 83, 85

Calaveras skull, 93–94
Campbell, Mr. and Mrs. W. H., 121–122, 128, 132
Cannibalism, 66
Capitan, L., 84, 87
Capsian, 83, *85, 86*
Carbon 14 test, 107, 135, 151
Cartailhac, Emile, 84
Carter, George F., 221
Caspian, 165
Catesby, Mark, 142
Cathoud, A., 223; work at Confins, 100–101
Catlin, George, 13
Central Texas. See Texas
Cephalic index, 156–157, *156, 157*
Cerro Pedernal, N.M., 132
Cerro Sota Hill, Chile, *139*
Chalco culture, Mexico, 134
Chancelade, France, 168

Charente, France, 63–64
Charney, Désiré, 26
Charpentier, 39
Châtelperron, 75
Cheekbones, Mongoloid, 162
Chellean, 54, 58, *59, 60, 62–64, 62, 78*; in New World, 132, 216
Chelles, France, 54
Childe, V. Gordon, 29, 32, 51, 90
Children of the Sun, 13, 181
Chinitna Bay, Alaska, 119–120
Chiricahua horizon, Ariz., milling stones, *127*
Chopping tools, in New World, 132; in Old World, 61, *217, 218*, 217–218
Choukoutien cave, China, 64, 77, 97
Christy, Henry, 53, 82
Chukchi, 30
Churchward, James, 181
Circle, Alaska, *139*
Clacton-on-Sea, England, 62, 63
Clactonian, 58, 59
Clarke, J. Grahame D., 111
Classification, difficulties of, 28–35; de Mortillet, 53–61
Clovis, N.M., 114–115, *138*
Coastal Chavin, 208
Coastal Texas. See Texas
Cochise culture, 126, *127*, 128, 134
Coffin, A. L., 114
Coffin, C. C., 114
Colbert, Edwin H., 141, 151
Collateral Yuma, *113*, 119
Collier, Donald, 127
Collins, G. N., 204
Collins, Henry B., Jr., 214
Combe Capelle, France, 77
Confins, Brazil, 100–101, *138, 160*
Conklin Cavern, N.M., *138*
Conyers, 51
Cook Inlet, Alaska, *139*
Coon, C. S., 216
Cordilleran glaciation, 42
Core industry, 57–61, 120–121. See also Hand axes
Corn, 202–209, *203, 205, 206, 207;* imported from Burma(?), 208–209; when first cultivated, 204, 207–209
Correâ, A. H. Mendes, 162, 169
Cotter, John L., 114
Count, Earl W., 169
Coup de poing. See Hand axes

Covarrubias, Miguel, 182, 190
Crawfurd, John, 30
Cressman, L. S., 135
Croll, James, 46
Cro-Magnon, 63, 68, 73, 75, 76, 77; skull types in New World, 98
Cromerian industry, 58
Cueva del Mas d'en Josep, Spain, 85
Cummings, Byron, 126
Cuvier, Georges L., 149

Daly, R. A., 41
Danubian glaciations, 39
Dating methods, by fossil associations, 61, 62; by glacial climates, 61, 62; by pluvials, 101, 129, 222–224; by river terraces, 42–44, 61, 62
Dating of early man in Old World disputed, 76, 79, 88–89
Daun glaciation, 40
Dent, Colo., 138
Díaz del Castillo, Bernal, 26, 105
Dick, Herbert W., 207
Dickeson, M. W., 92–93
Diffusion, evidences of, 21, 172, 176–179, 177, 178, 179, 182, 183–185; vs. independent invention, 175–198. See also Resemblances
Dighton Rock, Mass., 91
Dixon, Roland B., 26, 155, 162, 164–165, 167, 169, 171, 184–185
Dodoens, R., 205
Donnelly, Ignatius, 181
Dorsey, H. G., 15, 17, 41
Douglass, A. E., 40
Dubois, Eugène, 64, 65
Dugdale, William, 108
Durst Silts, 123–124

Early Central California Culture, 104, 161
Early man in Old World, dating in dispute, 76, 79, 88–89
Eberl, B., 46
Eden, Wyo., 116, 119, 139
Eden Yuma, 113
Eiseley, Loren C., 142–143, 145, 146, 148, 150
El Cauco, Managua, Nicaragua, 134
Elm Creek, Texas, 123
Elm Creek Silts, 123–124
Elmore, Frances, 179
Engravings, 87

Eoliths, 54–57, 55, 123–124
Eskimo, 174; skull traits, in Aurignacian, 76; in Magdalenian, 168, 212; in Peking Man, 77
European skull traits in New World, 163
Eustatism, 48, 50
Evans, Glenn L., 119
Evans, Sir John, 53
Extinction. See Mammals, etc.

Facial index, 157
Fairbanks, Alaska, 139
Falconer, Hugh, 53
Fell's Cave, Chile, 139
Figgins, J. D., 109, 110
Fisk, Harold N., 47
Flake industry, 57–58, 59, 61, 67; by percussion, 67, 70, 71; by pressure, 67, 72
Flat-sided skulls, Central Texas, 161; Early Sacramento, 161; Lagoa Santa, 100, 161; Melbourne, 103, 161; Pericú, 161; Punin, 101, 161
Fleure, Herbert John, 55, 77, 79, 88–89
Flint, R. F., 15, 17, 40
Folsom, N.M., 109; points, frontispiece, 24, 92, 109–116, 111, 112, 113, 122–123, 125, 132, 134, 138, 151, 173, 210; distribution, 112, 114; True, or Classic, Generalized, Clovis Fluted, Ohio Fluted, defined, 112
Font-de-Gaume Cave, France, 82; its art, 84
Font Robert, France, point, 80, 81
Food gatherer vs. hunter, 34–35
Forster, Johann R., 144
Fossils. See Mammals
Frankfurter, W. D., 125
Frederick, Okla., 110, 138
Frere, John, 52, 60
Fuchs, Leonhard, 203

Galley Hill, England, 63, 64
Gamio, Manuel, 134
Garcia, Fray Gregorio, 12
Gates, R. Ruggles, 167
Geer, Baron Gerhard de, 40
Geikie, James, 39
Generalized Folsom, 112, 113
Giant ancestors of man, 66
Gidley, J. W., 103
Gigantopithecus, 66
Gilluly, James, 37

Glaciation in general, 36–50; causes, 45–46, 48–50; due to astronomic conditions, 45–46; due to drop in summer temperature, 45; due to eustatism, 48, 50; due to rise in temperature, 48, *49;* end of, 40; extent of, *41,* 42, 44; in New World, 14, 16, 17, 18, 20, *22–23, 42;* in Old World, 38–45 *passim;* land bridges, 14–15, *15,* 17, 20, 42, 44, 45; pluvials, 44, 48, 101, 129, 222–224; raised beaches, 42, 44, 50; river terraces, 42–44, *43;* submerged beaches, 42, 44; summary in New World, 220–224. *See also* Cordilleran, Danubian, Daun, Günz, Labradoran, Mindel, Riss, Wisconsin, Würm

Gladwin, Harold S., 23, 40, 123, 126, 170–174, 183–184, 186–194, 201

Goguet, 28

Gravettian, 75, 76

Gray's Inn Lane, hand ax, 51, *52*

Great Ice Age. *See* Glaciation

Grimaldi, Gibraltar, 76, 77

Grotte du Pape, France, 74

Guayana River Pygmies, Venezuela, 171

Günz glaciation, 39, 46, 47

Gusinde, 162

Gypsum Cave, Nev., 121; points, 121, *121, 122,* 129, *138*

Haddon, A. C., 26, 162

Haeckel, Ernst, 64

Hagar, Stansbury, 21

Hand axes, 51, *52,* 53, 54, 57, 60, 62, 63, 67, 131–132, *131, 133,* 217–218, *217*

Hansen, 162

Harrington, John, 5

Harrington, M. R., 21, 83, 114, 121, 129, 168, 216, 218

Harrison, Benjamin, 56

Haury, Emil W., 126, 128

Heidelberg man, 63

Heizer, Robert F., 104, 161

Hellman, Milo, 161, 163

Henderson County, Texas, 130

Hibben, Frank C., 17, 119–120, 124, 125

Holmes, Arthur, 37

Holmes, W. H., 27, 70, 71, 72, 95, 132, 135

Homo eoanthropus dawsoni, 63

Homo neanderthalensis. See Neanderthal

Homo sapiens, 46, 63, 67, 73, 97

Hooton, Earnest A., 26, 37, 75, 96, 97, 102, 153–155, 158, 161, 162, 163–164, 165, 167, 168, 173, 175, 212

von Hornbostel, Erich M., 177

Howard, Edgar B., 5, 113, 114, 116, 118, 123, 147, 212, 214

Howe, Bruce, 124

Howells, W. W., 167–168

Howorth, Henry W., 149

Hoxne, Surrey, hand ax, 52, 60

Hrdlička, Aleš, 15, 17, 27, 94, 95, 96–98, 103, 110, 116, 161, 162, 181, 183, 210, 211, 216

Hueco, Tex., cave dwellers, 32

Hultkrantz, 162

von Humboldt, Alexander, 13

Huntington, Ellsworth, 21

Imbelloni, José, 170, *179*

Independent invention vs. diffusion, 175–198. *See also* Resemblances

Indian corn. *See* Corn

Inventions unique in New World, 197–198

Ipswich, England, eoliths, 56

Java man, 64, *65,* 67, 68, 73

Jefferson, Thomas, 92, 142, 144, 217

Jenks, A. E., 102, 116, 120

Johnson, Frederick, 18

Johnston, W. W., 15

Julius II, Pope, 10

Kalm, Peter, 92

ten Kate, C. F., 104, 161, 162

Kay, G. F., 102

Keeled vaults, Central Texas, *161;* Lagoa Santa, 100, *161;* Pericú, *161;* Punin, 101, *161*

Keewatin glaciation, 42

Keith, Sir Arthur, 26, 47, 73, 88–89, 100, 162, 163

Kent's Cavern, England, 53

Ketchikan, Alaska, 17, 119

Kidder, Alfred V., 110, 185

King, C. J., 134

Kingsborough, Lord, 13, 99

Koch, A. K., 92, 109; Missouri sites in Gasconade and Benton counties, *137*

von Koenigswald, G. H. R., 64, 66, 154

Köppen, W., 46

Krieger, Alex, 113, 120

Kroeber, Alfred L., 5, 185
Kuhn, 38

Labradoran glaciation, 42
Lacandon Indians, 153
Lagoa Santa Caves, Brazil, 92, 98, 99–
    100, *137, 161*, 167, 168, 170, 171
Lake Cochise, Ariz., 126–128, *127, 138*
Lake Lahontan, Nev., 110, *110, 137*
Lake Mohave, Calif., 121–122, *139;*
    points, 122, *122*, 129, 132,
Land bridges, 42, 44, 45; Antarctic, 21,
    169; over Bering Strait, 14–15, *15,* 17,
    20
Lankester, Sir Ray, 55, 57
Lansing, Kansas, 103, *137*
Larkin, Frederick, 144
Lartet, Edouard, 53, 82
Leakey, L. S. B., 32, 60, 78, 158
Lebzelter, 162
Leechman, Douglas, 18
Leighton, M. M., 26, 102, 123–124
Le Plongeon, Augustus, 181
Le Roc, France, 79
Levalloisian industry, 58, *59*
Lewis, Gilbert N., 195
Libby, W. F., 135
Liden, Ragnar, 40
Lime Creek, Nebr., 125–126
Lindenmeier, Colo., 112, 114–115, *138*
Lipscomb County, Tex., *139*
Little Lake, Calif., 129
Lone Wolf Creek, Texas, 110, *137*
Long-headed skulls, Confins, 100–101;
    Early Sacramento, 104, *161;* Lagoa
    Santa, 100, *161;* Melbourne, 103, *161;*
    Pericú, 103, 160, *161;* Punin, 101,
    161; Stanford, 104; Texas, central and
    coastal, 103–104, 160, *161*
Loomis, F. B., 103
Lothrop, S. K., 191
Low foreheads, central Texas, 103–104,
    161; Confins, 101; Melbourne, 103,
    161; Pericú, 103-104, *161;* Punin, 101,
    161
Lowie, Robert H., 180, 200
Lubbock, Sir John, 30–31
Lund, P. W., 92, 99–100
Lyell, Sir Charles, 93, 146

MacClintock, 102
McCurdy, George, 77, 78, 80, 81
MacEnry, Father John, 52–53

McGee, W J, 110
McGregor, J. H., 68
Magdalenian, *59, 74,* 77, 81–85, *82,* 151;
    artifact traits in New World, 216–217;
    skull types in New World, 97, 98
Maize. *See* Corn
Mammals, extinction of, in New World,
    140–151, in Old World, 90; extinct,
    relationship of, to artifacts and/or
    bones of early man, 92, 93, 100–103,
    105, 109–112, 114–116, 119, 121–
    122, 125, 126, 128, 130–131, 134,
    136–139, 145–146, 147–149, 151
Mangelsdorf, P. C., 204, 207
Marietta, Ohio, 92
Martin, Paul S., 127
Martin, Rudolf, 158
Martínez Hernández, Juan, 187
Mas d'Azil, France, 74
Mather, Cotton, 91–92, 142
Mather, Kirtley F., 46, 76, 79
Mattos, Anibal, 223; work at Confins,
    100–101
Meade, Grayson E., 119
Mediterranean, 165
Meganthropus, 66
Melanesian culture traits in New World,
    172, 191
Melanesian skull traits, in New World,
    21; in Peking Man, 77
Melbourne, Fla., 102–103, *137, 161*
Mendes Correâ, A. A., 162, 169
Mercati, M., 82, 108
Mesolithic Age, 31
Metallurgic Age suggested by Rickard, 30
Miami, Texas, *138*
Middle Aurignacian, 75
Middle Stone Age, 31
Migrations, early, estimates of time, 24,
    97–98, 101, 102, 104, 105, 114, 115,
    121, 123, 124, 125, 126, 210–211,
    219–222; routes, over Bering Strait,
    10, 11, 14–18, via Antarctic, 21; test
    of date by distance covered, 3, by dif-
    ferentiation of languages and phy-
    siques, 5, by development of civiliza-
    tion, 6. *See* Transpacific migration.
Milankovitch, Milutin, 46
Milling stones, 122, 126–129, *127,* 212–
    213
Milne-Edwards, 53
Mindel glaciation, 39, *47*

Minnesota Man, 102, 106, 160
Mochi, 162
Moir, J. Reid, 55, 56–57, 131
Mongoloid dominant traits, 153
Mongoloid fold, 153, *153*
Mongoloid skull traits, 152–174 *passim,*
    159; in Aurignacian, 76
Monument Site, Concord, Calif., 104,
    139
de Morgan, Jacques J. M., 118
Morley, Sylvanus G., 207
Morlot, Adolphe, 39
de Mortillet, Gabriel, 53–61 *passim,* 69
Mortlach, Sask., *139*
Mound Builders, 26, 92, 96, 144
Mount Carmel, Palestine, 73
Mousterian, 54, 58, *59, 62,* 64, 66–67,
    68, 69, 75, 78, 79, 85, 110, 124; arti-
    fact types in New World, 132; dates,
    69, *88–89*
Movius, Hallam L., Jr., 124, 217
Mu, 13, 14

Nasal index, 157–158
Natchez, Miss., 93, *137*
Neanderthal, 66–69, *68;* skull traits in
    New World, 167
Negroid skull traits, *159;* in Europe, 76;
    in New World, 26, 163–173 *passim;*
    in Peking Man, 77
Nelson, N. C., 5, 10, 76, 92, 120–121,
    153, 216, 218
Neolithic (New Stone) Age, 30–33
Nordenskiöld, Baron Erland, 27, 177,
    181, 186, 187–188, 191, 197–198

Oak Grove Culture, 104
Obermaier, Hugh, 85, 86
Oblique Yuma, *118,* 119
Okladnikov, A. P., 214
Old Stone Age, 30–31
Osborn, Henry Fairfield, 47, 60, 65, 74,
    76, 88–89, 150

Painting, 83, *84, 85,* 86
Paleolithic Age, 30–31
Palli Aike Cave, Chile, *139*
Paltacalo, Ecuador, 101, *137*
Paracas, Peru, corn in, 207
Parkinson, John, 206
Paterson, T. T., 217
Paviland, England, "Red Lady" of, 52,
    75

Peake, Harold, 55, 78, 79, 88–89
Pecos Pueblo, N.M., 163
Peking Man, 64, 66, 73
Pelican Rapids, Minn., *138. See also* Min-
    nesota Man
Penck Albrecht, 5, 26, 39, 46, 47, 221–
    222
Percussion flaking, 67, 69, 70, *71*
Pericú, Lower California, 103–104, 160,
    161, 162, 170
Perry, W. J., 13, 181
Peyroni, D., 84, 87, 131
Piltdown Man, 62, 63, 73
Pinto Basin, Calif., 122, 132; points,
    122, 128, 129
Pithecanthropus erectus, 64, *65,* 67, 68,
    73
Pithecanthropus robustus, 68
Plainview, Tex., 119, *139;* points, *113,*
    119–120, *120,* 151
Plant, Edith, 80, 118
Playfair, John, 38
Pleistocene period. *See* Glaciation
Pluvials, 44, 48; in New World, 101,
    129, 220–224
Points, 67, 69, 79, *80, 81,* 85, *109–113,
    118, 120–123, 125,* 213–215
Polynesian migrations, 21, 24, *182, 192*
Pottery, 32; Aurignacian, 86
de Pradenne, A. Vayson, 50
Pre-Chellean, 54, *60,* 63, 64
Pre-Dravidian, 64
Prescott, William H., 99
Pressure flaking, 69, *72,* 79
Prestwich, Sir Joseph, 53, 56
Primordial Age suggested by Rickard, 30
Prognathism, 158
Pueblo Indians, 125
Punin, Ecuador, 101, 102, *137, 161,* 163,
    167, 170
Putnam, F. W., 95
Putnam, Rufus, 92
Putnam, William C., 37
Pygmies, Guayana River, Venezuela, 171

Quatrefrages, 162
Quinby, George I., 127
Quito, Ecuador, *138,* 144
Qurunga tribe, Brazil, 168

Rainey, F. G., 119
Raised beaches, 42, 44, 50
Ranking, John, 144

Ray, Cyrus N., 123
Reeves, R. G., 204
Religion, first evidences of, 67
Renaud, E. B., 131–132
Resemblances in culture between Old
    World and New, 21, 26, 27, 117, 171,
    172, 176–196, 177, 178, 179, 182, 190
Rhodesian wall paintings, 83
Rickard, T. A., 29, 30
Rigollot, R., 53
Riss glaciation, 39, 47
River terraces, 42–44, 43
Rivet, Paul, 162, 169
Roberts, Frank H. H., Jr., 95–96, 97,
    110, 114, 120, 210–211
Romer, Alfred S., 150–151, 154, 155
Romero, Javier, 106
Rostrocarinates, 55, 57
Russell Springs, Kansas, 110, 137

Saltadora, Spain, 85, 86
Sandia Cave, N.M., 125, 139; points,
    124–125, 135
Sangamon interglacial, 20, 124
San Jon, N.M., 139
San Juan culture, Mexico, 134
San Luis Valley, Colo., 139
Sauer, Carl, 19, 49, 150, 168–169, 171,
    201, 204, 208, 224
Sauk Valley, Minn., 102, 138
Saussure, 38
de Sautuola, Marcelino, 84
Sayles, E. B., 123, 126, 132
Schimper, 39
Schmerling, 53
Schultz, C. Bertrand, 125, 220–221
Scott, William B., 146
Scottsbluff, Nebr., 138
Scrapers, 78
Sculpture, New World, 130–131, 130;
    Old World, 74, 79
Sellards, E. H., 103, 110, 130
Seton, Ernest Thompson, 148
Shell preceding stone, 29
Signal Butte, Nebr., 128, 138
Silver Lake points, 122, 122, 129
Simpson, Sir George Clark, 48, 49, 224
Simpson, George Gaylord, 214
Sinanthropus pekinensis, 64
Skull traits. See Australoid; Brow ridges;
    Eskimo; Keeled vaults; teeth; Long-
    headed skulls; Low foreheads; Melane-
    sian; Mongoloid; Negroid

Smith, C. Earle, Jr., 207
Smith, Sir Grafton Elliot, 13, 180–181
Smith, Joseph, 13
Smith, Philip S., 17
Smith, Reginald A., 131
Soan culture, 218, 218
Soergel, W., 46
Sollas, W. J., 117, 118, 168, 216
Solutrean, 54, 59, 77, 79, 80, 81, 82,
    118, 124; and Folsom and Yuma, 215–
    216
Spear point. See Points
Spear-thrower, 83
Spence, Lewis, 181
Spillman, Franz, 145
Spinden, Herbert J., 24, 180, 181, 201,
    218–219
Spitz, Austria, 74
Stahl, Willy, 129
Stanford University, 104
Stephens, John L., 99
Stewart, George R., 29–30, 78
Stewart, T. D., 103, 106
Stibbe, E. P., 158, 161
Stirling, Matthew W., 190
Strong, William Duncan, 128, 143, 208
Submerged beaches, 42, 44
Sullivan, Louis R., 161, 163
Sulphur Springs horizon, Ariz., 127
Swanscombe skull, 63–64, 73

Table Mountain, Calif., 135
Talgai skull, 165
Tanged points, 79–80, 80, 81
Taylor, Griffith, 154, 155, 157, 168, 169
Teeth, large, Minnesota Man, 102; Punin,
    101
Tello, Julio C., 207
Teotihuacan, Mexico, 134
Tepexpan Man, Mexico, 105–106, 139,
    160
Tequixquiac, Mexico, 134, 139
de Terra, Helmut, 105, 130, 131, 132,
    134, 218
Texas, central and coastal, skulls, 103–
    104, 160, 161, 170
Textiles, 32–33
Thompson, J. Eric S., 187
Thomsen, Christian Jurgensen, 28, 30
Totolzingo, Mexico, 139
Tournal, 53

Transpacific migration, 21, 24, 181, *182,* 188–195, *192*
Trenton, N.J., 95, 109, *137;* point, *109*
Tshon tribe, Patagonia, language of, compared with Australian, 169–170

Uhle, Max, 145

Vaillant, George C., 187, 190
Varves, 40
Vavilov, N. I., 201–202
Vedel-Simonsen, 28
Venetz, 39
Ventana Cave, Ariz., *139*
Venus of Willendorf, 74
Verneau, R., 68
Vero, Fla., 102–103, *137*
Virú Valley, Peru, 32, 208
Voltaire, 12–13

Walter, H. V., 223; work at Confins, 101–102
Wegener, A., 46, 169
Wegner, R. N., 168
Weidenreich, Franz, 68, 106
Weinert, Hans, 65, 85, 86

Wheel in New World, 26
White skull traits in Indian, 168
White Water Creek, Ariz., 126
Whitney, J. D., 94
Wickersham, James, 179
Wiener, Leo, 181
Wilford, A. L., 102
Wilson, Thomas, 82, 95, 131–132
Wisconsin glaciation, 20, 22–23
Wissler, Clark, 6, 210
Wood preceding stone, 29–30
Woodbury, Edna, 103–104
Woodbury, George, 103–104
Woodland pottery traced to Old World, 26, 173
Wormington, H. M., 113, 122, 123
Wright, Sewell, 150
Wright, W. B., 58
Würm glaciation, 39, 46, 47

Yuma County, Colo., 116, *138*
Yuma points, *113,* 116, *118,* 119, 134, 151

Zeuner, Frederick E., 46, 47, 48, 76, 79, 88–89

Date Due